George Matheson and Mysticism
—A Biographical Study

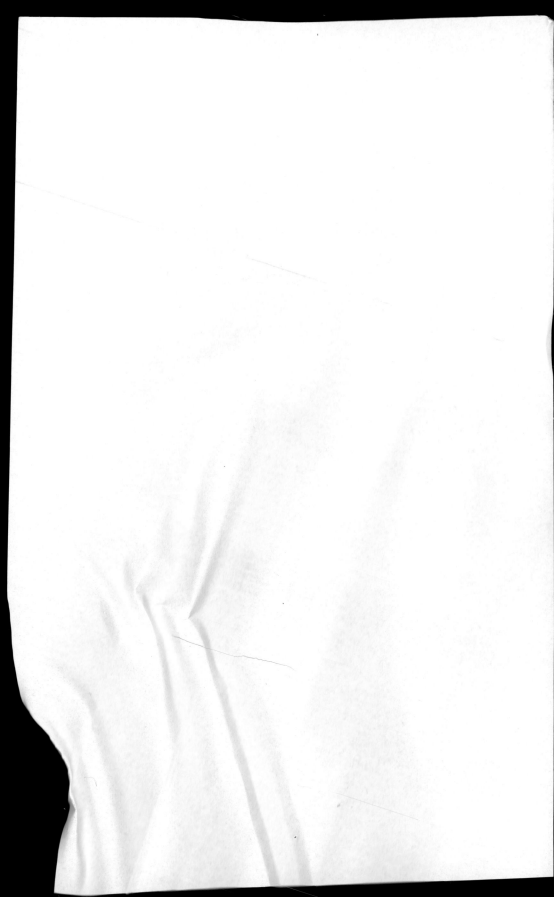

George Matheson and Mysticism —A Biographical Study

Mysticism in the Scottish Presbyterian Tradition

Scott S. McKenna

☙PICKWICK *Publications* · Eugene, Oregon

GEORGE MATHESON AND MYSTICISM—A BIOGRAPHICAL STUDY
Mysticism in the Scottish Presbyterian Tradition

Pickwick Publications
An Imprint of Wipf and Stock Publishers
199 W. 8th Ave., Suite 3
Eugene, OR 97401

www.wipfandstock.com

PAPERBACK ISBN: 978-1-7252-9891-0
HARDCOVER ISBN: 978-1-7252-9892-7
EBOOK ISBN: 978-1-7252-9893-4

Cataloguing-in-Publication data:

Names: McKenna, Scott S., author.

Title: George Matheson and mysticism—a biographical study : mysticism in the Scottish Presbyterian tradition / Scott S. McKenna.

Description: Eugene, OR: Pickwick Publications, 2022. | Includes bibliographical references.

Identifiers: ISBN 978-1-7252-9891-0 (paperback). | ISBN 978-1-7252-9892-7 (hardcover). | ISBN 978-1-7252-9893-4 (ebook).

Subjects: LSCH: Matheson, George, 1842–1906. | Mysticism. | Church of Scotland—Clergy—Biography. | Clergy—Scotland—Biography.

Classification: BX9225.M36 M35 2022 (print) | BX9225 (ebook)

01/10/22

For
Shelagh and Murdo

Contents

Acknowledgments

THIS BOOK HAS BEEN developed from my PhD thesis submitted to the University of St Andrews in Scotland. Above all, I would like to express my sincere and profound gratitude to my supervisor, the Revd Ian Campbell Bradley, Emeritus Professor of Cultural and Spiritual History. Ian's encouragement, guidance, enthusiasm, and friendship ensured that my work on Matheson was always stimulating and rewarding.

I am indebted also to others for their personal support during my research. In particular, I am grateful to Kirstine Baxter, Ian Campbell, Anette Hagan, and William Mearns.

I wish to acknowledge the extremely generous financial support which I received through the University of St Andrews. The sponsorship removed any financial stress that might otherwise have occurred. That tangible support was supplemented by the thoughtfulness and kindness of the Kirk Session of Mayfield Salisbury Parish Church in Edinburgh, where I was Minister during my years of study. Again, their generosity made a very real difference to me and my family.

Finally, I am truly grateful to my wise and devoted wife, Shelagh Laird, for her unfailing moral support, self-sacrifice, and love.

Scott S McKenna

Introduction

GEORGE MATHESON, A MINISTER OF WORD AND SACRAMENT in the Church of Scotland in the late Victorian period, was a mystic. While many see mysticism as "the hidden core at the heart of all religions,"[1] it is not commonly associated with Scottish Presbyterian ministers who stand in the Calvinist branch of the Reformed tradition. From at least the late second century CE Christians have sought the mystical or hidden meaning of the Bible, that is, "the inner message about attaining God that may be found beneath the literal sense of the scriptural texts and stories."[2] From the sixth century CE Christians have spoken of mystical theology and contemplation, that is, knowledge of God which is rooted not so much in rational effort or dialectical reasoning but "by the soul's direct reception" of the Divine.[3] In this book I shall discuss the extent to which Mathesonian theology reflects mystical theology, generally understood, and more specifically Hegelian mysticism. Drawing on a significant number of Matheson's appropriate writings, I have created a succession of foci which, taken together, encapsulate Matheson's mystical thought: union with God, the inner life, immortality of the soul, and self-forgetfulness. While a man of his time and indebted to his university teacher, John Caird, Matheson's insight into Scripture and overwhelming sense of the Divine dwelling in the human soul were mystical in nature and nurtured by his blindness, imagination and exceptional memory.

Definition of Mysticism

"Mysticism" is a broad term. Within the Christian tradition, it has meant different things at different times. For some, it is a matter of emphasis, for

---

1. McGinn, *The Essential Writings*, xiii.
2. McGinn, *The Essential Writings*, xiv.
3. McGinn, *The Essential Writings*, xiv.

1

example, focusing attention on the inner life. For others, it is regarded with suspicion or, worse, to be avoided as wholly disreputable, being the heretical beliefs of a sect which threatens orthodoxy. At the heart of mysticism is mystery. "Mystery" is derived from the Greek word "mysterion," a word and concept which the Church has appropriated from the mystery religions of the classical world in order to speak meaningfully of its sacraments.[4] Mysticism is often "portrayed as a path to knowledge of the divine or Absolute that begins with an initial stage of purification or initiation."[5] Generally understood, mysticism is a paradox: it stresses that God is unknown and unintelligible, yet God cannot remain completely unknown or unintelligible, otherwise we could know nothing of God. The mystery of God cannot be examined by the natural sciences but calls for "deep meditation or contemplation on some of our human experiences."[6] At its root, "mysterion" is derived from "muo," which means "to remain silent" or "to close the lips and eyes."[7] Literally and metaphorically, this is the practice Matheson lived out. Macquarrie describes the "cognitive claims" of mysticism as being "intersubjective," that is, they are "tested and supported by a very large number of people . . . not just the opinion of a few individuals."[8]

Bernard McGinn states that within the Christian tradition the "Father" or "Prince of Mystics" is Augustine. Augustine was:

> a doctrinal and speculative theologian, an educational theorist, a church leader, a monastic founder, a preacher and polemicist—but he was also an author who gave considerable attention to the mystical element in Christianity and to whom almost all later Western mystics appealed. It is in this sense that we can justify calling him not only a mystic, but "the Prince of Mystics" (to use Abbot Butler's term) or "the Father of Christian Mysticism" (to use John Burnaby's).[9]

Using quasi physical synesthesia, Augustine wrote of "the eye of the mind" or "the ear of the heart."[10] The inner or inward eye is a spiritual perspective and practice which Matheson used frequently.[11] In Augustine's work, we find

4. Macquarrie, *Two Worlds*, 4.

5. See McGee, 'Hegel and Mysticism', 265.

6. Macquarrie, *Two Worlds*, 2.

7. See Hamburger, "Mysticism and Visuality," 277.

8. Macquarrie, *Two Worlds*, 5.

9. McGinn, *The Foundations of Mysticism*, 231.

10. Miles, *Desire and Delight*, 36.

11. Matheson used the metaphor of the inner eye in *Moment on the Mount*, 54, 110; *Times of Retirement*, 92; *Spiritual Development*, 58.

intensity in his writing together with an emphasis on the inner life; on experiences the physical world, the world of sense, cannot give. Matheson valued and practiced daily meditation. Each evening he sought the seclusion and solitude of his study. Augustine practiced silent, private reading: he sat alone in God's presence.[12] In *Confessions* (X, 6), Augustine wrote: "I do have a kind of light, melody, fragrance, food, embracement when I love my God; for he is the light, the melody, the fragrance, the food, the embracement of my inner self—there where is a brilliance that space cannot contain, a sound that time cannot carry away, a perfume that no breeze disperses, a taste undiminished by eating, a clinging together that no satiety will sunder."[13]

Writing in 1856, Vaughan described mysticism as "everywhere synonymous with what is most visionary in religion and most obscure in speculation."[14] While he believed that mysticism to be defective, nevertheless he acknowledged that in every age there have been those "who pleaded the cause of the heart against prescription, and yielded themselves to the most vehement impulses of the soul."[15] In stark contrast to the "long conflicts of creeds," Vaughan pointed to the "unconscious unity of mystical temperaments in every communion."[16] This unity, even harmony, will have been spiritually attractive to a man of Matheson's outlook. Writing in 1860, Vaughan said: "If Mysticism be often a dream, it is consciously a dream in the right direction. Its history presents one of the most significant chapters in the story of humanity."[17]

In his Gifford Lectures of 1901–1902, William James offers four marks of mysticism. They are: ineffability, noetic quality, transiency and passivity. *Ineffability* means mystical states defy definition; they are more akin to feeling than the intellect. The *noetic quality* of mystical experiences means that, while such experiences offer a depth of truth, the mystic is unable to clearly articulate in detail the meaning of a mystical illumination or revelation. By nature, mystical experiences are *transient* and cannot be sustained for more than half an hour or, at the very most, an hour or two. Finally, the fourth mark is the *passivity* engendered in mystical encounter. The mystic enters a consciousness in which "his own will [is] in abeyance, and indeed sometimes as if he [is] grasped and held by a superior power."[18] James cites

---

12. Miles, *Desire and Delight*, 186.

13. Augustine, *Confessions*, 211.

14. Vaughan, *Hours with the Mystics,* xxvi.

15. Vaughan, *Hours with the Mystics,* xxviii.

16. Vaughan, *Hours with the Mystics,* xxviii.

17. Vaughan, *Hours with the Mystics,* xxxiii.

18. James, *Varieties of Religious Experience*, 322.

the experience of J. Trevor in his book, *My Quest for God* (1897), in which Trevor referred to the "Real Presence" and being "immersed in the infinite ocean of God."[19] Ocean is an image frequently used by Matheson, including in his hymn *O Love that wilt not let me go*.

Macquarrie helpfully offers a more detailed breakdown of marks, including directness, cognition, apophaticism, self-knowledge, a doctrine of God, individualism, passivity, a holistic view of reality and prayer.[20] Let me briefly describe each of these features. Often through visions, dreams or voices, mystics experience a direct relationship with God. We see this in the Buddha, Confucius, Moses, Jesus and Mohammed. Christian mysticism is most often Christ-mysticism, in which the mystics encounter the Holy through the mediation of Jesus. That said, some, like Eckhart, have sought "a direct relation to God that bypasses the persons of the Trinity."[21]

"Cognition" means that the mystical encounter is not an end in itself, but rather brings with it understanding. The mystical experience calls for verification by rational analysis. Mysticism is not a form of individual pleasure-seeking; rather, such experiences are "moments of joy" with "a sense of union with God or with all reality."[22] Instead of visions or physical sensation, the mystics often accentuate "intellectual visions" or "imageless revelations."[23]

As the Infinite, God is beyond our definition and the limitations of our language (apophatic theology). Believing God to be above space, time, name and conception, Clement of Alexandria said that we could only know God by what God is not. While light may be a favorite symbol of the mystics, it comes with a heavy qualification:

> Some would say that it was an inner light, intellectually perceived rather than sensibly; others with a love for paradox would say that this inner light so far transcends ordinary physical light that it is blinding and a kind of darkness. So darkness for the mystic is not simply a negative idea, for its symbolizes the unknowableness of God, and in the pilgrimage into God the soul is embarked on a journey into an ever-expanding awareness of God.[24]

---

19. James, *Varieties of Religious Experience*, 338.

20. Macquarrie, *Two Worlds*, 7.

21. Macquarrie, *Two Worlds*, 9.

22. Macquarrie, *Two Worlds*, 11.

23. Macquarrie, *Two Worlds*, 13.

24. Macquarrie, *Two Worlds*, 15.

Our ever-expanding awareness of the Divine suggests an eternal, unending exploration of the Mystery. Eckhart sought to "penetrate beyond even the Trinity to a region where all distinctions vanish."[25]

In a meditation on the Transfiguration in the Gospel of Mark, Matheson focuses on the cloud. Though Jesus' face and garments shine, and two celestial visitors are present, the words of revelation come from the cloud. It is from the corner of darkness that Christ's glory is revealed and, similarly, it is "the shadow of His Cross" in which we find God's greatest revelation.[26] If darkness is true of the biblical witness, for Matheson it is true also in our human experience. He wrote: "Is it possession of tabernacles of gold—the trappings of wealth, the homes of luxury, the gardens of pleasure? Not these. It is our cloud that reveals our origin. It is our wants that prove our birth. It is our thirst that betrays our aristocracy. It is the rent in our garment that shows how we in the body are not at home."[27] Matheson's interpretation of the story of the Transfiguration takes us to allegory and away from Scripture's literal meaning.

In knowing God, the mystic claims also to know the self. Self-knowledge, inwardness or the examination of the inner life is a key component for the mystic. Of the "inward self," Augustine wrote: "I entered, and with the eye of my soul saw above the same eye of my soul, above my mind, the unchangeable light. Not this common light, which all flesh may look upon, nor as it were a greater light of the same kind . . . but very different. It was above me, not as heaven is above earth, but it was above because it made me, and I was below because I was made by it."[28] Mysticism holds that God breathed life into humanity and God remains there. The image of the divine cannot be obliterated, not even through sin. Each human being is "the bearer of the divine image" and has "the possibility of growing more and more into the divine likeness."[29] Through examination of the soul, mystics trace their origin back to God: through introspective practice, revelation emerges from their "God-given core."[30] For Augustine, the highest form of (in)sight is intellectual vision which is seeing with the eye of the mind, that is, the perception of the intellect. It is the rational *soul* which alone is capable of receiving divine illumination and perceiving divine truth.

---

25. Macquarrie, *Two Worlds*, 15.

26. Matheson, *Rests by the River*, 202.

27. Matheson, *Rests by the River*, 202–203.

28. Augustine, *Confessions*, 10.

29. Macquarrie, *Two Worlds*, 17.

30. Macquarrie, *Two Worlds*, 18.

Meditation can lead mystics to blur the distinction between God and the human soul; language and, at times, theology, can "obscure the priority of God."[31] While Paul is careful to prioritize Christ (Colossians 1:15–20 or 2:8–9), "imagery of raindrops into a lake or a river running into the sea"[32] imply pantheism rather than panentheism or dialectial theism.[33] According to Macquarrie, in the late nineteenth century, at the time of the Anglo-Hegelianism, the mystical understanding of God, that is, the doctrine of God, was a "higher pantheism" rather than traditional theism.[34] We find this sentiment in Caird and Matheson.

Besides pantheism, mystics have been accused of individualism to the exclusion of care for others and the world. It is said that once mystics enjoy "the friendship of God," what else is there to want?[35] Plotinus wrote of mysticism as "The flight of the alone to the Alone." Critics of mysticism argue that the spiritual exercise of inwardness can lead to a "kind of spiritual hedonism."[36] By contrast, it may be argued that mystical insight sensitizes the mystic to the suffering of others and that, through meditation or, as Augustine wrote, intellectual vision, the mystic becomes deeply aware of the presence and life of the whole world. Mystical understanding of reality sees it in its "wholeness and interconnectedness."[37] Both Caird and Matheson sit comfortably within this perspective, at least to some extent. While many mystics throughout history have been at odds with doctrine, most of them have acknowledged the need for the Church.[38]

For mystics, prayer is both passive and passionate thinking.[39] In prayer, the mystic seeks to encounter a sense of reality which transcends everyday experience.[40] The act of prayer is "letting oneself be mastered, immersed in a power and wisdom transcending one's own."[41] Following Paul (Romans 8:26), the mystic understands prayer to be the Spirit of God praying in us: "we are caught up into God's own longing for the

---

31. Macquarrie, *Two Worlds*, 20.
32. Macquarrie, *Two Worlds*, 22.
33. Macquarrie, *Two Worlds*, 21.
34. Macquarrie, *Two Worlds*, 21.
35. Macquarrie, *Two Worlds*, 23.
36. Macquarrie, *Two Worlds*, 23.
37. Macquarrie, *Two Worlds*, 27.
38. Macquarrie, *Two Worlds*, 24.
39. Macquarrie, Two Worlds, 24.
40. Macquarrie, *Two Worlds*, 25.
41. Macquarrie, *Two Worlds*, 25.

final completion and perfection of the cosmos."[42] Prayer is an "opening of the self" that we may become "attuned to the divine will."[43] Meditative prayer involves not only receptivity to the Spirit but also imagination: through imaginative engagement in inward reflection, the mystic becomes a "participant."[44] While the words "meditation" and "contemplation" are often used inter-changeably, meditation has "definable content" while contemplation, perhaps through the use of a mantra such as the Jesus Prayer, aims to lead the mystic to awareness of God's presence or be present to the whole of creation. In such moments, mystics speak of being "infused by God."[45] In contemplation, the mystic moves beyond images to nothingness, though nothingness is not a blank state of mind.[46]

"Mysticism" in the Victorian Period

To some extent, mystical experience may be "conditioned by historical context."[47] By the end of the eighteenth century and the beginning of the nineteenth century, the narrow rationalism of the Enlightenment was giving way to Romanticism, which accentuated "aspects of experience that had been ignored or underestimated in the Age of Reason."[48] The term "mysticism" did not appear as a category until the early eighteenth century; previously, the classification had been "mystical theology." "Mystical theology" was often misunderstood, unappreciated and often regarded with suspicion, particularly within the churches of the Protestant Reformation. In fact, it became a term of "abuse as of approbation."[49] In 1896, an unsigned essay in the *Edinburgh Review* stated that "mysticism" was a term that defied definition because its use was wide and varied.[50]

Chambers' *Cyclopaedia* (1728) associated "mystic theology" directly with biblical exegesis. The mystical sense of Scripture involved seeking the "internal, hidden senses of scriptural texts, the spiritual and arcane elements behind the surface of the literal."[51] In the *Encyclopaedia Britannica* (1797),

42. Macquarrie, *Two Worlds*, 27.
43. Macquarrie, *Two Worlds*, 31.
44. Macquarrie, *Two Worlds*, 31.
45. Macquarrie, *Two Worlds*, 32.
46. Macquarrie, *Two Worlds*, 34.
47. Hamburger, "Mysticism and Visuality," 277.
48. Macquarrie, *Two Worlds*, 215.
49. See Amy Hollywood, *Companion to Christian Mysticism*, 6.
50. Schmidt, "The Making of Modern Mysticism," 276.
51. Schmidt, "The Making of Modern Mysticism," 277.

"mystics" are defined as a kind of sect.[52] The understanding that mysticism or mystical theology was a sect can be found throughout the eighteenth and nineteenth centuries. In addition to the *Encyclopaedia Britannica*, Webster's *American Dictionary* (1828) defined "mystics" as "a religious sect who profess to have direct intercourse with the Spirit of God," while "mysticism" was rendered as "the doctrine of the Mystics, who profess a pure, sublime and perfect devotion, wholly disinterested."[53] In his work, *Religious Denominations of the World* (1872), Vincent Milner, classified mystics as a small sect, as clearly defined as Buddhists or Baptists.

Besides the misunderstanding that mystics formed a sect, when finally in 1858 the *Encyclopaedia Britannica* admitted the term "mysticism," it did so only to say that it was a "form of error . . . which mistakes the operations of a merely human faculty for a Divine manifestation."[54] However, it acknowledged that mysticism had a global presence; it manifested itself in numerous forms, including Oriental mysticism, Greek mysticism, German mysticism, Spanish mysticism and French Quietism. Suspicion of mysticism had long held that it was nothing more than "disappointed love." Henry Coventry (1761) said that the frustrated passion is "transferred from mere mortals to a spiritual and divine object, and love . . . is sublimated into devotion. That divine object was necessarily 'an imaginary and artificial' contrivance, a mistaken substitute, a product of the 'wantonest appetites and wishes.'"[55]

As a man of his time, Coventry claimed that the emotional nature of the mystic meant that it was predominantly to be found in women. The "divine object" was, he said, nothing more than "a spirituality of sublimated sexuality," a craving for "connubial love;" the cure from mysticism being a "timely application" of the male sex.[56] At a superficial level, the charge that mysticism is a presenting symptom of emotional (or sexual) distress may be attributable to Matheson but this analysis does not allow for the possibility that the claims of the mystic are true, namely, that God is found in the darkness. It may be that the doorway into darkness is personal experience, particularly emotional experience, but that does not preclude an encounter with the Divine in the darkness. The claim or basis of dialectical theology is no stronger than that of mystical theology: both are experienced within the mind or consciousness and, therefore, subjective.

---

52. Schmidt, "The Making of Modern Mysticism," 280.

53. Schmidt, "The Making of Modern Mysticism," 281.

54. Schmidt, "The Making of Modern Mysticism," 282.

55. Schmidt, "The Making of Modern Mysticism," 278.

56. Schmidt, "The Making of Modern Mysticism," 278.

At the very end of the eighteenth century and the beginning of the nineteenth century, mysticism started to grow in strength, not least nature mysticism. We see this in the work of Wordsworth and Coleridge. Wordsworth moves from "a youthful sympathy with nature to a more mature mystical sense of a divine presence."[57] The cultural critic, Matthew Arnold, said that it was Wordsworth's ability to raise the reader to a higher level of self that set him apart from his contemporaries. The poet, he said, was possessed of "a force greater than himself" which articulated "a truth far beyond any philosophic truth."[58] Able to convey the deepest sense of joy, Wordsworth arouses feelings which release the reader from "the clutches of our appetite-satisfying lower self" in order that the higher self may "rise to the level of moral conduct."[59] He wrote:

> I felt the sentiment of Being spread
>
> O'er all that moves, and all that seemeth still,
>
> O'er all, that, lost beyond the reach of thought
>
> And human knowledge, to the human eye
>
> Invisible, yet liveth to the heart . . .

In one sense, nature mysticism may represent a shift from an inward light to a light that shines in all things. In another sense, it is the inward light which perceives the light shining in all things. In the decades after Wordsworth, Tennyson writes in a manner reminiscent of Julian of Norwich:

> Flower in the crannied wall,
>
> I pluck you out of the crannies,
>
> I hold you here, root and all, in my hand,
>
> Little flower—but if I could understand
>
> What you are, and all, and all in all,
>
> I should know what God and man is.

The English cleric John Keble (1792–1866), described as "a modern mystic," published *The Christian Year* in 1827. The festivals and seasons of the liturgical calendar are interpreted by his mystical imaginative poetry. It passed through ninety-five editions and sold over 265,000 copies. Expressing his spirituality, the book had a "tremendous influence": Keble followed

---

57. Macquarrie, *Two Worlds*, 216.

58. Collini, *Victorian Thinkers*, 308.

59. Collini, *Victorian Thinkers*, 309.

the meditations of the life of Christ composed by Ignatius of Loyola.[60] For Keble, the "open sky" does not speak of infinity or nothingness,[61] but of love:

> The glorious sky, embracing all,
>
> Is like the Maker's love,
>
> Wherewith encompassed, great and small,
>
> In peace and order move.

At the time Keble employed his mystical imagination to interpret Scripture, many of his contemporaries read the Bible in a literal sense. Besides the fundamentalists, many "studied the text in a more scientific manner."[62] In his defense, Keble argued that, following the Early Church Father, Origen, the meaning of Scripture "cannot be simply read off from the words like a piece of information."[63] Scripture was comprised of many layers of meaning which required meditation, contemplation and prayer. "There could be no glib or easy talk of spiritual realities. They have to be safeguarded, even sometimes by silence."[64] For Keble, the whole of creation, the material universe, was a sacramental reality: a vehicle for perceiving God's presence.[65]

In 1856, Robert Alfred Vaughan published his seminal work, *Hours with the Mystics*. In two volumes, with the fifth edition printed in 1888, Vaughan established mysticism in the popular mind as "a conduit into 'the highest form of spirituality.'"[66] He believed mysticism to be "the romance of religion."[67] Described as "an English Dissenter of a literary, meditative, and melancholy cast," Schmidt says that Vaughan "had come round to the ministry by way of his father's example and 'the lone dark room of the artist.'"[68] During this period, some, like Frothingham,[69] argued that the attraction and temptation of mysticism is that it offers poetry rather than politics, the inward life and not the outward; ethics and social obligation are of little interest to the mystic. This charge represents another misunderstanding of mysticism. It is wholly refuted, not least by William James.

60. Macquarrie, *Two Worlds*, 219.

61. Macquarrie, *Two Worlds*, 220.

62. Macquarrie, *Two Worlds*, 222.

63. Macquarrie, *Two Worlds*, 222.

64. Macquarrie, *Two Worlds*, 222.

65. Macquarrie, *Two Worlds*, 223.

66. Schmidt, "The Making of Modern Mysticism," 283.

67. Schmidt, "The Making of Modern Mysticism," 284.

68. Schmidt, "The Making of Modern Mysticism," 283.

69. Schmidt, "The Making of Modern Mysticism," 288.

For James, the "consistent measure of religious experience was its fruits, its production of saintliness and active habits . . . [it was] a way to unleash energy, to find the hot place of human initiative and endeavor, and to encourage the heroic, the strenuous, and the vital."[70]

It is into this evolving and unstable climate with its shifting definitions, misunderstandings and appreciations of mysticism that Matheson was born and exercised his professional ministry. Matheson's "crisis of faith" may have been brought on by Rationalism, the claims to absolute truth by the Church, the impact of comparative religions on Christian doctrines or an emotional crisis in his private life. However, "the invention of an historical, poetic, intuitive, and universal mysticism served religious liberals well."[71] It offered an intellectual response to "the fierce onward current of purely scientific thought."[72] William James cannot be understood without taking full account of his breakdown, philosophical melancholy and the deepest spiritual yearning.[73] For James, mysticism had value because it addressed directly the "lacking and loss," the "emptied space of longing for 'a heightened, intensified way of life'" and a search for "an undivided whole of experience . . . [in] a world of serialized and alienated selves."[74] The personal breakdown of James is not unlike the crisis of faith suffered by Matheson.

Hegelian Mysticism

Matheson was a student of the Idealist John Caird. In lecture, university address and sermon, Caird followed Hegel. It is not clear if John Caird read Hegel himself or relied on his younger brother, the philosopher Edward, to instruct him in Hegelian thought. There are almost no direct quotations from Hegel in Caird's work and, similarly, no quotations of Hegel or Caird in Matheson's work. What can be established is that John Caird stood within the tradition of mysticism, but specifically Hegelian mysticism, which itself is dependent on the work of Jakob Boehme (1575–1624). Hegel was born into Protestant Pietism and was "steeped in its theosophy and mysticism."[75] Hegel read the works of Boehme, Eckhart and Tauler; "it was Boehme who made the greatest impression on him."[76] For many of

70. Schmidt, "The Making of Modern Mysticism," 292.
71. Schmidt, "The Making of Modern Mysticism," 288.
72. Schmidt, "The Making of Modern Mysticism," 288.
73. Schmidt, "The Making of Modern Mysticism," 293.
74. Schmidt, "The Making of Modern Mysticism," 294.
75. See Magee, "Hegel and Mysticism," 254.
76. See Magee, "Hegel and Mysticism," 255.

Hegel's generation, Eckhart and Boehme were a "liberating release from the deadness of Enlightenment rationalism."[77] In Hegel, Caird and Matheson, we find Boehme's central conception of God, namely, that God is dynamic and evolving. Boehme rejected the idea of God as Transcendent, outwith creation and complete and perfect within God's Self. For Boehme, God develops God's Self through creation. Most significantly, Boehme said that without creation God is not God. God needs creation to realize God's Self. It is through creation that God achieves self-consciousness. Magee writes: "Boehme wrote, 'No thing can be revealed to itself without opposition'. Thus, God must 'other' Himself in the form of the world. The process of creation, and of God's coming to self-consciousness, eventually reaches consummation with man."[78]

Extrapolating from self-consciousness to the nature of the Divine, to love, Caird made the same point in his Gifford Lectures (1890–1891, 1896): "God reveals Himself to Himself in nature and in the finite spirits He has made in His own image. The capacity of love in the heart of God may be said to find a new channel for its outflow in every human soul; and in the responsive love which that love awakens there is something which we can think of as adding a new sweetness and joy to the very blessedness of the Infinite."[79]

During his lifetime Hegel was criticized for the mysticism in his thought. Despite that, in his 1824 *Lectures on the Philosophy of Religion*, Hegel quoted Eckhart, and here again we find that creation is necessary for God to be God: "The eye with which God sees me is the same eye by which I see Him, my eye and His eye are one and the same. In righteousness I am weighed in God and He is in me. If God did not exist nor would I; if I did not exist nor would he."[80]

Within the mystical tradition, hermeticism is the belief that human life is necessary for God's being. Alongside Eckhart, Boehme, Hegel and Caird, it can also be found in Kabbalism and Sufism. However, Hegel departs from the broad mystical tradition in two ways: first, mystics typically argue that knowledge of the Divine is mysterious, ineffable and beyond the capacity of language to express or reason to comprehend; second, mystics often say that their knowledge is ineffable because it is non-rational, immediate, and an intuition of the Absolute. Hegel and Caird rejected both of these. Hegel said that it was through speculative philosophy that human

77. Magee, "Hegel and Mysticism," 256.

78. Magee, "Hegel and Mysticism," 257.

79. Caird, *Fundamental Ideas of Christianity*, 73.

80. Hegel, *Lectures on the Philosophy of Religion*, I: 347–48; Werke, 16:209.

beings rise above nature and "complete the actualization of God."[81] In his Gifford Lectures, Caird said:

> Philosophy seeks to lead us to a higher point of view, from which the seeming contradictions vanish, from which reason, following in the wake of faith, grasps the great conception that the religious life is a life at once human and divine—the conception that God is a self-revealing God, that the Infinite does not annul, but realises Himself in the finite, and that the highest revelation of God is the life of God in the soul of man; and, on the other hand, that the finite rests on, and realises itself in, the Infinite; and that it is not the annihilation, but the realisation of our highest freedom, in every movement of our thought, in every pulsation of our will, to be the organ and expression of the mind and will of God.[82]

Hegel had emphasized *coincidentia oppositorum*: "the idea that all difference and opposition in the world is really only apparent, and that 'beyond' this all is one in God."[83] Through discursive, rational form we can know the nature of the Absolute. We discern the identity of the Absolute through its unfolding in creation, in the life of humanity and moral action. Caird said: "It is the prerogative of man's spiritual nature that he can rise above himself as this particular being, that he can cease to think his own thoughts, or be swayed by his own impulses, and can yield himself up to a thought and will that are other and infinitely larger than his own."[84]

Eckhart, Boehme, Hegel and Caird represent the philosophical background to Matheson's mystical theology. It is important to stress that Matheson does not make direct quotations from any of them but his work reflects their theology. What is more, in his work Caird does not concern himself with the minutiae of Hegel's philosophy, and neither does Matheson. Their interest was solely concerned with the broad direction of travel. Even as a disciple of Caird, Matheson does not directly cite the importance of speculative philosophy. Matheson's expression of mysticism is more experiential, spiritually sensual and pastoral in nature. It is also reasonable to assume that, as a parish minister working in a rural parish in Argyll, Matheson would not easily have had the ability to study Hegel in depth. The study of Hegel would have been additionally difficult due to his blindness: he could not have read Hegel for himself.

81. Magee, "Hegel and Mysticism," 267.

82. Caird, *Fundamental Ideas of Christianity*, 54.

83. Magee, "Hegel and Mysticism," 271.

84. Caird, *The Philosophy of Religion*, 236.

Spiritual Practice

It was Matheson's practice to sit alone each evening in his room for an hour, undisturbed. Unable to read, he sat silently in his darkness and meditated: it was for him "an hour of communion."[85] MacMillan said of Matheson that he lived most of his life "in close fellowship with the Father of Spirits."[86] On one hand, Matheson was typical of his generation in using mysticism, in its broad sense, as a response to the challenges of his day but, on the other hand, he grew into it and, in so doing, lived a mystical life. Vaughan (1856) described mysticism as "an internal manifestation of the Divine to the intuition or in the feeling of a secluded soul."[87] It is in a general sense, informed by themes of hiddenness, darkness, solitude, silence and, as we will see in his meditations, imaginary explorations in interpreting Scripture that we can say Matheson was a nineteenth century mystic.

As his thought matured, Matheson increasingly focused his attention on "the spiritual life,"[88] the "personal experience in religion [emphasizing] the nature of its spiritual inwardness."[89] "Laying hold of the inward essential element in religion"[90] was Matheson's primary concern. Increasingly, he sought to penetrate the "outward fetters of dogma" in order to see God face to face in "His self-revelation in nature, history, providence, and the Bible."[91] With the blood of a Celtic Highlander as well as a Lowland Scot, Matheson comfortably blended imagination and reason[92]; there was never a day in which he did not spend time in reading, reflection and writing.[93] In his Preface to *Times of Retirement*, Matheson said his purpose was to compose meditations which appealed to "the instinct of prayer."[94] His biographer goes further: not only was Matheson almost entirely absent from church courts and the work of ecclesiastical administration, but, in preference, Matheson strove "to discover those deepest springs of religious thought and feeling which are common to all and which explain and reconcile the outward differences."[95] In true mystical fashion, Matheson

85. MacMillan, *The Life*, 303.
86. MacMillan, *The Life*, 241.
87. Vaughan, *Hours with the Mystics*, 21.
88. Matheson, *Times of Retirement*, 8.
89. Matheson, *Times of Retirement*, 30
90. Matheson, *Times of Retirement*, 31.
91. Matheson, *Times of Retirement*, 31.
92. Matheson, *Times of Retirement*, 10.
93. Matheson, *Times of Retirement*, 24.
94. Matheson, *Times of Retirement*, 6.
95. Matheson, *Times of Retirement*, 8.

sought the spirituality which lies "beneath creeds and forms of church government, and [which makes] all believing one."[96] In his preaching and published works, the "spirit of Matheson's teaching goes beneath all outward
distinctions and divisions of Christian theology."[97] Matheson sought to "do
justice to all forms of belief which have manifested themselves, not only
during the Christian era, but since reflection on Divine things began."[98] In
and through the great world religions, Matheson believed he could find the
"Person and Life of Christ," the Cosmic Christ.[99]

After a brief biographical chapter, in chapter two I shall discuss Matheson's crisis of faith, which he suffered in the first year or two following his
ordination, and his spiritual recovery. Matheson's ministry was exercised
in a particularly stimulating and unsettled period of church history: the
new discoveries of the sciences, the claims of biblical criticism, and comparative religion were understood by many to challenge the foundations
of Christianity. For some, scientific materialism accounted for the whole
of life, while biblical criticism and the stories of other world religions cast
doubt on Christian claims to absolute truth. In chapter three, I shall discuss
Matheson's contribution to the debate between science and religion and
specifically his engagement with the doctrine of transcendence proposed
by Herbert Spencer. Matheson saw in Spencer's defense of transcendence
the point of union between new scientific discoveries, the new faith, and the
traditions of Christianity, the old faith.

In chapters four, five, and six, I shall discuss the four central themes of
Matheson's work: union with God, the inner life and immortality of the soul,
and self-forgetfulness (kenotic theology). In chapter four, I shall discuss
Matheson's sense of union or oneness with the Divine in his Baird Lectures
and biographical study of Jesus, *Studies of the Portrait of Christ*. Christ in us,
Christ in you, was the lived experience which molded Matheson's spiritual
life, theology and meditations. An intense sense of union with the Divine
is the key characteristic of a mystic and we find this quality throughout
Matheson's work. For the mystic, encountering God is like meeting a friend
or loved one. In his meditations, prayers and elsewhere, Matheson spoke
directly and intimately to Jesus.

In chapter 5 I shall discuss Matheson's focus on the inner life, the
importance of silence and solitude, and immortality of the soul. Matheson
believed that Jesus' attention was focused on the soul and the urgent need

---

96. Matheson, *Times of Retirement*, 9.

97. Matheson, *Times of Retirement*, 32.

98. Matheson, *Times of Retirement*, 31.

99. Matheson, *Times of Retirement*, 31.

to overcome the ego, the small self. The spiritual journey is a wrestling within. Matheson followed the example of Jesus: he sought the benefits of silence and solitude. Communion with the Father was a determinative factor in the life of Christ and so too in Matheson. I shall also discuss the importance of immortality. In a remarkable departure from orthodoxy, Matheson said that it is through union with God, oneness with the Immortal Spirit, that our immortality is secured: the concept of resurrection is meaningless. In chapter 6 I shall discuss Matheson's kenotic theology. Matheson understood death and suffering, like eternal life, to be integral to the Divine. Holiness means sacrifice: a daily dying to self and salvation requires human participation. Christ's death was an atoning death, but no more so than His life, His daily outliving of self-forgetfulness.

Matheson's mystical insight flowed from his physical blindness. The darkness which enveloped his existence was the darkness in which he saw and felt the mystery of God. From inescapable darkness, he saw God in all things. Matheson's imagination was animated and his spirit vibrant, both nourished by his sense of the Immortal living in him, an awareness encountered in silence and solitude:

> I said to my soul, be still, and let the dark come upon you
> Which shall be the darkness of God. As, in a theatre,
> The lights are extinguished, for the scene to be changed
> With a hollow rumble of wings, with a movement of darkness on
> darkness . . .
>
> . . .
>
> But the faith and the love and the hope are all in the waiting.
> Wait without thought, for you are not ready for thought:
> So the darkness shall be the light, and the stillness the dancing.[100]

---

100. Eliot, *Collected Poems*, 199.

1

Biography

Early Years

GEORGE MATHESON WAS BORN in the parish of St David's Church, Glasgow on 27 March, 1840.[1] Married in 1838, his parents were second cousins, George Sr. and Jane; Matheson was their oldest son and second child. There were eight children in all, born between 1839 and 1854,[2] seven of whom lived into adulthood and, of those, only two married. George Sr., who worked as a merchant, was a native of Dornoch and throughout his life Matheson made much of his Highland ancestry. The Matheson family attended worship at Sandyford Church, one of the largest and wealthiest in the city. The minister was John Ross MacDuff. Matheson was indebted to MacDuff for his sense of the poetic: "Dr MacDuff gave me my first sense of literary beauty, my first experience of oratory, my first real conviction of the beauty of Christianity."[3] He was later to become the assistant minister at Sandyford Church alongside MacDuff.

Matheson was fortunate in that his family was reasonably affluent: Matheson's mother was born into a "cultured, talented family, not without commercial success."[4] Matheson's education began with a private tutor at home. In 1853, at the age of 13, Matheson started at Glasgow Academy. Academic excellence was to follow him through his school years and into university. A school friend, James Hotson, who often accompanied Matheson

1. Matheson's biographer, Donald Macmillan, cites Matheson's date of birth as 27 March, 1842. However, the Old Parish Record shows that Matheson was born on that day in 1840. This is substantiated because the third child, Margaret, was born on 22 June, 1842. Again, the Old Parish Record confirms this.

2. George and Jane Matheson's children: Jane Gray (1839–1925), George (1840–1906), Margaret (1842–1922), John (1844–1915), Ellen (1845–1915), Henry Donald (1849–1890), James Charles (1851–1853) and William Wilson (1854–1894).

3. Moffatt, *The Church Hymnary*, 414.

4. MacMillan, *Life of George Matheson*, 6.

from St Vincent's Crescent along Kent Road to the Academy, told of their
shared passion for Byron's *Corsair*, and how they would steal time together,
during which he would read aloud from the poem to Matheson.[5] Of all his
subjects, Matheson excelled most at English Composition. He wrote a poem
about the death of Lazarus, *Bethany Tears*, which his classmates paid to be
printed. Hotson quotes an extract:

> Once when the world in pomp and pride swept by,
>
> And 'Raise up Mammon' was its ruling cry,
>
> When man in sin's embrace had fallen asleep,
>
> The God-man Jesus was constrained to weep.
>
> Time has flown on with wings of speed arrayed,
>
> Empires have risen, flourished, and decayed;
>
> Great kings and warriors in oblivion lie,
>
> But those embittering tears can never dry.[6]

At this early age, we begin to hear Matheson's spiritual and pastoral
sensitivity emerging as well as his empathy for God's suffering. Written in
his middle teenage years, this poem reveals a mastery of language, a rich vo-
cabulary and a growing self-confidence. While still at school, Matheson on
occasion would "preach" a sermon to his family at home, one entitled "The
Children Playing in the Streets of Jerusalem"[7] and another "Our Father
which art in Heaven."[8] He also wrote a play about Theseus, the mythical
founder of Athens, which he had performed in the family drawing-room,
with his brothers and sisters taking the leading roles.[9] There can be little
doubt that Matheson's parents encouraged him and provided him with a
safe and stimulating environment in which to grow up. His mother was a
gifted singer and pianist and Matheson was "indebted [to her] for his gift of
imagination and spiritual insight."[10]

It was at the very early age of eighteen months that his mother noticed
her son's defective eyesight. The family consulted Dr Mackenzie, the leading oculist in Glasgow; he determined that the cause was an inflammation
at the back of the eyes. Matheson's eyesight deteriorated throughout his
childhood and adolescence. During his early schooling, he was permitted

5. MacMillan, *Life of George Matheson*, 17.

6. MacMillan, *Life of George Matheson*, 18.

7. MacMillan, *Life of George Matheson*, 8.

8. Tyler, *The Blind Seer*, 1.

9. Macmillan, *Life of George Matheson,* 20.

10. MacMillan, *Life of George Matheson*, 7.

always to sit near a window and, with the aid of very strong glasses, he was able to read and write. By the age of eighteen, he was almost totally blind. Years later, while minister at Innellan, he said he sometimes saw the shadow of the steamers passing up and down the Clyde. When the sunlight was very bright, he could occasionally make out signboards above shop windows in Glasgow.

Drawing upon the opinions of many who knew Matheson, Macmillan suggests that Matheson's blindness was "the making of him."[11] This natural disability "threw him back upon himself, compelled him to meditate on Divine things, and thereby enabled him to produce those works which by their depth, insight and suggestiveness have been the joy and comfort of so many."[12] His blindness was, at the very least, a contributing factor in the growth and maturation of his spiritual insight into Scripture. The darkness in which he lived much of his life not only shielded his attention from superficial distraction but it opened the way into a mystical appreciation of reality. Matheson's preaching and academic and spiritual writing were shaped by his immediate sense of the Sacred.[13]

University

In 1857, after four years at the Academy, aged seventeen, Matheson matriculated at Glasgow University.[14] Had he not been blind, Matheson's hope had been to go to the Bar. Macmillan suggests he would have been a "distinguished advocate" with his "natural ability, mental alertness, and the gift of speech."[15] However, it was to the High Street campus that Matheson went and in 1861 he graduated B.A. with Honorable Distinction in Philosophy and M.A. in 1862.

With ever-poorer eyesight, Matheson was increasingly dependent on others to read to him. His eldest sister, Jane Gray, became his lifelong companion and aid. They grew increasingly close and throughout his studies and later in his congregational and parochial work, she was always with him, sharing his burdens and guiding him through the "quicksand and pitfalls" of life in a parish church.[16] Described as a "gentle and gifted lady," it is

11. MacMillan, *Life of George Matheson*, 12.

12. MacMillan, *Life of George Matheson*, 12.

13. MacMillan, *Life of George Matheson*, 12.

14. Macmillan states that Matheson first matriculated at the age of fifteen, but this is because he has the wrong birth date.

15. Macmillan, *The Life of George Matheson*, 23.

16. MacMillan, *Life of George Matheson*, 21.

important in acknowledging the achievements of Matheson that Jane Gray smoothed his path by attending to so many of the practical tasks required each day. [17] She freed him from the daily duties that would otherwise have exhausted him and denied him the time and energy for study.

Jane Gray is described by Macmillan as Matheson's "alter ego."[18] In Matheson's scrapbook, which dates from 1868, written on the very first page, there was a sonnet by Richard Chenevix Trench (1807–1886), the Archbishop of Dublin, entitled "Brother and Sister." In the poem, we read of the tender love brother and sister have for each other and the extent to which their hearts are bound together. The poet expresses the fear that, in time, one will die and the other will be left alone. However, the poem ends with God taking both brother and sister at the same time and, says Macmillan, that was the wish of Matheson and Jane Gray.

After graduating with Honours in Philosophy in 1862, Matheson entered the Divinity Hall. At the Graduation Ceremony for his M.A., when Matheson was handed his scroll, the Principal remarked, "We are all proud of you, George."[19] He started the same year as the new Professor of Divinity, John Caird, who would go on to become principal of the university. Together with his brother, Edward, who was Professor of Moral Philosophy, the Cairds brought the spirit of Hegel to Glasgow University and, in particular, to those training for the ministry in the Church of Scotland. One student remembered Caird for his eloquence and the centrality of Christ in his thought. He wrote of Christ being "burned into the minds of the students with a power which they can never forget."[20] Matheson listened to Caird with "rapt attention . . . drinking it in with avidity, and silently assimilating it."[21] Matheson's fellow students believed Matheson to be the Caird of the next generation.[22] On Caird's death in 1898, it was said, "Caird is dead, but Matheson is still with us."[23]

17. MacMillan, *Life of George Matheson*, 80.

18. MacMillan, *Life of George Matheson*, 21.

19. Tyler, *The Blind Seer*, 3.

20. Macmillan., *Life of George Matheson*, 48.

21. MacMillan, *Life of George Matheson*, 49.

22. MacMillan, *Life of George Matheson*, 51.

23. Tyler, *The Blind Seer*, 6. Tyler draws on material not included in Macmillan's biography. In particular, he is grateful to R. S. Calderwood, Marshall Lang and T W McAndrew, all of whom knew Matheson well. Lang had served as an assistant with Matheson, while Calderwood and McAndrew were his private secretaries and lived in the manse with him.

Assistant Minister

Matheson was licensed by the Presbytery of Glasgow on 13 June, 1866. During this first summer after university, Matheson spent his time studying "the great masterpieces of English literature."[24] Every sermon he ever preached, from the very first one as an assistant to his last at St Bernard's Parish in Edinburgh, Matheson recorded in large notebooks, each book and sermon carefully numbered with details of where and when it was preached. Each sermon ends with a summary of its contents. From the outset, Matheson was determined to be an outstanding preacher. Either in honesty or with a hint of hagiography, Macmillan says that "No man that attained to [Matheson's] supreme position ever provoked so few jealousies."[25]

Matheson was surrounded and influenced by distinguished preachers, each one bequeathing different qualities or gifts to him and each one noted for their thought, eloquence and spiritual life. Macmillan, who had been an assistant to Matheson, suggests that Matheson was "the representative of all their special qualities:" John Caird for his "speculative genius," Norman Macleod his "humanitarianism," William Pulsford his "mysticism," Arthur Hamilton Charteris[26] his "fervor" and John Ross MacDuff his "poetry." Matheson readily acknowledged that he owed his spiritual awakening to the mystic Pulsford. Of Pulsford, Matheson wrote: "The man of all others that shaped my personality was Pulsford. I met him only once, but I never heard a man who so inspired me; He set me on fire, and, under God, he was my spiritual creator."[27] Pulsford was minister at Trinity Church, which was situated very near to the Matheson family home in St Vincent's Crescent. Pulsford was not a popular preacher and he made no attempt to attract larger numbers. Macmillan recalls that Pulsford was a "true son of consolation; he was surrounded by a spiritual atmosphere which gave comfort and imparted peace to the afflicted."[28] Pulsford was the catalyst for Matheson's sense of the mystical. Pulsford was a friend to John Caird and greatly admired by him.

Macduff is described as a "sweet preacher, an exponent of the devout life [who possessed] a gentle radiance."[29] He wrote many books, some of

24. Macmillan, *Life of George Matheson*, 70.

25. MacMillan, *Life of George Matheson*, 73.

26. Charteris was a minister in the Church of Scotland, Professor of Biblical Criticism at the University of Edinburgh and is credited with the formation of The Women's Guild.

27. MacMillan, *Life of George Matheson*, 75.

28. MacMillan, *Life of George Matheson*, 76.

29. MacMillan, *Life of George Matheson*, 76.

which sold over three million copies.[30] As minister of Sandyford Church, Macduff had been Matheson's minister in his earliest years. Matheson knew the congregation well and was known by them. On leaving university, Matheson was asked by Macduff to become his assistant at Sandyford Church, which he was reluctant to do. However, he was appointed to the post on 8 January 1867. Matheson's preaching was noted for its empathy with the human condition. He sought to discover and illumine the presence of God in the commonplace and, in particular, in the suffering and personal trials faced by members of the congregation; his preaching had a definite pastoral emphasis to it. Macduff's daughter said that Matheson's appeal lay in his "individuality and originality of thought," which he brought to bear on his theme.

Matheson acknowledged Pulsford as his "spiritual creator" but MacDuff he considered "a father."[31] MacDuff, he said, gave him his sense of literary beauty, impressed him with his oratory, introduced him to the idea of sanctity and inspired him with the beauty of Christianity. Matheson wrote: "The tones of his voice are even now unconsciously reproduced in my own. I have retained more of his pulpit influence than that of any other teacher."[32]

Innellan

Matheson was ordained at Innellan, a Chapel of Ease in the Parish of Dunoon, on 8 April, 1868. Not surprisingly, there was considerable opposition to the appointment of a blind minister. While he was acknowledged as the best preacher of the possible candidates, there was concern that he would be unable to fulfill his pastoral duties adequately. It seems that he succeeded in being chosen because he and his family were already known within the Innellan community. They had holidayed there many times and knew many of the villagers. Years earlier, Matheson had expressed the wish to be the minister in the village.

The church in Innellan was built fifteen years before Matheson's appointment. It was opened in the autumn of 1853. Although not large, it was sufficient to hold the numbers attending worship regularly. Innellan sits on the shores of the River Clyde with the hills of Cowal to the east and the Irish Channel to the west. In the fifteen years before Matheson, Innellan had had

---

30. Macduff's books include *Memories of Bethany*, *Grapes of Eshcol*, *Memories of Olivet*, *Morning & Night Watches* and *Palms of Elim*.

31. MacMillan, *Life of George Matheson*, 80.

32. MacMillan, *Life of George Matheson*, 81.

four previous ministers. His predecessors were Robert Horn, Martin Peter Ferguson, William Porteous[33] and James Donald.

On the evening of his induction, Matheson skillfully paid tribute to his predecessors—their "indelible footprints"—and, in particular, Porteous.[34] He spoke of looking back and looking forward and said that, in the Church and in preaching, there was an urgent need for "intellectual enlightenment" and for the rediscovery of reason. He spoke of his understanding of the ministry of Word and Sacrament within the ministry of the Church:

> The preacher of our day must be a man not only of universal knowledge, but, to some extent, of universal nature too. In him must be blended something of the lives of all men. There must be the depths of the philosopher's thought, with the simplicity of the child's expression . . . There must be argument for the doubting and confirmation for the trustful, encouragement for the fearing and approbation for the brave, gentleness for the erring and sympathy with the strong, and boundless, deathless charity for all.[35]

While the sentiment of the address has an idealistic tone to it, he believed that the Christian faith had the resources to meet the needs of every age and understood ministry to mean entering the "noblest academy . . . the university of souls."[36] He was introduced or "preached in" to his charge by MacDuff, who commended Matheson to the people of Innellan for his "inner sunshine" and, above all, for his spiritual radiance and piety.[37]

During the winter months, the population of Innellan was just a few hundred. For eight months of the year, there was only one weekly service. However, for the remaining four months, there was a morning and evening diet of public worship.[38] With the increased means of transport by train and steamboat, Innellan became a popular summer resort for city

33. MacMillan, *Life of George Matheson*, 94. Porteous was a young minister appointed in 1862. He was accused of plagiarism by the minister of Govan, Matthew Leishman (of the Middle Party of 1843). Leishman pursued Porteous through the courts of the Church. After three years of dispute, Porteous was cleared of the charge but it was a pyrrhic victory: he died in 1865 the day before he was due to be inducted into his new charge, the Parish of Bellahouston.

34. MacMillan, *Life of George Matheson*, 97.

35. MacMillan, *Life of George Matheson*, 97–98.

36. MacMillan, *Life of George Matheson*, 98.

37. MacMillan, *Life of George Matheson*, 101.

38. Tyler, *The Blind Seer*, 7. Tyler notes that during the winter months attendances were around 40—50 worshippers, while in the summer months numbers soared to around 300.

merchants and their families.[39] Matheson's sermon preparation began on the Sunday afternoon once he returned home from worship in the morning. He selected his text and reflected on it over the next couple of days. By the middle of the week, he dictated his thoughts to his secretary and by Saturday morning the sermon was ready to be preached. So as not ever to be found unprepared, even on holiday he worked on his sermon in the same manner. In the summer months, his evening congregation was largely made up of visitors and so he preached sermons that he had prepared and used in the winter months at the morning diet.

The introduction of an evening service was necessary because of Matheson's increasing popularity. He very soon became a household name in Scotland and beyond, known as "Matheson of Innellan." Families would return to the Argyll village year after year in the hope that they would hear him preach. In periodicals of the day, a writer spoke of the "moral wrong" that Matheson should be in some remote village, instead of Glasgow, Edinburgh or London.[40] Another writer compared Matheson more than favorably to Guthrie, Caird, Macleod and Tulloch, saying that Matheson excelled all of them in "originality of conception, and forcible, quaint expression."[41] Within two or three years of Matheson's arrival, plans were put in place to build a manse and lift the charge into parish status.[42] £3000 was raised and by the end of 1873 Innellan had become a parish in its own right. In the following year, a spire was completed, a bell was presented and, by the time Matheson was ready to leave to go to Edinburgh, further plans were in place to extend the church.

During the summer months, many students made a pilgrimage to Innellan. Inspired in the lecture hall by the Idealist philosopher Edward Caird, they came to hear Matheson out of term time. Comparing Caird and Matheson favorably, Macmillan said:

> We cannot forget those Sundays at Innellan when, with the teaching of one of the deepest thinkers that then filled a university chair fresh in our mind, we attended worship in that little country church and listened with rapt admiration to sermons which were as profound, suggestive and stimulating as the lectures of the renown professor. We felt that Matheson

39. See Macmillan, *Times of Retirement*, 20.

40. MacMillan, *Life of George Matheson*, 111.

41. MacMillan, *Life of George Matheson*, 111.

42. Matheson first lived at Labrador House, Innellan before occupying the new manse.

discovered by the flash of genius what Edward Caird found by a long process of thought.[43]

Writing at the beginning of the twentieth century, Macmillan said, "To be a Mathesonian is a growing characteristic of many of our rising pulpit orators."[44]

Spiritual or Personal Crisis

A year or two into his ministry his faith was shaken to its core and he declared himself an "absolute atheist."[45] Matheson tendered his resignation to the Presbytery. Fortunately, the request to demit was handled by the Revd Dr Cameron of Dunoon who, it seems, did not raise the matter with the Presbytery. There is no record of the Presbytery dealing with such a matter. Matheson was told that he was a young man and that he would change. He did change and his route back into faith was the philosophy of Hegel, which he had heard years earlier articulated eloquently by his professor, John Caird. Matheson said he returned to preach "all the old doctrines and . . . old forms, but with deeper meaning."[46] As is common in the spiritual life, those who suffer such a crisis or similar often emerge into a more profound, deeper spirituality. It is worth noting that Matheson not only mentioned God in his statement of unbelief, but immortality. Throughout his ministry and in his writing, immortality was to be a pivotal and significant theme. Matheson meant immortality of the soul, not resurrection (traditionally understood).

With fresh eyes, Matheson stressed the centrality of Christ. In a sermon preached in 1878, he said he believed in a broad Church founded on Christ and in the "all-transcending truth of the Gospel." The Gospel, he said, "throws its light upon everything . . . It will reveal stars in many a night that appeared without a ray."[47] The presence of God perceived in and through suffering is another pivotal and significant Mathesonian theme. From the depths of his spiritual breakdown, he said: "If you have reached the foundation, you have come to that charity which believeth all things, and hopeth all things, and endureth all things; for you have entered into union with the source of infinite love, and you have looked upon the world

43. See Macmillan, *Times of Retirement*, 22.
44. See MacMillan, *Times of Retirement*, 33.
45. Macmillan, *Life of George Matheson*, 121.
46. MacMillan, *Life of George Matheson*, 124.
47. MacMillan, *Life of George Matheson*, 127.

with His light. Thine is the boundless compassion, and the worldwide sympathy, and the endless hope."[48]

Union with the source of infinite love is a characteristic of the mystical life, and to spiritually journey in this way following a life crisis is not unusual. Matheson concluded saying that the whole universe, the whole of creation, will be included in God's redemptive love. Matheson spoke of union, wholeness and the embrace of all things in the love of God. Born out of a crisis, Matheson's newfound spirituality followed a well-established pattern and he was now possessed of an intimacy and immediacy of the Spirit which he did not have before. The redemptive love of God was, for him, all-consuming: he said, "Calvary is older than Eden."[49] Following the idealism and preaching of Caird, he said: "All things shine by passing into the life of others: the seed into the flower, the sun into nature, the sea into the reflection of the light. Each stage of human life expands by sacrifice of self-will . . . When the will is surrendered the work is practically done."[50] Taken together, the sacrifice of self-will alongside the presence of God in suffering are hallmarks of Matheson's theology. Similarly to Caird, Matheson saw the foreshadowing of Christian truths in other world religions. Matheson was "the great reconciler of his age."[51] Matheson's crisis of faith was a vital moment for much of what was to follow and almost certainly led to a significant deepening and maturing of this faith.

Crathie

In October 1885, Matheson attended the Queen at Balmoral Castle. Matheson's book on religion and science was given to the Poet Laureate, Lord Tennyson, and to the Queen by the Bishop of Ripon. Tennyson and his wife were admirers of Matheson's work, not least for his command of the English language. In private correspondence afterwards, Matheson wrote to his friend Stevenson, telling him of the Queen's immense delight at his preaching and prayers. His text had been from James 2 entitled "The Patience of Job." The theme of the sermon was the spirit of endurance through all suffering and trial without asking "Why?" While alone with the Queen, she said to him, "Your life has been a sorely tried but a very beautiful one."[52]

48. MacMillan, *Life of George Matheson*, 127.
49. MacMillan, *Life of George Matheson*, 128.
50. MacMillan, *Life of George Matheson*, 128.
51. MacMillan, *Life of George Matheson*, 129.
52. See Macmillan, *Times of Retirement*, 19.

St Bernard's, Edinburgh

As a son of Glasgow, Matheson felt "thoroughly at home" among the people of the West of Scotland. However, within three years of celebrating his fifteenth anniversary at Innellan, Matheson accepted a call to St Bernard's Parish Church, Edinburgh. Despite his reputation as a preacher, theologian and poet, it seems that many congregations were reluctant to approach Matheson during his years at Innellan. Due to his blindness, many wondered if he would be able to perform his pastoral duties adequately if the prospective charge was larger than Innellan.[53] Macmillan bemoaned the fact that the Church of Scotland had no place for a preacher within its Presbyterian structure whereas, had Matheson been a priest in the Church of England, he would have "found his proper sphere long before," perhaps as a Canon of St Paul's Cathedral.[54]

Jane Gray went on to be a source of strength to Matheson in his new ministry. She took a leading part in the social life of the congregation and "her tactful and gentle manner smoothed over every difficulty."[55] One of his younger sisters, Ellen, known affectionately as "Miss Maggie," occasionally offered respite to her older sister now that she and her brother George had moved to Edinburgh. There is no doubt that the care and personal commitment to their brother made Matheson's life a happy one. In addition to his sisters, Matheson employed private secretaries over the years. William Smith served as Matheson's private secretary for ten of his thirteen years at St Bernard's, after which Matheson, from his own funds, employed an assistant minister to help with parish duties. He was revered and respected by his secretaries.[56]

At the age of 46 years, Matheson was inducted into his new charge on 12 May, 1886. His ministry lasted thirteen years.[57] Macmillan describes it as "One of the richest and most brilliant ministries of which the Church of Scotland bears record."[58] It did not take long before St Bernard's was "full

53. That said, in 1880, Matheson received a unanimous Call from Crown Court, London, to succeed the Rev Dr John Comming. Matheson declined because the managers would not permit him to "exchange freely with the other Presbyterian and Non-Conforming ministers in London." Tyler, *Blind Seer*, 12.

54. Macmillan, *Life of George Matheson*, 222.

55. MacMillan, *Life of George Matheson*, 289.

56. MacMillan, *Life of George Matheson*, 290.

57. MacMillan, *Life of George Matheson*, 287. For most of that time, Matheson lived in his own home at 19 St Bernard's Crescent. The Crescent was build on the estate of the painter, Sir Henry Raeburn and, over time, the neighbourhood boasted such names as Sir James Simpson, Sir John Watson Gordon, Robert Chambers and Thomas Carlyle.

58. MacMillan, *Life of George Matheson*, 228.

to overflowing."[59] The congregation was socially mixed: it was comprised of clergymen, advocates, academics, scientists as well as manual workers. Many of those who attended worship at St Bernard's were "eager seekers after truth—among them not a few whose faith was distressed, and who found in his sermons the message for which their souls had been waiting."[60] Matheson's eloquence, spiritual depth, boldness of Scriptural interpretation and humor were all contributing factors to his popularity in the pulpit. "His daily reading and profound study of the Bible"[61] shone through.

One minister who, as a former student attended St Bernard's, spoke of being "caught up into the seventh heaven" by Matheson's preaching.[62] The Rev Sydney Smith of Keith said that Matheson would acknowledge traditional exegesis before moving on to his own more speculative and imaginative insight. Matheson used "bold metaphors" and "illustrations drawn from present-day fiction."[63] He drew also from art, science and history.[64] Another worshipper, the Rev T R Barnett, said that Matheson would draw into his prayers and preaching the weather of that day: the glorious sunshine to illustrate God's eternal Light and a day of cloud to reflect all that is dark in human experience.[65] Along with others, Barnett said that Matheson's first prayer was "often the finest part of the service."[66] Of the first prayer, Barnett wrote: "A lifting up of the heart and upraising of the Spirit, a reaching out after God, an outpouring of the soul, like the rapturous song of the lark, mounting higher and higher into the blue, to find in the limitless skies the satisfaction of its whole nature. I confess that it was the first prayer that often lifted us up into the *mystic presence* more than any other part of the service."[67] It was Matheson's rich inner life which enabled him to elevate his listeners to the Divine. Matheson, Barnett said, was reaching out and up into his own illumined darkness, as if trying to catch something of the mystery of God and draw it down to man.[68] Barnett is not slow to criticize Matheson: he said that the congregation would smile at the preacher's humor rather than laugh and his interpretation of Scripture was, at times,

---

59. MacMillan, *Life of George Matheson*, 230.
60. See Macmillan, *Times of Retirement*, 26.
61. Macmillan, *Life of George Matheson*, 229.
62. MacMillan, *Life of George Matheson*, 232.
63. MacMillan, *Life of George Matheson*, 233.
64. MacMillan, *Life of George Matheson*, 241.
65. MacMillan, *Life of George Matheson*, 235.
66. MacMillan, *Life of George Matheson*, 235.
67. MacMillan, *Life of George Matheson*, 235.
68. MacMillan, *Life of George Matheson*, 235–236.

"wayward,"[69] but he wrote also of Matheson drawing tears from the eyes of the congregation by his prayers and of Matheson's "divine imagination" which "revealed the beauties of many a hidden truth." Matheson "infected us all with a sense of God's very self."[70]

According to Barnett, Matheson's broad preaching theme throughout was threefold: reconciliation, the perfecting of humanity through suffering and the harmony between faith and reason. By reconciliation, Matheson saw the mercy of God in all things: "pain and joy, sorrow and mirth, light and gloom."[71] He encouraged his hearers to learn the patience of faith and to believe in "the Great End of God."[72] By the perfection of humanity through suffering, Matheson understood that God "meant us to overcome the pains of life, not by avoiding them, but by taking them to our hearts and passing them through our souls." Pain was not to be seen as an enemy but rather as a friend in disguise. "Man was made by God to become perfect through sufferings, not to be made perfectly free from sufferings."[73] There is in this approach a sense of the unity of all things and all things being in God. To the mystic, even the darkness is a blessing, for it is in those experiences that God is closest to us. By faith and reason, Matheson sought to show that they were "twin sisters"[74] and not in opposition to each other. Faith, he said, transcended reason but they went hand in hand.

An American visitor, the Rev Charles Parkhurst, like many others, testified to the depth, spirituality and effect of Matheson's first prayer. He wrote, "Though his visual sight is entirely eclipsed he does 'see God' and he does see into the souls of his hearers . . . In that [first] prayer we have been to the mount of worship, and we could go away content even if we heard no more."[75] These sentiments are echoed by Norman MacLean.[76] On one Sunday in November 1889, MacLean attended public worship at St Bernard's. Writing almost sixty years later, he said of his experience: it was "as if a door were suddenly opened into the Infinite."[77] It was the first prayer and, in the sermon, the humane rendering of the doctrine of atonement that stood out.

69. MacMillan, *Life of George Matheson*, 237.

70. MacMillan, *Life of George Matheson*, 236.

71. MacMillan, *Life of George Matheson*, 236.

72. MacMillan, *Life of George Matheson*, 236.

73. MacMillan, *Life of George Matheson*, 236.

74. MacMillan, *Life of George Matheson*, 237.

75. MacMillan, *Life of George Matheson*, 240.

76. Norman MacLean (1869-1952) was minister at St Cuthbert's Parish Church, Edinburgh and Moderator of the General Assembly of the Church of Scotland in 1927.

77. MacLean, *Set Free*, 108.

Of the first prayer, MacLean wrote: "What struck me first was his prayer. 'Bow Thy heavens also and come down,' he prayed, and his right hand rose stretched straight to heaven and was withdrawn again quickly. This was repeated through the prayer. It was as if he were laying hold on the Infinite and bringing Him down from the highest heaven to the lowest earth."[78]

As if from within his own soul, Matheson reached up to the Divine. The prayer was nothing less than a poem delivered in Matheson's "pleading musical voice."[79] MacLean cites the prayer:

> Let Thy beauty be upon us as we trust in Thee. Help us to wear it everywhere. Where Thou goest may we also go. May we go with Thee to the marriage feast without being soiled; may we enter the house of mourning without despair. In the power of Thy Divine beauty may we be able to see beauty in all things, in the crowded streets and in the solitary fields until at last we are brought to the land that is afar off and see the King in His beauty.[80]

Maclean concludes, "On the wings of inspiration we were lifted and soared as to the very gates of heaven."[81]

In his sermon that day, Matheson reflected on the doctrine of atonement. MacLean said that Matheson was a "unique preacher who, far back in his career, had buried the dry bones of Calvinism."[82] For Matheson, atonement meant that humanity could be "at one with God, thinking the same thoughts, loving the same things and working for the one end."[83] This sense of mystical union could only be achieved when humanity "willed what God willed;" we see this supremely in Jesus' sacrifice in the Garden of Gethsemane.[84] This day in Maclean's life was so memorable because he said that it was "the beginning of my deliverance from a theology that had ceased to satisfy the questing mind."[85] Repulsed by Calvinist theology, the representation of God the Father "pouring out punishment for all the sins of humanity on His Son . . . was [for MacLean] a travesty of justice . . . For how could justice be appeased by transferring its judgement to the

---

78. MacLean, *Set Free*, 108–9.

79. MacLean, *Set Free*, 109.

80. MacLean, *Set Free*, 109.

81. MacLean, *Set Free*, 109.

82. MacLean, *Set Free*, 108.

83. MacLean, *Set Free*, 109.

84. MacLean, *Set Free*, 109.

85. MacLean, *Set Free*, 110.

innocent? And the God who was thus presented to men was devoid not only of justice but of love."[86]

The service closed with a hymn written by Horatius Bonar of the Free Church, a sign in itself of Matheson's refusal to fuel the fire of sectarian turmoil.

Matheson's daily routine was governed strictly by time; he had a clearly defined timetable to which, on the whole, he adhered. This may have been necessary due to his blindness. If he suffered from irritation at all, it was when his schedule was interrupted by an unexpected visitor or there was a delay forced upon him. In what can only be an overstatement of the case, Matheson once remarked that interruptions were "the only clouds that even temporarily darkened his life."[87] Matheson took breakfast at 9am during which he had his correspondence and the newspapers read to him. Unless a letter required a theological response, his correspondence was handled by his secretary; he liked the replies to be sent by return of post and he did not settle until his secretary assured him that he had done so.[88] From the daily newspapers, Matheson particularly liked notices of interesting literature as well as news from politics, conflicts and wars, and criminal trials. He also "drank in" articles on matters of mechanism, such as turbines or motors, trains or steamships.[89] From correspondence and the newspapers, Matheson turned to his studies of French and German followed by theology, philosophy, science, history and literature. From his morning reading, he dictated articles for the Press and worked on his compositions. In the afternoon, he read fiction.[90]

Matheson's popularity was considerable. He received many more requests to preach at special events than he was able to accept. In fact, he declined most of them, not least because he had to satisfy the demands of his own congregation. The invitations came from across the United Kingdom and bookings usually had to be made two years in advance. During his first year at St Bernard's, Matheson delivered the inaugural addresses to the theological students at New College in the University of Edinburgh,

86. MacLean, *Set Free*, 110.

87. MacMillan, *Life of George Matheson*, 298.

88. MacMillan, *Life of George Matheson*, 292.

89. MacMillan, *Life of George Matheson*, 292.

90. His reading included the works of George Meredith, Elizabeth Braddon, Hall Caine, W E Norris, Thomas Hardy, George Eliot, J M Barrie, Anthony Hope, Humphrey Ward, Henry Seton Merriman (Hugh Stowell Scott), E F Benson and, from the United States, Gertrude Atherton, Mary Wilkins and James Lane Allen. Smith says of the 'school farther back', Matheson read the works of Thackeray, Dickens, Trollope and Kingsley. He did not care very much for Scott or Lytton.

the United Presbyterian Hall, the Free Church College in Glasgow and at the University of Aberdeen.

Retirement

Freed from the burden of preaching every week, Matheson was able to concentrate more of his attention on his writing. His first book in retirement was *Studies of the Portrait of Christ*. For Macmillan, this marked the final stage in Matheson's theological development and became the most popular of all his books.[91] The book, which is a substantial work, was produced in two volumes (published in 1899 and 1900). Volume One sold over 11,000 copies in the first year. In the summer of 1901, Matheson was the guest preacher in the University Chapel of Aberdeen and in December that year he delivered the Murtle Lectures. He was again praised for his opening prayer during his conduct of worship at the Chapel services.[92] The Murtle lectures comprise five or six lectures delivered in the Mitchell Hall, Marischal College. In previous years, the lectures had been given by former moderators of the General Assembly of the Church of Scotland, the Bishops of Salisbury and Stepney, Canons Scott Holland and Hensley Henson, Professor Margoliouth of Oxford and Principal Rainy, among others. Matheson was offered the Gifford Lectureship by the Senatus at Aberdeen but he declined on medical grounds. In 1902, the University of Aberdeen conferred on him the honorary degree of D.D. Macmillan says that Matheson already had the material prepared which he would have used in the Gifford Lectures; he said that he had prepared a volume on natural religion for publication but that it never saw the light of day. Matheson was already a Fellow of the Royal Society of Edinburgh (1890).

During his time at St Bernard's, Matheson enjoyed two full months holiday each year, in the months of August and September. In later years, he holidayed at North Berwick and made a good friend in Hately Waddell, the former minister of Whitekirk in East Lothian. Waddell wrote of Matheson's overwhelming sense of the immanence of the Divine (that God was in all things): that, through many conversations, he felt that Matheson's faith was more than a philosophy; it was a "spiritual conviction, learned direct from Christ."[93]

91. MacMillan, *Life of George Matheson*, 327.
92. MacMillan, *Life of George Matheson*, 336.
93. MacMillan, *Life of George Matheson*, 352.

Death

By June 1906, Matheson's appearance had noticeably changed and, Macmillan observed, that "It seemed to me that the hand of Death was upon him."[94] His secretary, William Smith, had seen a deterioration in Matheson over the previous two years or so. Matheson's final preaching engagement was in Morningside Church, Edinburgh on 14 February, 1904.[95] Three weeks before his death, he remarked to Smith that he was a "poor creature" and that "I don't think you will have me long."[96] Matheson died at Avenell House, North Berwick, in the early hours of Tuesday 28 August, 1906.

Between 8pm and 9pm in the evening, Smith had been reading to him from the Napoleonic Volume of the Cambridge Modern History and then a little light reading from one of the novels of W E Norris. Finally, he asked for his Braille so that he could work for a short time on his forthcoming book, *Representative Women of the Bible* (published posthumously). He was in good spirits when he retired to bed at 11.15pm. At 1.30am, his sister, Jane Gray, heard a "slight groan" and together with another sister, Nellie, hurried downstairs into his room. He was lying on his bed smiling but unable to speak. He knew that they were there. Once summoned, the doctor told the sisters not to disturb him and that he thought that he would recover. Sometime later, Jane Gray went into Matheson's room: he lay there, she said, with a "radiant glow" that no photograph could capture.[97] Matheson died peacefully shortly afterwards.

In newspapers through Scotland, England, the British Empire and America, notices appeared of Matheson's death. At Sunday worship, reference was made in almost every church in Scotland and, not surprisingly, congregations sang his great hymn, "O Love that wilt not let me go." Special resolutions of sympathy were minuted by the Presbyteries of Edinburgh and Glasgow and by the Royal Society of Edinburgh. His sister received correspondence from across the world, not least from many people similarly afflicted by blindness and for whom Matheson had been an inspiration. On Saturday 1 September, a short service was conducted by the Rev James Robert Burt, the parish minister of North Berwick, and Scripture was read by the Rev Alexander Fiddes of St Bernard's (who succeeded J J Drummond) at Matheson's new address at 14 Belgrave Crescent, Edinburgh, a home he

94. MacMillan, *Life of George Matheson*, 354.

95. Tyler, *The Blind Seer*, 16. The Minister of Morningside Church remarked on Matheson's reputation as a preacher well-known for his "spiritual meditations of a high excellence."

96. Macmillan, *Life of George Matheson*, 356.

97. MacMillan, *Life of George Matheson*, 359.

never occupied. Thereafter, his body was taken to the Glasgow Necropolis to be placed in the family vault. It was a gloriously sunny day and a large crowd gathered to pay their respects. The Free Church minister, W Robertson Nicoll, expressed one of the most eloquent tributes: "George Matheson, we verily believe, was potentially the greatest man given to the Scottish Churches since the days of Dr Chalmers. He was a great orator, a powerful thinker, a man born with the instinct of scholarship, a master of expression, overflowing with love and vehement ardour, and dauntless courage . . . He did great things, but greatest of all was the living of his life."[98]

98. Tyler, *The Blind Seer*, 19–20.

2

Crisis of Faith and Recovery

Introduction

IN THIS CHAPTER I shall discuss Matheson's 'crisis of faith' and his intellectual and spiritual recovery. As a writer, at least at this early stage in his career, he was derivative, synthesizing from a very broad range of theological and other material. I shall discuss the cultural and religious context of the mid-nineteenth century and the factors which may have come to bear on Matheson's faith which, for a time, he lost completely. I shall discuss his recovery of faith and, in particular, his dependence upon his university teacher, the Idealist John Caird, and the Hegelian method. By the beginning of the twentieth century, Idealism had fallen out of favour but, in the time of Caird and Matheson, its presence was strongly felt, not least in Glasgow. Finally, I shall briefly discuss two of Matheson's early publications, both of which indicate his sympathy for the inner life, for religion of the heart.

'Crisis of Faith': Historical Context

In 1869 or 1870, in the first or second year of his ministry at Innellan, Matheson suffered "a temporary unhinging, a threatened collapse, of his religious beliefs."[1] His crisis of faith does not appear to have been triggered by any single event; rather, as a man of considerable intellect living at this time in Victorian Britain, it is perhaps no surprise that he subjected his traditional, childhood faith to rigorous scrutiny. In its early months, that scrutiny appears to have precipitated the collapse of his faith. As an ordained minister, responsible to a congregation for the nourishing of faith, it is possible that, in the turbulent if not hostile, religious climate of the time, that he did not believe what was required of him. Looking back on this

1. MacMillan, *Life of George Matheson*, 120.

period, Matheson described himself as an atheist.[2] He wrote: "At one time, with a great thrill of horror, I found myself an absolute atheist. After being ordained at Innellan, I believed nothing; neither God nor immortality. I tendered my resignation to the Presbytery."[3]

The nineteenth century has been described as "the evangelical century" and "the golden age of church attendance."[4] Many Victorians attended public worship each Sunday, though for some that may have been "more a matter of custom than a matter of deep faith."[5] Religion permeated the air: it was "both manifestly public and intensely private."[6] There was a strong, if not universal belief, that "religion and religious institutions were good for the individual, and good for society."[7] The sales of devotional books providing Scripture readings and daily meditations "indicated that Victorians set aside time for private devotions."[8] Matheson's own devotional books were part of this buoyant market. In a further instance, William Holman Hunt's painting "The Light of the World" was "the most familiar image of Christ in the Victorian era: it became a part of people's daily lives."[9] While many bemoaned the "irreligious nature of the working classes" for "not attending Sunday Services on their one day of freedom from the drudgery of daily work," a substantial number of Victorians observed the commandment to "keep the Sabbath holy."[10] If not Sabbatarians, many Victorians spent their Sunday by attending morning worship, followed by a family walk in the afternoon, a time for private reading of religious literature and, to close the day, attending another service in the evening.[11]

The nineteenth century was a time of great change, in which the world of work, industrial production and "leisure, play and consumption"[12] were revolutionized. From 1855 onwards, daily newspapers came within the "economic grasp of the lower middle classes for the first time,"[13] while from 1843 the first Sunday newspaper, the *News of the World*, with its

---

2. MacMillan, *Life of George Matheson*, 121.

3. MacMillan, *Life of George Matheson*, 121.

4. Larson, *Crisis of Doubt*, 1.

5. Melnyk, *Victorian Religion*, 64.

6. Melnyk, *Victorian Religion*, 64.

7. Cox, "Worlds of Victorian Religion," 435.

8. Melnyk, *Victorian Religion*, 79.

9. Melnyk, *Victorian Religion*, 65.

10. Melnyk, *Victorian Religion*, 77.

11. Melnyk, *Victorian Religion*, 77.

12. Bailey, "Leisure: Merrie to Modern," 619.

13. Law, "Periodicalism," 538.

fondness for crime and scandal became a staple of the working-class diet.[14] Throughout the country, with the help of local government and philanthropists, "art galleries, museums, libraries and concert halls" appeared in ever-increasing numbers: Glasgow listed its "commercial entertainments . . . among its foremost attractions."[15] With the professionalization of football, "Saturday afternoon at the match became a sacrosanct secular ritual for working-class males."[16] While journalist, W T Stead, denounced music halls as "drivel for the dregs" and philosopher, Herbert Spencer, called football "the rebarbarization of society,"[17] urbanization, the shifting patterns of work, extensive poverty in the city slums, and the whole world of leisure, increasingly led people towards democratization, greater franchise and into a different world from that in which they grew up and in which their parents had lived. The rapid rate of change made it difficult for institutions to keep pace with changing social attitudes and lifestyle, not least the churches. Big towns struggled to provide drainage, sanitation, housing and parks for the rising number of city dwellers.

Together with other forms of mass entertainment and education, the advent of the zoo attracted tens of thousands of visitors each year. To an extent never before encountered, at a metaphysical level, people viewed the apes' fingers and hands, their attentive expressions . . . their fussy attention to their young offspring and saw that they were not as "alien as one could wish."[18] In light of such changes, it is remarkable that the churches fared so well, not least because of their dogged intransigence in a more literal interpretation of Scripture and a theology which, in many ways, was no longer credible when stacked up against scientific inquiry. The educated younger generation, particularly from the 1860s and 1870s onwards, preferred to "find faith for themselves, and [were] no longer [prepared] to inherit serenely the faith of their parents."[19] The young thought of the church and world of religion as "somber" or "narrow."[20] In contrast to the feeling of change pervading society, its progress and liberalization, "all forms of orthodoxy were associated with an austere view of self-restraint."[21] Matheson was a young man during this period; this was his generation. While "most

---

14. Bailey, "Leisure: Merrie to modern," 626.
15. Bailey, "Leisure: Merrie to modern," 626.
16. Bailey, "Leisure: Merrie to modern," 629.
17. Bailey, "Leisure: Merrie to modern," 631.
18. Wilson, *The Victorians*, 94.
19. Chadwick, *Victorian Church Part II*, 112.
20. Chadwick, *Victorian Church Part II*, 118.
21. Chadwick, *Victorian Church Part II*, 119.

preachers continued to assume that a real fish swallowed Jonah,"[22] in his book, *History of the Rise and Influence of the Spirit of Rationalism in Europe* (1865), Lecky argued that reason was slowly conquering superstition in society: "victorious over magic and witchcraft and religious persecution, promoting tolerance and causing dogma to decline."[23] Such was the temperature around 1870 that Bendyshe, a Fellow of King's College, Cambridge, was described as "a raging and devoted atheist at whose talk God trembles on his tottering throne."[24] The poet Swinburne felt "Christianity to be a fetter upon human life."[25] It would have been almost impossible for Matheson, as a man open to intellectual inquiry, to have been immune to the influences at work on his generation.

Wilson suggests that, throughout the nineteenth century, the loss of faith in Christianity can be attributed to the loss of belief in Jesus as Son of God, that is, with each passing decade, from both academic and popular writers, more and more people entertained the possibility that Jesus was a man, no more and no less.[26] It seemed to many that Christianity was not quite as true as previous generations had believed.[27] If the Gospels were no longer literal reality but an expression of the beliefs of the early Christian communities, it increasingly seemed that the faith of the Church was "like other religions in human history, a human construct, rather than a divine revelation."[28]

Initially a Roman Catholic seminarian, Ernest Renan published his *Life of Jesus* in 1863. Described as a "landmark" and "written by a master of the evidence," it was the first time that a biography of Jesus had been written without any reference to the supernatural.[29] Renan interpreted the Gospels as a "genre comparable to mediaeval saints' lives—crammed with legendary material . . . basically true, though with liberal additions of magical or miraculous folk tales in which we need not believe."[30] While New Testament scholarship largely ignored the book, it was accessible and nothing short of "a sensation in England"[31] and, in particular, for the middle classes.[32] It

22. Chadwick, *Victorian Church Part II*, 113.

23. Chadwick, *Victorian Church Part II*, 114.

24. Chadwick, *Victorian Church Part II*, 115.

25. Chadwick, *Victorian Church Part II*, 117.

26. Wilson, *God's Funeral*, 163.

27. Wilson, *God's Funeral*, 164.

28. Wilson, *God's Funeral*, 165.

29. Chadwick, *Secularization*, 219.

30. Wilson, *God's Funeral*, 172.

31. Wilson, *God's Funeral*, 174.

32. Chadwick, *Secularization of the European Mind*, 219.

may be that the wide appeal of this style of writing was the inspiration for Matheson's later biography or human "portraits" of Jesus. While he believed that the Sermon on the Mount "will never be surpassed," Renan argued that the Christ who stands outside of history cannot be a human,[33] but as a man, he could therefore be wrong in his views.[34]

The following year, in 1864, the English Judicial Committee allowed a clergyman in the Church of England to teach ultimate salvation, that is, even the wicked could have hope of being saved. In challenging the existence and prospect of hell, many feared that the authority of the Bible was being undermined. 11,000 clergy signed a public declaration affirming their belief in hell.[35] In 1865, in his *The Ethics of the Dust*, John Ruskin argued that Christians can no longer assume "that their way of looking at life was superior to that of the 'pagans.'"[36] In 1869, drawing on mythology in his book, *The Queen of the Air*, Ruskin wrote of Demeter and Poseidon and, without saying as much, his intention was to critique the unique claims of Christianity.

The reasons for the secularization of British (and European) culture are far from certain. During the 1850s, the first "Secular Societies" were founded in various towns,[37] though secularists were always a small minority.[38] The emergence of cities with their large populations, their increasing anonymity and less social accountability than in villages, has been offered as a possible cause, though we ought not to romanticize village life.[39] By contrast, within cities, churchgoing within the more prosperous areas rose.[40] It is also suggested that churchgoing was an activity for the respectable in society and the poor, without good clothes, did not feel respectable.[41]

In declaring himself to be an atheist, Matheson drew particular attention to his disbelief in immortality. Although published anonymously around twenty years earlier, Tennyson's poem, *In Memoriam*, articulates doubt about the after-life. T S Eliot said that the poem was "not religious because of the quality of its faith, but because of the quality of its doubt."[42]

33. Chadwick, *Secularization of the European Mind*, 220.

34. Chadwick, *Secularization of the European Mind*, 225.

35. Wilson, *God's Funeral*, 104.

36. Wilson, *God's Funeral*, 348.

37. Wilson, *God's Funeral*, 91.

38. Wilson, *God's Funeral*, 89.

39. Wilson, *God's Funeral*, 95.

40. Wilson, *God's Funeral*, 100.

41. Wilson, *God's Funeral*, 102.

42. Melnyk, *Victorian Religion*, 140.

Written as a reflection on spiritual pilgrimage, on what Tennyson called "the way of the soul,"[43] the poem commemorates the death of Tennyson's close friend and religious mentor, the historian, Arthur Henry Hallam. Rather than expressing an individual or esoteric view in the poem, Tennyson said that he wrote for "the whole human race."[44] He transformed the mood of the age into "haunting lyrics."[45] Aware that the universe "might be a mindless machine,"[46] the work "explores the agonizing processes of religious doubt."[47] To Tennyson, it seemed that not only the dinosaurs, but that we too face extinction and the erstwhile comforting poetic prayers of the psalmist were now rendered "fruitless." Devastated by the loss of his friend, Tennyson speculated that human life and human aspiration might now have lost all meaning: "Humanity, like the dinosaurs—'the dragons of the prime'—can one day go extinct, becoming no more than a part of a fossil record, 'seal'd within the iron hills.'"[48]

Published in 1867, just a year before Matheson was ordained, Matthew Arnold in his "master narrative,"[49] *Dover Beach*, "finds human love the only anodyne against the pain and uncertainty of human existence."[50] "Nowhere in Victorian poetry are the sadness and regret at lost faith expressed more poignantly than in this poem."[51] The mood is somber: for Arnold, the ebb and flow of the waves moving the pebbles to and fro on the beach "bring the eternal note of sadness in." The "sea of faith" which once was full makes its "withdrawing roar, retreating, to the breath of the night-wind." In this world, Arnold said, there is no "joy, nor love, nor light, nor certitude, nor peace, nor help for pain." The 1860s, the decade of Matheson's call and formation for ministry, is perhaps the most dangerous and challenging of the century for people whose faith was uncritical.

Several factors conspired to create personal crises in sufficient numbers to precipitate what came to be a national "crisis." Victorians wrote about the "crisis" they were living through. These factors included the challenge of scientific naturalism to teleology, the advent of higher biblical criticism from Germany, the crystalizing of the theory of evolution, the

43. Brett, *Poems of Faith and Doubt*, 53.

44. Wilson, *The Victorians*, 99.

45. Wilson, *God's Funeral*, 99.

46. Wilson, *God's Funeral*, 99.

47. Wilson, *God's Funeral*, 192.

48. Melnyk, *Victorian Religion*, 139.

49. Cox, "Worlds of Victorian Religion," 433.

50. Brett, *Poems of Faith and Doubt*, 49.

51. Brett, *Poems of Faith and Doubt*, 49.

appearance of comparative religion, the disunited and competing "array of aggressive alternative Christian denominations"[52] and, most significant of all, the tenacity with which the Church defended its doctrine and its claims to absolute and literal truth found in the Bible. The Victorian crisis of faith was, in part, a by-product of the religiosity of the Victorians and, in particular, the influence of evangelicalism.[53] So much is public record. But Larsen offers a corrective to the overwhelming impression that many or most Victorians lost their faith. He argues that "Those most interested in faith are often the ones who are most preoccupied with doubt."[54] Equally, many of the most vociferous advocates of atheism or the loss of faith had begun their journey as evangelicals, for example, George Eliot. Of those that lost their faith, a number reconverted to Christianity or, at the very least, to Spiritualism or Theosophy. Reconverts included some of the high profile leaders of the Secular Movement. Larsen states, "As a percentage, it is very apparent that a very much higher percentage of Secular leaders reconverted than ordained Christian ministers lost their faith."[55] Notwithstanding Larsen's critique, faith in the nineteenth century faced challenges it had not encountered before and Matheson's own crisis can be viewed against this backdrop of extensive upset and unease.

Within the context of an evangelical century, the Victorian "crisis of faith" was a "Protestant problem."[56] In the shadow of the Enlightenment, texts which otherwise had been unquestionably accepted were now found to be too incredible to believe or morally repugnant. In John's Gospel, the historicity of the Wedding Feast at Cana in Galilee or in Matthew's Gospel the dead in Jerusalem rising from their tombs on the day of crucifixion defied credibility.[57] Stories from the Old Testament called into question the morality of God. In First Samuel, in a story of divinely ordered genocide, God commands Saul to slaughter the Amalekites; men, women, children, infants and livestock (1 Samuel 15:3). In Joshua, God causes the sun to stand

52. Cox, "Worlds of Victorian Religion," 434.

53. Smith, "Religion," 342. Smith defines evangelicalism as having four components: conversion, biblicism, crucicentrism and activism. Evangelical conversion was the defining characteristic of a Christian; it meant 'a direct experience of being justified by grace through Jesus Christ'. Biblicism was a 'commitment to the idea that the Bible was the authoritative source of spiritual truth in matters of faith and practice'. Crucicentrism placed 'an emphasis on the cross of Christ and the doctrine of atonement usually understood in substitutionary terms . . .'. Finally, activism meant a commitment not only to spreading the gospel but also philanthropy and political causes.

54. Larsen, *Crisis of Doubt*, 8.

55. Larsen, *Crisis of Doubt*, 235.

56. St Aubyn, *Souls in Torment*, 23.

57. St Aubyn, *Souls in Torment*, 176.

still in order to give His Chosen People more time to annihilate their enemies (Joshua 10:13–14). Altholtz described this conflict as the "warfare of Conscience with Theology."[58] In other words:

> The most fundamental challenge to Christianity in the late Victorian period was a principled ethical objection to its doctrine and its view of human nature. In particular, the apparently vengeful picture of God that emerged from a reading of the Old Testament, the doctrines of everlasting punishment in hell and the substitutionary atonement of Christ came under fire from people who regarded them as objectionable and unjust . . . Orthodox presentations of the faith were being judged and found wanting against moral standards largely formed by Christianity itself.[59]

Taken together, for many at the time the very concept of God was called into question.

Alongside this array of problems and upsets, comparative religions introduced the Victorians to the mythology of other ancient cultures: myths of incarnation unsettlingly were found described in other religious systems.[60] Besides biblical criticism, Victorians were increasingly uncomfortable with the doctrines of predestination and substitutionary atonement. What sort of God would exclude most of humanity from salvation[61] and "What sort of Father would demand the death of His Son to placate His wrath against the Human Race?"[62] The Church historian and theologian Aubrey Moore has written that it was "important to distinguish clearly between faith in Christ and the immorality of Calvinism."[63] Yet the credibility and reliability of the Bible had been challenged, and with it its moral code. With the challenge to authority of Scripture came a similar challenge to the authority of the clergy. Agnosticism was gaining an ever-higher profile.[64]

Of the 1860s, Macmillan wrote: "The deeper religious and intellectual needs of the times could not be satisfied by a formal and, in the main,

---

58. Altholz, J. L., "The Warfare of Conscience with Theology."

59. Smith, "Religion," 346.

60. Aubyn, *Souls in Torment*, 175.

61. Aubyn, *Souls in Torment*, 19.

62. Aubyn, *Souls in Torment*, 179.

63. Aubyn, *Souls in Torment*, 23.

64. The principles of Agnosticism were introduced through four publications: Mansel's *Bampton Lectures* (1858), Herbert Spencer's *First Principles* (1862), Huxley's *Lay Sermons* (1870) and Leslie Stephen's *An Agnostic Apology* (1877).

scholastic handling of theology."[65] This sentiment may be seen nowhere more clearly than in the writing of Matthew Arnold. Critic of politics, religion, and literature, Arnold triumphed in the art of challenging assumptions. More persuasive, perceptive, and readable than Coleridge, Carlyle, Mill, and other contemporaries, Arnold sought to draw society back from abstract, obtuse systems of thought which, on the whole, he believed amounted to no more than a showy edifice, a pyramid of eggs, in which the "original intuition" had been lost.[66] Arnold said that "man is a just and fruitful object of contemplation much more by virtue to what spirit he is of than by virtue of what system of doctrine he elaborates."[67] The individual's "cast of mind," that is, one's emotional, intellectual and psychological disposition is more crucial than abstractions demanding orthodoxy.[68]

While much of Arnold's criticism of the religious outlook appeared after 1870, two important literary pieces were published during the time of Matheson's "crisis of faith." Arnold's *Culture and Anarchy* was published in 1868, in which his Preface challenges the central claims of Christianity and, expanding on this theme, his book, *St Paul and Protestantism* appeared in 1870. Although his religious work drew criticism from almost every quarter of the Church, Arnold said his intention had been to offer the Church hope for the future. In his view, unless the Church departed from the literal interpretation of the Bible and its over-reliance on theory and doctrine, it would terminally decline. His "constant concern for the spirit in which a belief is held rather than the letter of dogma," his desire for "inclusivity and unity" rather than sectarianism and partisanship, were what shaped his thinking. He said: "To reinthrone (sic) the Bible as explained by our current theology, whether learned or popular, is absolutely and forever impossible!—as impossible as to restore the feudal system, or the belief in witches."[69] For Arnold, it was orthodox theology and the literal interpretation of the Bible which would bring about the decline of Christianity. The language of the Bible was not to be understood as "rigid, fixed and scientific" but rather "fluid, passing and literary."[70] He stressed the importance of metaphor, symbol and poetry and said that the word "God" was not an exact or scientific term but something to be apprehended in the human consciousness.[71] Drawing on the

65. See Macmillan, *Times of Retirement*, 15.

66. Collini, "Arnold," 206.

67. Collini, "Arnold," 207.

68. Collini, "Arnold," 207.

69. Wilson, *God's Funeral*, 337.

70. Collini, "Arnold," 300.

71. Collini, "Arnold," 301.

Fourth Gospel, he said that Jesus brought an "inwardness" to the legalistic world of Jewish Law and that the Fourth Evangelist confounds the literalists with "the soaring style of his mysticism."[72] In preference to the accretions of the supernatural and superstitious, Arnold said that the kernel of faith is righteousness; it is an inward experience. He described religion as "morality touched by emotion," an emotion which lifts us to an "awareness of something 'not ourselves',"[73] an emotion which may be found equally in Sophocles as in Isaiah.[74] In 1865, in his Bampton Lectures, the Regius Professor of Divinity at Oxford, J B Mozley, argued that miracles are supernatural truths and that they go hand in hand with Christianity: they "stand or fall together."[75] By contrast, in seeking to secure the centrality of the Bible, Arnold said: "To restore the use of the Bible to those (and they are an increasing number) whom the popular theology with its proof from miracles, and the learned theology with its proof from metaphysics, so dissatisfy and repel that they are tempted to throw aside the Bible altogether."[76]

Arnold's critique of biblical interpretation and his departure from the traditional understanding of miracles, is potentially devastating for those who had simply accepted an inherited faith at face value. Arnold's motives may have been to secure the future life of the Church but, initially, it was seen as an attack on all that Christians' believed. Filled with the religious outlook of his childhood, it is no surprise that Matheson and many besides found the emerging intellectual climate to be anything other than hostile to all that he had been taught and believed. While Cardinal Newman said that Protestantism was "inherently destructive,"[77] others sought to rescue the Church from its troubles. Coleridgeans stressed that "spiritual truth is spiritually discerned"[78] and together with liberals and rationalists, they said that the proof of Christianity did not rest on miracles. Undermined by the "worship of science and progress,"[79] an interesting and important case is the novel by Mrs Humphry Ward, *Robert Elsmere* (1888), which is set in the 1870s; selling over one million copies, it is one of the most popular books of the nineteenth century and it picked up the themes which must have been active in Matheson's mind at this crucial time. Defenders of religious belief, like the

72. Collini, "Arnold" 302.

73. Collini, "Arnold," 302–303.

74. Collini, "Arnold," 303.

75. Livingston, *Religious Thought*, 115.

76. Collini, "Arnold," 304.

77. St Aubyn, *Souls in Torment*, 26.

78. Livingston, *Religious Thought*, 119.

79. Richter, *The Politics of Conscience*, 24.

eponymous Elsmere, had to contend with a host of challenges: Comtism, rationalism, agnosticism and materialism. The novel underlined the position that suggested people had to choose between reason and faith. What is interesting about *Robert Elsmere* is that, like Matheson, Elsmere is a young clergyman in his first parish who, having been challenged by rationalism, loses his faith. Elsmere resigns his living; Matheson tried to do so.

Romanticism

In the Victorian period, religious thought, together with that of art, music, literature and philosophy was shaped by the work of the German Romantic circle. In both Germany and Britain, panentheism is the defining characteristic of Romanticism. Seeking a third or middle way, the Romantics sought to avoid, on the one hand, "a traditional understanding of a personal God" and, on the other, nihilism and atheism.[80] Atheism meant that everything is finite and conditioned and that all talk of the Infinite and the unconditioned was meaningless.[81] The German philosopher, Lessing, said, "The orthodox concepts of the Divinity are no longer for me: I cannot stomach them . . ."[82] In part, the Romantics found their inspiration in Spinoza, if not in the detail of his doctrine then, at least, in their poetic interpretation of his work. Drawing on the mysticism of the Kabbala, Lessing said, "The One was the soul of the All."[83] The Neo-Spinozaism of the Romantics avoided a dualism of "the transcendence of the living God . . . over against the inert matter and mechanistic causality of nature;" they sought "livingness."[84] The divine attributes became "organic forces" and, said Herder, "We swim in an ocean of omnipotence."[85] Schleiermacher spoke of "the sensibility and taste for the infinite;" the Romantics "drink the absolute like water."[86] The Romantics understood the Infinite as immanent, an "organic monism;" Schleiermacher described immanence as a "marriage of the infinite with the finite."

The late Victorian period exuded "an aura of Romanticism to a greater or lesser degree."[87] The French literary critic, Emile Faguet, argued that Romanticism was an attempt to escape from the "horror" of reality by

---

80. Lamm, "Romanticism and Pantheism," 166.

81. Lamm, "Romanticism and Pantheism," 170.

82. Lamm, "Romanticism and Pantheism," 168.

83. Lamm, "Romanticism and Pantheism," 169.

84. Lamm, "Romanticism and Pantheism," 173.

85. Lamm, "Romanticism and Pantheism," 173.

86. Lamm, "Romanticism and Pantheism," 175.

87. Reardon, *The Age of Romanticism*, 2.

submerging oneself in the imagination, "to liberate oneself . . . through solitude and by retiring into the sanctuary of personal feeling."[88] He failed to see that Romantic dissatisfaction was not an escape from reality but rather an escape from the Enlightenment view of reality, namely, its reductionism to rationalism. In essence, the Romantic perspective penetrates beneath the surface of all life: "[It] lies in the inexpugnable feeling that the finite is not self-explanatory and self-justifying, but that behind it and within it— shining, as it were, through it—there is always an infinite 'beyond,' and that he who has once glimpsed the infinity that permeates as well as transcends all finitude can never again rest content with the paltry this-and-that, the rationalized simplicities, of everyday life."[89]

In 1799, Friedrich Schleiermacher described religion as having a "sense and taste for the Infinite;" it is "to lie in the bosom of the Universe and feel its boundless life and creative power within your own."[90] The Romantics believed that, while rationalism and the empirical sciences yielded knowledge, they did "not necessarily or readily [yield] wisdom."[91] They "stood for a religious interpretation of the universe."[92]

Spiritual Recovery

Matheson resolved to leave his post but the "leader" of the Presbytery handled the crisis sympathetically, believing that Matheson was "a young man and would change."[93] Despite this crisis, Matheson remained in his charge. Perhaps under the guidance of a co-Presbyter, Matheson found his way back to faith, but it was not to the faith he inherited from his childhood, of MacDuff or Pulsford. During his student years at Glasgow University, Matheson was introduced to the philosophy of Hegel by John Caird, then Professor of Divinity, later principal of the university. Although Caird's initial influence appears to have been slight, it was Hegel's system which enabled Matheson to take the first steps in the rebuilding of his shattered faith. MacMillan, who had served for a time as one of Matheson's secretaries, wrote that it was not possible for "a spiritually-minded man like Matheson to remain for any length of time an atheist."[94] MacMillan wrote:

88. Reardon, *The Age of Romanticism*, 3.
89. Reardon, *The Age of Romanticism*, 3.
90. Reardon, *The Age of Romanticism*, 5.
91. Reardon, *The Age of Romanticism*, 16.
92. Reardon, *The Age of Romanticism* 26.
93. MacMillan, *Life of George Matheson*, 122.
94. MacMillan, *Life of George Matheson*, 123.

"The darkness could only be temporary; new light was sure to dawn upon the troubled mind. This new light came from the philosophy of Hegel. Matheson's first introduction to the system of the great German thinker was at the hands of Dr. Caird."[95] For Matheson, the philosophy of Hegel was "the key to the mystery; and he rejoiced with joy unspeakable when what was dark was illumined, and when his faith was restored in a new and living form."[96] Writing at a much later date, Matheson said:

> I am every year more persuaded that the ideal is the reality, and that the study of Church History ought to be the study of the genesis and development of the Christian ideal. I believe that the ideal of the Christian life is itself the supernatural creation in the heart of man, and that it must have existed before the historical Christ. Because without its previous presence the beauty of the Christ of History would have been unintelligible.[97]

As Caird did in his Gifford Lectures, Matheson traced the organic or evolutionary history of religion in his two early works, *Aids to the Study of German Theology* and *Growth of the Spirit of Christianity*.

Hegel

In his philosophy, G. W. F. Hegel (1770–1831) was acutely aware of the intellectual challenges which faced Christian intellectuals in the wake of the Enlightenment. These included "the problem of reconciling revelation to reason, the relationship of Christianity to other religions, the veracity of reported miracles, and the historical challenge to the claims of Scripture."[98] Hegel's rational theology is informed by his interest in mysticism because he believed that "the goal of all striving is the presence of God indwelling in all things . . . and all things indwelling God."[99] Hegel understood unity with the Divine as the climax of human history and the history of creation. Human fulfillment is to be found "not in some distant eschatological future but in the everyday world of family life, civil society and the church."[100] Hegel wrote: "All the distinctions of the arts and sciences and of the endless interweavings

---

95. MacMillan, *Life of George Matheson*, 123.

96. MacMillan, *Life of George Matheson*, 125.

97. MacMillan, *Life of George Matheson*, 126.

98. Fergusson, "Hegel," 59.

99. Fergusson, "Hegel," 59.

100. Fergusson, "Hegel," 60.

of human relationships, habits and customs, activities, skills, and enjoyments find their ultimate center in the one thought of God."[101]

For Hegel, history is "the medium of philosophical truth" and reality is "a continuum rather than an aggregate of disparate entities."[102] Hegel's concept of spirit or *Geist* is central to his philosophy. The spirit is "self-communicating" and denotes "movement, energy and dynamism."[103] The whole "embraces all otherness, everything finite and determinate."[104] There is no place in Hegel's theology for "the asceity of God,"[105] for the Kantian view of God in God's Self. For Hegel, his theology is concerned with humanity's union with God and God's union with humanity. In the Eucharist, "our existential separation from God is overcome in a double movement toward God and from God"[106] and the "Kingdom of God is a universal community which can unite races, nations and peoples."[107]

It is through creation that the spirit or *Geist* knows itself. For Hegel, Christian doctrine is discerned "through historical forces and movements" as the spirit realizes itself.[108] In what Fergusson describes as "highly unorthodox," Hegel's doctrine of the Trinity departs from the Three Persons as co-equal, co-eternal and consubstantial to "a dialectical progression toward the advent of Spirit as the final form of God."[109] The Incarnation is, for Hegel, the "high point in the historical development of religion, for here in the person of Christ is reconciliation of God with the world."[110] However, though Jesus was an exceptional individual, "it could not be said that he was God in any sense other than that in which we are all identical with God."[111]

Hegel saw a progression in other world religions which ultimately led to Christianity. The insights of Judaism and the Greco-Roman religion, together with the religions of other cultures, such as Chinese, Indian, Persian, Syrian and Egyptian, all had their part to play as human history moved towards the Incarnation in Christianity.[112] For example, in

101. Fergusson, "Hegel," 59.

102. Fergusson, "Hegel," 60.

103. Fergusson, "Hegel," 62.

104. Fergusson, "Hegel," 62.

105. Fergusson, "Hegel," 62.

106. Fergusson, "Hegel," 63.

107. Fergusson, "Hegel," 64.

108. Fergusson, "Hegel," 65.

109. Fergusson, "Hegel," 65.

110. Fergusson, "Hegel," 64.

111. Fergusson, "Hegel," 65.

112. Fergusson, "Hegel," 66.

Indian religion Hegel found the absolute asserted as beyond all conceptual determination while deities are manifested in a plethora of natural forms.[113] While he had a difficulty in accounting for Islam because it appeared much later than Christianity, he was very sympathetic to the "religion and culture of ancient Greece because . . . in the form of a plurality of gods appearing in human form, reconciliation and unity are achieved albeit in a limited way."[114] It is not credible today to maintain that other faiths ultimately lead to Christianity.

Hegel sought the inner meaning of Christianity. His work is "a landmark in the history of the modern Western mind."[115] His critics, however, came to believe Hegel's re-working of Christian teaching had the potential to refine it to such an extent that it no longer resembled Christianity. Hegel understood human consciousness in two ways: firstly, it was through human consciousness that creation became conscious of itself; and, secondly, it is through that same human consciousness that God has consciousness of God's Self. Like the mystic, Meister Eckhart, "The eye with which God sees me is the same eye with which I see him; my eye and his eye are one."[116] For Hegel, perfect or absolute religion is the one in which "the divine self-consciousness is fully attained; it is absolute because it is here and here alone that Absolute Being finds its complete reflection."[117] God reveals God to God's Self.

While standing firmly in the Romantic movement, Hegel believed that, through philosophical reflection, humanity must move beyond "a purely imaginative and emotional acceptance of religious truth."[118] Hegel understood the Fall of humanity to be the moment of its birth, the birth of human self-consciousness; this is a view shared by Matheson. No longer an animal, humanity could not live in the Garden of Eden. The emergence of human self-consciousness, however, was, at the same time, our moment of separation from God: "The Fall is . . . the Mythus of Man—in fact, the very transition by which he becomes Man."[119] For Hegel, religion must be "in our hearts" and, equally, our intellect must remain "continually active."[120]

Hegel believed that philosophy superseded religion because it is through philosophical reflection that humanity is able to "grasp the truth

113. Fergusson, "Hegel," 66.

114. Fergusson, "Hegel," 67.

115. Reardon, *The Age of Romanticism*, 60.

116. Reardon, *The Age of Romanticism*, 65.

117. Reardon, *The Age of Romanticism*, 66.

118. Reardon, *The Age of Romanticism*, 66.

119. Reardon, *The Age of Romanticism*, 70.

120. Reardon, *The Age of Romanticism*, 81.

concerning God."[121] It is not that philosophy is able to discern new and otherwise unobtainable knowledge but that it is able to move beyond the historical particularity of religion. In this regard, it is no surprise that he met with criticism. Christianity's central claim is rooted in human history, in the birth, life, death and resurrection of the man from Nazareth. On the face of it, Hegel's thought appears to be fatal to the Christian faith.[122]

Hegel's criticism of Eucharistic theology is particularly insightful. Through the celebration of the Eucharist, in "a sensible, immediate way," humanity becomes conscious of its "reconciliation with God and of the Spirit directly within" us.[123] He rejected the Roman Catholic doctrine of transubstantiation, of its belief that Christ is present solely in the consecrated host but, equally, he believed that the Reformed churches had reduced the rite to a "bare commemoration—an unspiritual and merely lively remembrance of the past."[124] For Hegel, the truth of the sacrament had been "lowered to the prose of the Enlightenment."[125] Matheson's teacher, John Caird, was a Hegelian, though Hegel is almost never cited by Caird. It is difficult to be certain to what extent Caird read Hegel. It is at least possible that most or all of what Caird knew of Hegel he learned from his younger brother, Edward.

John Caird

John Caird, who was one of a number of British philosophers to follow Hegel, was one of Matheson's teachers. Others included T H Green (1836–1882), E Caird (1835–1908), H Jones (1852–1922), F H Bradley (1846–1924) and Bernard Bosanquet (1848–1923). The Hegelian dialectic, as applied to theology by John Caird, underpins Matheson's philosophical system of thought. Hegelianism belongs to the speculative or metaphysical school of thought. In 1880, Caird published his first major work, *An Introduction to the Philosophy of Religion*, "a book depending on Hegel's *Philosophie der Religion* and for which there was no Scottish precedent."[126] T. H. Green said that "it represented a thorough assimilation by an eminent Scottish theologian . . . of Hegel's philosophy of religion."[127] Together with his brother, Edward, Caird offered a way forward in natural theology and

---

121. Reardon, *The Age of Romanticism*, 83.

122. Reardon, *The Age of Romanticism*, 85.

123. Reardon, *The Age of Romanticism*, 78.

124. Reardon, *The Age of Romanticism*, 78.

125. Reardon, *The Age of Romanticism*, 78.

126. Drummond, *Late Victorian Scotland*, 243.

127. Caird, *The Fundamental Ideas*, cxx.

biblical criticism which was not a mere repetition of dogma, but rather what Bulloch termed "a growing religious life."[128]

Caird's philosophy held that religious ideas, their facts and figurative representations, are subject to philosophic scrutiny, what he called "scientific reflection,"[129] no less than any other field of human inquiry. Caird disliked popular religion because it retained "traces of its origins and so betrayed the mind to illusions and errors."[130] In his *Introduction*, Caird confronts the "inadequacy of materialism."[131] In 1894, A Mair said that the positive theory of materialism more than agnosticism or even atheism *per se*, has the potential to "alter all our institutions, and abolish those it dislikes."[132] Increasingly, through matter and force, materialism was understood to be the "ultimate source and explanation of all things."[133]

By the middle of the previous century, three hundred years of the reign of Calvinism had come to an end.[134] By the end of the nineteenth century, "under the aegis of Edward and John Caird there was to be a radical reorientation of philosophical teaching in Scotland."[135] In 1875, T. M. Lindsay defined natural theology as "the sum of the knowledge which man, apart from revelation, has about God."[136] Luther and Calvin, and again in the twentieth century with Barth, believed that the Church and salvation were "founded on the Word of God alone, on God's revelation in Jesus Christ as it is attested in Scripture, and on faith in that Word."[137] Acknowledging the presence of God in all things, the natural theology taught by the Cairds believed it would have been "an impoverishment of Christian theology if it may not embody in its witness for God traces of the divine Father's presence in the natural world discerned by many a reflective spirit, and that cannot but enter into the Christian consciousness."[138]

---

128. Drummond, *Late Victorian Scotland*, 238.

129. Caird, *The Philosophy of Religion*, 1. Caird's use of the word 'scientific' has been criticised by Fergusson in *19th century Theology* because Caird nowhere defines the term. For Caird, it seems that because it is derived from science, he imbues it with high authority.

130. Drummond, *Late Victorian Scotland*, 243.

131. Drummond, *Late Victorian Scotland*, 243.

132. Drummond, *Late Victorian Scotland*, 224.

133. Drummond, *Late Victorian Scotland*, 223.

134. Drummond, *Late Victorian Scotland*, 216.

135. Drummond, *Late Victorian Scotland*, 229.

136. Drummond, *Late Victorian Scotland*, 221.

137. Drummond, *Late Victorian Scotland*, 221.

138. Drummond, *Late Victorian Scotland*, 221.

For Caird, much of the language of the Bible was "obviously figurative and cannot be interpreted as literal fact."[139] Moreover, though regarded as the inspired written Word of God, the Bible "does not address us simply as an authoritative message from heaven which we are to believe at our peril."[140] The Bible "elicits, educates and appeals to all that is highest in our nature."[141] We are to imaginatively engage with Scripture and let it inform and shape our consciousness or soul. This is the methodology adopted by Matheson. Like Caird's reliance on Hegel, Matheson never cites Caird, which makes it difficult to be certain which sources Matheson used. Caird was influential during the period of Matheson's ministry and there can be little doubt that from his university days Caird shaped Matheson's thought.

Union in Caird's Theology

For Caird, union with God was humanity's religious imperative but it was also in the nature of God to desire union. He suggested that the nature of God would be imperfect "if it did not contain in it relation to the finite world."[142] More than that, failure of God to reveal God's Self would mean, for God, an "unrealized potential: the full grown plant is something more or higher than the seed or germ."[143] The essential spiritual element in God is love and, as such, God is therefore relational in nature.

Caird's dialectic of unity is echoed in his sermons. In his sermon on John 3:7, "Marvel not that I said unto thee, Ye must be born again," Caird spoke of finding our fulfillment in God. Our perfection lies in achieving self-denial, which will be: "the sweetness and joy of our life, a frame and temper of mind in such harmony with the mind and will of God that duty passes into spontaneity and becomes the manifestation of an inward impulse, the gratification of the deepest passion of the soul."[144] At the heart of his sermon on John 3:7, Caird describes union with God in near mystical terms:

> I believe that if we could reach a spiritual state in which the di-
> vine mastery of the mind, heart, will of man were so absolute
> that we should no longer think our own thoughts or desire our
> own ends or do our own will, but have our whole spiritual being
> suffused, permeated, inseparably blended with the spirit and life

139. Drummond, *Late Victorian Scotland*, 246.

140. Drummond, *Late Victorian Scotland*, 239.

141. Drummond, *Late Victorian Scotland*, 239.

142. Caird, *The Philosophy of Religion*, 239.

143. Caird, *The Philosophy of Religion*, 240.

144. Caird, *University Sermons*, 90.

of the Eternal, —that then, instead of the leveling down of our spiritual life to nature, there would be reached the highest conceivable pitch of spiritual elevation, that liberation, expansion, perfection, which is involved in being sharers of the infinite life of Him in whose image we were made.[145]

In his sermon on mind and body, Caird preached of our hearts being touched by a Being who captivates our affections and binds Himself to us by "a profound yet passionate self-surrender."[146] Christ comes to us with "a voice of personal love and forgiveness"[147] and, in response, "we cast ourselves into the embrace of One in whom law and love, the righteousness we reverence and the tender compassion we need, are blended in perfect unity."[148] Religion is "the absolute self-surrender of the soul to God. It means the giving up or annulling of the private, particular self, of every interest or satisfaction that belongs to me as this particular individuality, and the blending or identification of my will, and potentiality of my whole life and being, with the will of the Infinite."[149]

Our faith in Christ is "the inward witness to the perpetual presence and operation of the ever-living spirit of Christ."[150] The ever-living spirit which purifies and hallows with love, incarnate in Christ, "is still and for ever, if we will but open our hearts to receive it, living and breathing within us."[151] If we will allow it, "the ever-present, inexhaustible fountain of spiritual life and strength" will penetrate and suffuse our souls.[152] In every Christian heart, we find "the irrefragable witness to the abiding, life-giving presence" which is "a living, operating spirit and power in the present life and experience of men."[153] Drawing on Hegelian mysticism, Caird most often used names for God such as "the Absolute," "the Eternal," "the Universal," and 'the Infinite."

Publications

Like Matthew Arnold, Matheson preferred the spirit within rather than any "pyramid of eggs." Matheson drew his reader back to the inwardness, the life

145. Caird, *University Sermons*, 79.
146. Caird, *University Sermons*, 99.
147. Caird, *University Sermons*, 101.
148. Caird, *University Sermons*, 102.
149. Fergusson, *Nineteenth Century*, 72.
150. Caird, *University Sermons*, 107.
151. Caird, *University Sermons*, 107.
152. Caird, *University Sermons*, 108–109.
153. Caird, *University Sermons*, 110.

of the Spirit, the inner life. Besides his first two major publications, Matheson's other works include *Natural Elements of Revealed Theology (the Baird Lecture), Landmarks of New Testament Morality, The Spiritual Development of St Paul, The Lady Ecclesia, The Distinctive Message of Old Religions, Can the Old Faith Live with the New, The Psalmist and the Scientist* and *Studies of the Portrait of Christ*. He produced a number of works which offered a more subtle interpretation of the inner life: *My Aspirations, Moments on the Mount, Words by the Wayside,* and *Voices of the Spirit*. Some of his works were translated for a wider market: *My Aspirations* and *Words by the Wayside* were translated into German, *The Originality of the Character of Christ* in French and *Studies of the Portrait of Christ* into Chinese. His works were sold in Britain and America. Many who never heard Matheson preach were able to benefit from his thought through the printed word. Like his sermons, his publications possessed "originality and lucidity, depth of thought lit up by beauty of style, a fresh setting of an old truth, a subtle distinction followed by a hitherto unseen resemblance."[154]

Aids to the Study of German Theology

Hegel's Idealism offered a philosophical and theological response to the Victorian "crisis of faith." Idealists sought to "satisfy both people's spiritual needs and the intellectual rigours of the new scientific way of thinking."[155] Alongside Idealism, others responded in different ways. G J Holyoake, who coined the term "secularism" in 1851, and Charles Bradlaugh, who founded the National Secular Society in 1866, opted for dogmatic atheism. The Oxford Movement sought refuge in traditional faith. There was "confused soul-searching"[156] from the cleric, E B Pusey, the theologian, F D Maurice, and others in *Essays and Reviews* (1860) and a celebrated lament by the English poet, Matthew Arnold in "Dover Beach" (1867).

In *Aids to the Study of German Theology*, Matheson presented a "desideratum."[157] It is in the form of "thought-translation;"[158] in other words, rather than his focus being on the minute detail of German theology or the problem of translating the German language, Matheson offered to "disregard the word and describe the thing."[159] There is an introduction

154. Macmillan, *Times of Retirement*, 29.

155. Mander, *British Idealism*, 138.

156. Mander, *British Idealism*, 138.

157. Matheson, *Study of German Theology*, 1.

158. Matheson, *Study of German Theology*, 4.

159. Matheson, *Study of German Theology*, 4.

followed by sixteen chapters. His main subjects are the work of Kant, Schleiermacher, Fichte, Hegel, Schelling, and Strauss. In *Growth of the Spirit of Christianity . . . to the Lutheran Era*, Matheson demonstrates in thirty-eight chapters what he describes as the spirit of Christianity, though sometimes obscured, working through, within and often despite Christianity's form and its ecclesiastical structures.

In both works, Matheson aligns mysticism with Protestantism, at least to some extent. Matheson believed that the spiritual progress of humanity had much to do with the spirit we find in mysticism and Protestantism. At the beginning of his first major work, Matheson highlighted the vital importance of mysticism as well as that of the Protestant spirit. Against "Romanism," he wrote: "The Church was the sole medium of revelation, and it was only through the united body of believers that God would speak to the world. Against this one-sided tendency mysticism and Protestantism alike protested, both sought to vindicate the importance of each separate soul, both vehemently struggled to defend the possibility of a personal communion with God."[160] Matheson described the mystics—Tauler, Ruysbroeck, Staupitz, and Wesel—as "men who saw in God something more than could be represented in a pageant or imaged in a crucifix, who sought deeper life than that of sensuous worship.[161] Matheson names four mystics as laudable examples, all of whom he described as being "misunderstood and unappreciated" in their own time.[162]

For Matheson, Kant's "essential work was to destroy, to prove that all the efforts of reason to explain the mystery of life had been vanity of vanities."[163] Kant's system had given prominence to the authority of conscience: "it has even indirectly shown that the ideas of Christianity are eternal ideas, that the historical framework is the expression and embodiment of the deepest instincts of the human heart."[164] It is "the heart" not human reason that is the doorway into the Divine. The tragedy for Christianity had been that it attached itself to Rationalism. Rationalism had been the 'handmaid of Christian truth' so that when Rationalism fell, so too did all belief.[165]

From Kant, Matheson turned to Schleiermacher. Helmer describes Schleiermacher's system as "a paragon of modern theology."[166] Matheson

---

160. Matheson, *Study of German Theology*, 183.

161. Matheson, *Study of German Theology*, 3.

162. Matheson, *Study of German Theology*, 3.

163. Matheson, *Study of German Theology*, 10.

164. Matheson, *Study of German Theology*, 31.

165. Matheson, *Study of German Theology*, 6.

166. Helmer, "Schleiermacher," 31.

regarded Schleiermacher's work as "a sad piece of patchwork,"[167] "a mass of inextricable inconsistencies"[168] in which there was nothing "distinctively new."[169] He doubted that Schleiermacher could have any sense of a personal redeemer.[170] Despite these severe criticisms, Matheson believed that Schleiermacher spoke to the heart, to the intuition. Schleiermacher "felt, and rightly felt that the spirit of religion was deeper than all religions."[171] More than that, for Schleiermacher, Christianity brought "a new and higher life into the world', one which would 'assimilate everything to itself'" and that, in "the religion of Christ," "all intellectual differences would be merged in the unity of love."[172] Schleiermacher spoke to Matheson's mystical sentiment.

The Spirit of Christianity in and through History

Matheson's second major work, *Growth in the Spirit of Christianity from the First Century to the Dawn of the Lutheran Era*, is written in two volumes. Spanning sixteen centuries of history, Matheson considers Judaism, the Caesars, Saul of Tarsus and Paul, Gnosticism, Irenaeus, Montanism, Tertullian, Cyprian, Origen, Augustine, Benedict, the Council of Ephesus (in particular, the doctrinal development of Mary), the prophet Mohammed and Islam (Mohammedanism), the relationship of Church and State, the merits of monasticism, the papacy, the Waldenses, indulgences, the Inquisition and Francis of Assisi.

Matheson's work is derivative because it is drawn from the Hegelian system which he received from Caird. Matheson sought to show the growth or progress of the spirit of Christianity *in and through* events and individuals. He begins by establishing the principle of the evolution of religious thought. Christianity "must be viewed, not as conflicting periods of good and evil, but as progressive stages of an ever growing life."[173] To claim a disjunction would be to denigrate the Author of Revelation: every insight prior to Christianity would need to be considered false and erroneous.[174] The theory of development meant that Christianity was rooted in the spiritual consciousness of the world.

167. Matheson, *Study of German Theology*, 39.

168. Matheson, *Study of German Theology*, 36.

169. Matheson, *Study of German Theology*, 39.

170. Matheson, *Study of German Theology*, 54.

171. Matheson, *Study of German Theology*, 37.

172. Matheson, *Study of German Theology*, 37.

173. Matheson, *The Spirit of Christianity*, 4.

174. Caird., *The Philosophy of Religion*, 333.

Following Hegel and Caird, Matheson argued that Paul, John, Justin Martyr, Tatian, Iraeneus and Clement of Alexandria brought the wisdom of previous eras into the service of Christianity.[175] Of Augustine, he wrote: "None has done so much to exhibit the points of union between the religion of Christ and the highest features of those religions which went before Him; none has succeeded so well in finding for Christianity a meeting place with the philosophy of Plato."[176] Matheson said that Christianity appealed to the ancient world because it took to itself the very best spiritual insights that the world had to offer while, at the same time, offering the world the virtue of unselfishness and the honoring and elevation of the weak. Platonism valued the unseen and eternal over the seen and temporal; Stoicism taught the all-pervading presence of the divine spirit in the universe; many valued a religion in which the gods took on human likeness; victims of political oppression were attracted to a religion "whose keynote was brotherhood, whose watchword was self-sacrifice, and whose essence was the communion of soul with soul."[177] The attributes were gathered up in Christianity. Evolving beyond them, Christianity brought a new spiritual insight. The ancient world had valued above all those who had physical power and the opulent, but this left no room for the weak, destitute or infirm. By contrast, Christianity said that "the highest marks of glory" were "those which the old world had despised: poverty of spirit, meekness, endurance of persecution, forgiveness of injuries, the returning of good for evil."[178]

Looking back to the beginning of the Church's history through the fifteen centuries that led to the Reformation, for Matheson, the relationship of Church and State was problematic. The desire on the part of church leaders to align themselves with the emperor brought unwelcome religious and theological developments. It opened the door to portraying God in the image of the emperor. For Matheson, the cost to the Church of seeking to extend the kingdom of God through its relationship with the empire was too high: it cost the Church *the sacrifice of the inner life*. Matheson argued that Irenaeus favored outward forms of religion over "its inward life" and that Tertullian, Cyprian and Augustine all in different ways compromised the inner life of the Church "binding it to a worldly life."[179] Looking for the spirit within, Matheson said that the ever-closer relationship of Church and State, together with the emergence of the pope as priest *and* king, a

175. Matheson, *The Spirit of Christianity*, 6–7.

176. Matheson, *The Spirit of Christianity*, 7.

177. Matheson, *The Spirit of Christianity*, 9.

178. Matheson, *The Spirit of Christianity*, 14.

179. Matheson, *The Spirit of Christianity*, 66.

"dread theocracy," while "outwardly calamitous," "may be inwardly only the stages of a progressive development."[180] Matheson said that, though there be "persecutions, heresies, superstitions, barbarisms, the undue predominance of worldly influence" and the "temporary hiding of *spiritual intuition*," these are but the school days of Christianity, preparing it for mature and "riper years."[181]

Matheson singled out the openness of the apostle Paul to finding God in all things. On the Damascus Road, "Saul of Tarsus fell to the earth, and Paul the apostle arose in his room."[182] There had been no struggle when he encountered the Risen Christ face to face: "the old nature of the man died instantaneously."[183] Matheson wrote of death and resurrection, of inner death, the death of the old nature. This is the language of the mystic. Paul quoted the poetry of Grecian literature and spoke of "a Being *pervading* all His works, *participating* in the very nature of the objects He has made, and Himself a *sharer* in the life of His whole creation."[184] The emphasis is mine: it reveals not only Paul's sense of the Presence or immanence of God but that same sense in Matheson. Paul's martyrdom was the crown of an unselfish life.[185]

Of all the biblical writers, Matheson most admired the writer of the Fourth Gospel, the Gospel Clement of Alexandria called "the spiritual Gospel." It was also the Gospel favored by Matthew Arnold. Matheson acknowledged that there is intolerance in the Gospel towards the writer's Jewish contemporaries but that, years later, "the greatest of all changes is that which has been accomplished in himself."[186] Matheson drew attention to this inner change: "His mind was driven ever more and more inward upon itself, and taught ever increasingly to seek for its highest good in the deepening of its own spiritual nature."[187] Matheson explained what he saw in John's inner change: "If hitherto men had looked chiefly at what Christianity had done for them, John *meditated intensely* on what Christianity had done *in* them, and sought amidst the disciples of the Master for the evidence that His own life was *present within their souls*; this he regarded as

180. Matheson, *The Spirit of Christianity*, 67.

181. Matheson, *The Spirit of Christianity*, 69.

182. Matheson, *The Spirit of Christianity*, 101.

183. Matheson, *The Spirit of Christianity*, 100–101.

184. Matheson, *The Spirit of Christianity*, 106.

185. Matheson, *The Spirit of Christianity*, 123.

186. Matheson, *The Spirit of Christianity*, 126.

187. Matheson, *The Spirit of Christianity*, 127.

the goal of Christianity."[188] Again, the emphasis is mine. Matheson saw that John's reflection was no mere intellectual exercise but a deep soul-searching. Through meditation, the author of the Fourth Gospel found God within. He observed that John's writing was "so profound in its spirituality, and so intense in its pathos, that it has become pre-eminently the most precious relic of early Christian literature."[189]

Gnosticism, Tertullian, Origen, Augustine, and Monasticism

Matheson went on to comment on Gnosticism, Montanism, Tertullian, Origen, Augustine and Monasticism. While he acknowledged shortcomings, he drew out the spiritual life present in each of them. Gnosticism looked for "an inward meaning;" "the grandeur of its inward depths" was greater than any grandeur which the world could offer.[190] Montanism, like Methodism in the 18th century, sought to turn our thoughts inwards and away from the "life of outward ecclesiastical forms."[191] The Carthagean, Tertullian, is praised for the spiritual power of his writing. Matheson said: "Tertullian wanted direct communion with God. He desired a living, personal union with the Divine Spirit—a union not consummated by the mediators of church or priesthood, but wrought out by the surrender of his own will to the will of the Supreme; and he was ready to welcome any channel of communication through which such a privilege could flow.[192] Matheson chose to focus on Tertullian's desire and search for personal union and communion with God, whom he referred to as "the Divine Spirit" or "the Supreme." To a large extent, Matheson too avoided anthropomorphic terms and stressed imagery or names which are not external, but can be conceived of as being within the worshipper.

In a time of ever-increasing worldliness, ambition and materialism, Matheson believed that Origen stood almost alone. Though he regarded some of Origen's views as "grotesque" or "fantastic," owing more to poetry than reason, nevertheless, he found "flashings of real light," light intended to guide and "through them all there shines the spirit of a genuine man, high in aspiration, deep in devotion, in purpose earnest, in imagination pure."[193] Origen sought to "render to the world the things which were the world's, and

188. Matheson, *The Spirit of Christianity*, 127.
189. Matheson, *The Spirit of Christianity*, 127.
190. Matheson, *The Spirit of Christianity*, 133.
191. Matheson, *The Spirit of Christianity*, 162.
192. Matheson, *The Spirit of Christianity*, 176.
193. Matheson, *The Spirit of Christianity*, 198.

to the spirit the things which belonged to the spirit."[194] Origen appealed to Matheson because he had "imagination behind his judgement."[195] Matheson later said that imagination is the most real.[196] Origen had within his heart "an ideal of what the sacred portrait should be."[197] Matheson would later adopt the word "portrait" for his life of Jesus: *Studies of the Portrait of Christ*. Portrait suggests immediacy, emotion, warmth, personality, and life itself. Doctrine is best understood "through the medium of the heart;" under the light of pure reason, it is deprived of its energy.[198] Rationalism robs the Church of its consciousness or perpetual sense of the divine presence.[199]

Like Origen, Matheson saw in Augustine a life utterly "spiritual . . . independent of time"[200] and indebted to his mother, "a living representation" of the Christian religion.[201] For ten years, Augustine found the views of the Manichaeans to be persuasive; they said that there were two rulers in the universe, one good and one evil. Then, with an autobiographical tone to it, Matheson wrote: "And so at length there came to Augustine that which at some times comes to most of us—a period, we shall not say of intellectual darkness, but of intellectual voidness, when the old belief had passed away, and left not new faith to fill the blank."[202] Matheson's choice of the word "voidness" suggests more than emptiness, but also bereavement, a painful loss. Perhaps Augustine's own darkness took Matheson back to his own dark night. In Christianity, Augustine found that liberation from self will, from unrest and unhappiness, must flow from the "breath of the Divine Spirit."[203] In this inner journey, Augustine found "great calm" and a "profound peace."[204] Matheson's insight into Augustine clearly spoke to his own experience: "[Augustine] seemed to have his being in a new world, to have risen from the grave of his former self, and to be living a life which was in him but not of him, possessed by his soul, yet issuing from another heart."[205] Matheson wrote persuasively of Augustine's inner spiritual ex-

194. Matheson, *The Spirit of Christianity*, 202.
195. Matheson, *The Spirit of Christianity*, 204.
196. Matheson, *Times of Retirement*, 188.
197. Matheson, *The Spirit of Christianity*, 204.
198. Matheson, *The Spirit of Christianity*, 206.
199. Matheson, *The Spirit of Christianity*, 207.
200. Matheson, *The Spirit of Christianity*, 252.
201. Matheson, *The Spirit of Christianity*, 253.
202. Matheson, *The Spirit of Christianity*, 256.
203. Matheson, *The Spirit of Christianity*, 261.
204. Matheson, *The Spirit of Christianity*, 261.
205. Matheson, *The Spirit of Christianity*, 261.

perience; he is comfortable with this language of intimacy. The record of Augustine's mystical experience at Ostia will have inspired and nourished Matheson's own theology.

Writing as a Presbyterian in the late Victorian period in a Protestant country torn by religious division, Matheson commends the work of the mediaeval monasteries. While he accused them of corruption, he said that they had started out with a Protestant spirit against the worldliness and excesses of the papacy. In the pope, Christianity had sought a representative monarchy, not an absolute ruler. The monastery became the school, "the training place of the spirit of Christianity."[206] Spiritual obedience led to "some of the brightest virtues to which the Christian religion can lay exclusive claim."[207] Matheson was critical of the Protestant Reformation for its suspicion of all that was mediaeval. He accepted that for the three centuries before the Reformation the monasteries had become houses of licentiousness, hypocrisy, deception, extortion and bribery, nevertheless, he believed that they had gifted much to Christianity.

In praise of Benedict and the Benedictine monasteries, Matheson described the monk as a "man of prayer" who combined the "duties of meditation" and of "secular labor."[208] "Labor was ennobled, it was lifted from the dust and set upon a throne."[209] The monastery was "higher than the Papacy"[210] and a place of refuge for "the vanquished," an "asylum for the weak," and a place of "calm retreat to which the laboring and the heavy-laden might repair for rest."[211] They were open to all: from the most frail and infirm of women and men to the highest in the land. Matheson said, "The monasteries descended as a gift from God."[212] They carried the spirit of Protestantism against Rome and, in an age of despotic power, "they kept alive in many souls the sense of personal piety and individual responsibility . . . they held aloft the ideal of humanity, and proclaimed aloud the brotherhood of souls."[213] It is Matheson's appreciation of the inner life, the life of prayer, meditation and contemplation that predisposed him towards such profound sympathy, an unusual appreciation in the Church of Scotland.

206. Matheson, *The Spirit of Christianity*, 289.

207. Matheson, *The Spirit of Christianity*, 290.

208. Matheson, *The Spirit of Christianity*, 303.

209. Matheson, *The Spirit of Christianity*, 304.

210. Matheson, *The Spirit of Christianity*, 311.

211. Matheson, *The Spirit of Christianity*, 312.

212. Matheson, *The Spirit of Christianity*, 312.

213. Matheson, *The Spirit of Christianity*, 312.

Mohammed

Matheson's spirituality and openness to the Spirit of God wherever it may be found is perhaps seen nowhere more clearly than in his sympathetic handling of Islam, or Mohammedanism. He was interested in the spiritual experiences of Mohammed. For Matheson, Mohammedanism was a Christian heresy; it was borne out of the failings of Christianity, not least the squabbling with Christianity but also Christianity's slide back towards Paganism and the worship of many gods. Mohammedianism made two claims: there is one God and Mohammed is His apostle.

Mohammed had grown up in Mecca and from being the status of a camel driver he rose to become the husband of a wealthy woman. Mohammed undergoes "a silent stage of inward death."[214] At the age of 40, Mohammed was subject to "terrible visions, in which he is to abandon the belief of his fathers. Old forms are shaken, old associations broken, old ties severed, and he seems to hear a voice calling him . . . he feels his individual life to be crumbling into nothingness." Matheson was drawn to the spiritual break-through which often comes through spiritual or worldly breakdown. Of Mohammed, he wrote: "He is humbled to the dust, bowed down by the perception of human insignificance, appalled by the majesty of that power before which men are as grasshoppers. He goes forth from the haunts of men, and on the mountain, in the desert, and in the cave he spends long days alone. He becomes subject to fits of epilepsy, he is assailed by paroxysms of nervous excitement, his frame is shaken by the force of the inward man."[215]

Matheson did not deny the Prophet's revelation. On the contrary, he believed that "truth is to be found in all systems."[216] It is noteworthy that he wrote about Mohammed at all. Like Paul on Mars Hill, Mohammed was stirred within "when he beheld the city wholly given to idolatry;" "we need not be afraid to concede to him the honor of a special place in history . . . he was indeed an instrument of the hand of God."[217] At a time when Victorians were beginning to learn more about other world faiths and some in the churches were resorting to claims of superiority and absolute truth, Matheson honored the spiritual life of the Prophet. More than the adoption of the Hegelian method, Matheson's acceptance of Islam may demonstrate his sense of oneness with all things, including the Spirit

214. Matheson, *The Spirit of Christianity*, 331.
215. Matheson, *The Spirit of Christianity*, 332.
216. Matheson, *The Spirit of Christianity*, 334.
217. Matheson, *The Spirit of Christianity*, 338.

in Islam. Like Arnold, Matheson may be comfortable to find the Spirit in Sophocles as well as Isaiah, so to speak.

Late Middle Ages

Matheson expressed sympathy for the doctrine of transubstantiation, the life of Francis of Assisi and mysticism. Quite remarkably, Matheson acknowledged the genuine, heartfelt desire which lies behind the doctrine of transubstantiation. In the Church of Scotland, even today, praise and sympathy for this doctrine is extremely rare. Not at all concerned with sectarian squabbles, Matheson saw transubstantiation as a deep desire to re-create within the Church "the presence of the Master,"[218] who had become so divine as to become entirely remote from human experience. While he regretted that the power to dispense the sacrament was reserved for the hierarchy and therefore open to abuse, the doctrine sprung from spiritual hunger. It is the experience of the inner life that interested and excited Matheson, not doctrinal purity.

As with Augustine and Mohammed, Matheson recited in vivid terms the "crisis of faith" faced by Francis. After the crisis passed, for Francis the world had changed: it no longer held the attraction for him that it once did. From pride, Francis journeyed to "the profoundest humility, into the deepest conviction of utter nothingness."[219] He served lepers, "stooping to the most menial offices"[220] and his friars heroically, at great cost, tended to men on the battlefields of Europe.[221] In a mystical experience, an "ecstasy of prayer, in a moment of rapt enthusiasm" Francis met "a heavenly stranger, bearing a sword in his hand."[222] The stranger imprinted on Francis five wounds, the same as those suffered by Christ on the cross. While acknowledging the subjectivity of the vision, Matheson saw in this vision "the desire to go back to the earthly life of the Master, and to see Him as He was in the fashion of a suffering man."[223] Suffering is central to Matheson's understanding of the Eternal. Francis "glowed with the spontaneous fervor of a life which had awakened to the joys of a personal religion."[224]

218. Matheson, *The Spirit of Christianity*, vol. 2, 20.

219. Matheson, *The Spirit of Christianity* vol. 2, 165.

220. Matheson, *The Spirit of Christianity*, vol. 2, 166.

221. Matheson, *The Spirit of Christianity*, vol. 2, 167.

222. Matheson, *The Spirit of Christianity*, vol. 2, 167.

223. Matheson, *The Spirit of Christianity*, vol. 2, 168.

224. Matheson, *The Spirit of Christianity*, vol. 2, 170.

The Franciscans took sin seriously; they did not believe that the practice of indulgences could affect the inner life, the spiritual nature. Spiritual growth is an inner struggle. Matheson wrote: "The struggle is fierce and keen, sometimes inclining to the flesh, and sometimes to the spirit. But if the spirit faint not, it will conquer at the last, and the virtue will become no longer meritorious, but natural—as natural as breathing of the air, as natural as the vision of the sunbeams.[225] Filled with the Spirit, Matheson chose first a metaphor which placed God within breath itself, as the very source of our life: God is within us. The second metaphor draws on the importance of light, but also warmth: the Spirit gives light, casting away our blindness but, as warmth, it is also near, tenderly touching our skin, our face.

Mysticism

Of Mysticism, Matheson, the Protestant, Presbyterian minister, made the most astounding claim: for him, mysticism brings us "almost within sight of the promised land . . ."[226] There has never been an age in any religion, he said, which did not possess within it lives dedicated to the mystical spirit. It is there in the hymns of Brahmanism, the aspirations of Platonism, the writings of Paul, the Alexandrian School of the second century, Origen, Dionysius, Scotus Erigena, Bernard of Clairvaux, Bonaventura, Eckhart, Tauler and Ruysbrock. For the period of which Matheson is writing, he states that the mystical spirit culminates in the work of Thomas à Kempis: the *Imitation of Christ* stands next to the Bible.[227] In mysticism, Matheson sees the spirit of Protestantism, that is, the desire for the individual life to thrive against the collective authority of the Church. Mysticism is a revolt, a "silent protest," a "dissent expressed inwardly in the secret places of the heart."[228] Mysticism "craved the liberty to think in solitude, to commune with its own heart, to stand face to face and alone with those mysteries in which it lived and moved and had its being."[229] Christ was not to be found in the heavens, but within: "He whom ye seek is already nigh you; dwelling in your hearts, and waiting for recognition by them! Ye have only to turn your eyes inward, and you will behold His glory; ye have only to look on Him,

---

225. Matheson, *The Spirit of Christianity*, vol. 2, 185.

226. Matheson, *The Spirit of Christianity*, vol. 2, 191.

227. Matheson, *The Spirit of Christianity*, vol. 2, 214. Matheson does later say that this work is essentially an ascetic work and suited men of prayer in the desert.

228. Matheson, *The Spirit of Christianity*, vol. 2, 194.

229. Matheson, *The Spirit of Christianity*, vol. 2, 195.

and immediately you will be likened unto Him."[230] Or, again: "There is a life which is touching your life—the life of infinite love; receive it, and it will become your own! Gaze upon it, and in your gaze you will be transfigured into its glory—you, and the world with you."[231]

Similarly, while acknowledging that even in the holiest of persons, absolute assimilation to Christ is a "far-off attainment," nevertheless, Caird described the "first, faint breath of a living faith" as "intensively and in essence, the perfect union of the soul with Christ."[232] Caird describes the relationship of Christ with His followers as being "a presence . . . infinitely more intimate and profound than that of His outward contiguity as an individual person."[233] He taught that the goal of a finite life is reached when it is "suffused with the presence and life of the Infinite."[234] Caird defined religion as:

> The surrender of the finite will to the infinite, the abnegation of all desire, inclination, volition, that pertain to me as this private individual self, the giving up of every aim or activity that points only to my exclusive pleasure or interest, the absolute identification of my will with the will of God. Oneness of mind and will with the Divine mind and will is not the future hope and aim of religion, but its very beginning and birth in the soul. To enter on the religious life is to terminate the struggle between my false self and that higher self which is at once mine and infinitely more than mine, it is to realize the latter as that with which my whole spiritual being is identified, so that "it is no longer I that live"—not any "I" that I can claim as my own—"but God that liveth in me."[235]

For Caird, prayer is to rise above ourselves. In prayer, we leave behind the outer world, as unreal, and enter "the true, the real, the world of unchangeable and eternal reality."[236] In the lecture room, Matheson listened to Caird's every word, enthralled by his voice, insight and teaching. Combined with the mystical insight of his childhood minister, Pulsford, Caird's lectures helped shape Matheson, a man who often spoke of his Highland blood. Matheson said, "He whom ye seek is already nigh you; dwelling in your hearts . . ."[237]

230. Matheson, *The Spirit of Christianity*, vol. 2, 195.

231. Matheson, *The Spirit of Christianity*, vol. 2, 196.

232. Caird, *The Fundamental Ideas*, 232.

233. Caird, *The Fundamental Ideas*, 237

234. Caird, *The Philosophy of Religion,* 281.

235. Caird, *The Philosophy of Religion*, 283.

236. Caird, *The Philosophy of Religion*, 288.

237. Matheson, *The Spirit of Christianity*, vol. 2, 195.

Mysticism relied on "inward evidence."[238] We are drawn into "the very heart of the divine life:" the pride of the human spirit is broken and its selfishness is crucified. The kingdom of God is to be "seen by an inward sense"[239] which was "irrational, not because reason was opposed to it, but because reason was beneath it."[240]

Conclusion

The story of Matheson's "crisis of faith" is a complex one. Behind him lay the unquestioning faith of his early years, and the earthquake brought by the challenges of the Victorian era. Behind his personal struggle for faith and understanding lay the complex subject headings of Idealism and Mysticism: Matheson's importance lies in part not only in his being subject to those conflicting influences, but being capable of speaking and writing about them in ways which provided not only the public experience of worship under his ministry, but a unique personal record of the struggle of an intense, intelligent, well-informed and sensitive Christian mind to reconcile them into a personal faith which was workable and able to sustain a long ministry.

Throughout these mature years, Matheson was explicit in his support of the mystical sense or the mystical interpretation of Scripture. He was attracted to those theologians whose religion appealed to the heart or intuition, to those that sought the hidden meanings in Scripture. A product of his time, influenced by Caird certainly, and perhaps others, such as Arnold, Matheson was a mystic who had survived his "crisis of faith," who was to have decades of strongly original thought to express and to convey to his contemporaries, and to preach to his congregation. His inner battle fought, he was able to continue his ministry in ways which were original, sometimes troubling, always indicative of a strong mind facing up to some of his century's most appealing and troubling enigmas.

238. Matheson, *The Spirit of Christianity*, vol. 2, 198.
239. Matheson, *The Spirit of Christianity*, vol. 2, 202.
240. Matheson, *The Spirit of Christianity*, vol. 2, 203.

3

Evolution

Introduction

IN THIS CHAPTER, I shall discuss Matheson's contribution to the religion and science debate that took place in the second half of the nineteenth century. I shall begin with scientific and religious background information in order to place Matheson's work in context. Matheson's major work on the doctrine of evolution is his book *Can the Old Faith Live With The New? Or The Problem of Evolution and Revelation* (1885). I shall briefly discuss the thought of some of the main protagonists from both sides during this period, such as Huxley, Spencer, Drummond, Temple and Moore. In his book Matheson critiqued the work of Herbert Spencer. I shall discuss in detail Matheson's understanding of how the doctrines of creation and evolution relate to each other. I shall explore his interpretation of the first two chapters of the Book of Genesis in relation to Spencer's doctrine of evolution. I shall discuss Matheson's theology of union and immortality of the soul in light of evolution. Matheson strove to maintain the unity of all things and so the complementarity of religion and science.

Historical Context: Scientific Developments

In the period from the late eighteenth century to the middle of the nineteenth century, geology, paleontology and zoology "opened up a vast and unfamiliar history of the earth, of the animal kingdom, and of the human race itself."[1] Victorian society was introduced to a new vision of the earth's history, an altogether larger timescale and humanity's close relationship with the nonhuman world. By the 1830s, in geology the discovery of dinosaur fossils similarly raised a question concerning the accuracy of the

---

1. Livingston, *Religious Thought*, 150.

biblical account of creation in Genesis. Melnyk notes that, not only was fossil hunting a popular pursuit for the amateur, it was one of the few areas of science which afforded women the chance of meaningful participation.[2] Throughout the 1830s, *The Evangelical Christian Lady's Magazine* carried articles and letters on geology and its possible implications.[3] In the early 1830s, the Scottish geologist Charles Lyell (1797–1875), "the foremost paleontologist of the century," published his *Principles of Geology* in which he established uniformitarianism, which assumes that natural laws and processes in the universe apply everywhere and in the past. Lyell demonstrated "the sheer impossibility of believing that the world had been created all in one go, some thousands of years BC."[4] The traditional interpretation of the six days of creation in the Bible could not be true.

In 1844, the most explicit pre-Darwinian publication which proposed the idea of development was that of Robert Chambers (1802–1871) in his *Vestiges of the Natural History of Creation*. Although ridiculed by many scientists for its simplistic Lamarckianism and though it caused a public outcry, nevertheless Chambers' book proved very popular running to four editions in the first six months. While some thought it to be from the pen of Prince Albert, Chambers argued that humanity, which to the Author of Nature was no more than "a consideration of inferior moment," was left to take its "chance amidst the melee of the various laws affecting him . . . The system has the fairness of a lottery, in which every one has the chance of drawing the prize."[5] Adam Sedgwick, Professor of Geology at Cambridge, wrote of Chambers' book: "If the book be true, the labors of sober induction are in vain; religion is a lie; human law is a mass of folly, and a base injustice; morality is moonshine; our labors for the black people of Africa mere works of madmen; and man and woman are only better beasts."[6]

The perception of rivalry or even hostility between religion and science in large measure arose from the popular works of James William Draper (1811–1882) and Andrew Dickson White (1832–1918). Draper, a rationalist and professor of chemistry, published his *History of the Conflict between Religion and Science* in 1874, while White, the first president of Cornell University, "an intrepid defender of intellectual freedom and an opponent of sectarianism," published his two-volume *A History of the Warfare of*

---

2. Melnyk, *Victorian Religion*, 137.

3. Melnyk, *Victorian Religion*, 138

4. Wilson, *God's Funeral*, 236.

5. Wilson, *God's Funeral*, 237

6. Melnyk, *Victorian Religion*, 138.

Science with Theology in Christendom in 1896.[7] Of both publications, Livingston notes: "While neither author opposed a theology open to scientific advance, their choice of examples and their militant rhetoric belied the fact, and their books incited a combative polemic on both sides, producing the image of two discordant, contending powers."[8] Published in 1859, Darwin's *Origin of Species*, explained his theory of natural selection. While Darwin played down "the metaphysical implications of his theory,"[9] it "removed any necessity for a metaphor of purpose when discussing natural history."[10] At this early stage in his work, Darwin chose to frame his theory of natural selection in religious language. There was no need to make any reference to the existence of a Creator, but Darwin's closing paragraph reads: "There is a grandeur in this view of life with its several powers, having been originally breathed by the Creator into a few forms or into one; and that, whilst this planet has gone cycling on according to the fixed law of gravity, so from so simple a beginning endless forms most beautiful and most wonderful have been, and are being, evolved."[11] In 1868, the Austrian monk, Gregor Mendel, through his experiments in breeding pea-plants, established "the existence of what he called hereditary particles and are now called genes."[12] In a discovery which may be more important than that of Darwin, Mendel "demonstrated that natural forms can be subdivided into discrete traits which are transmitted genetically from one generation to the next."[13] Wilson notes: "Father Mendel showed no unwillingness, day after day, to rise before dawn and sing a psalm which proclaimed that it is God 'who hath made us and not we ourselves;' he died in his monastery."[14] The cumulative impact of Chambers, Lyell, and Darwin did not lead to widespread unbelief, but in 1871, shortly before he died, H. L. Mansel, philosopher and Dean of St Paul's Cathedral, warned that theology will soon need to defend the existence of God and human free will.[15] The period 1850 to 1870 was described as the age of the "cult of science" or the "worship of science."

In his work *Evidence as to Man's Place in Nature* (1863), T H Huxley sought to show that there was "no absolute structural line of demarcation"

7. Livingston, "Natural Science and Theology," 141.

8. Livingston, "Natural Science and Theology," 141.

9. Wilson, *God's Funeral*, 237.

10. Wilson, *God's Funeral*, 240.

11. Wilson, *God's Funeral*, 238.

12. Wilson, *God's Funeral*, 242.

13. Wilson, *God's Funeral*, 242.

14. Wilson, *God's Funeral*, 242.

15. Wilson, *God's Funeral*, 241.

between animals "which immediately succeed us in the scale" and our-selves.[16] For Huxley, Darwinism implied "a mechanistic materialism."[17] In 1870 Huxley, Darwin's bulldog, was anointed "pope" by Richard Holt Hut-ton, theologian and editor of *The Spectator*, in view of Huxley's tendency to dogmatism. Hutton used the word "pope" to suggest that Huxley's appar-ent intellectual openness was a sham.[18] By 1880, though he later qualified his remarks, in a public lecture Huxley claimed that "for the purpose of attaining real culture, an exclusively scientific education is at least as ef-fectual as an exclusively literary education."[19] Hutton's view was that the scientific naturalists, when in power, behaved no differently from those they had displaced. Huxley's anointing came a year following the declara-tion by the Roman Catholic Church that Pope Pius IX was infallible. In an attempt to undermine pantheism, materialism and atheism, the First Vati-can Council sought to defend religion in its declaration. Throughout the nineteenth century, the Vatican assaulted "every development in scientific knowledge, every glimmering of light shed in the field of biblical scholar-ship, [and] every advancement of technical skill (it even issued condemna-tion of the electric light)."[20] Huxley referred to himself as "the Bishop of the church scientific." He said: "Whenever science and [religious] orthodoxy have been fairly opposed, the latter have been forced to retire from the lists, bleeding and crushed if not annihilated . . . Extinguished theologians lie about the cradle of every science as strangled snakes besides that of Hercules."[21] Huxley often used his satirical gifts to attack Christian ortho-doxy and to "seize the high moral ground for a progressive intellectual culture associated with the sciences."[22] It was Huxley who termed the de-scription "agnostic." Hutton said that it was a reference to the Unknown God cited by Paul in the Book of Acts. However, Huxley insisted that the term meant that, unlike the Gnostics, he had no knowledge of God.[23] For thirty-five years, Huxley was "the most eloquent public defender of the notion that Science and Christianity—anyway, orthodox Christianity, as popularly understood and officially defended by the Establishment—were

16. Livingston, *Religious Thought*, 158.

17. Livingston, *Religious Thought*, 167.

18. Lightman, "The Creed of Science," 456–57.

19. Otis, *Literature and Science*, xviii.

20. Wilson, *God's Funeral*, 286.

21. Livingston, "Natural Science and Theology," 142.

22. Lightman, "The Creed of Science," 456.

23. Wilson, *God's Funeral*, 256.

incompatible."[24] In 1888, in an article entitled "The New Dogmatism," the poultry, pigeon, and animal expert Lewis Wright described the materialistic system of evolution as a new creed, saying, "It explicitly claims to be sufficient for all the concerns and conduct of human life."[25]

In 1872, in his last work, *The Old Faith and the New*, Strauss said that the "only choice is between the miracle—the divine hand of the Creator—and Darwin."[26] While Matheson does not refer to Strauss in his work on evolution, nevertheless the titles are very close. William Kingdon Clifford (1845–1879), described as a mathematical genius, argued that truth is no greater than the proofs upon which it is built. He said, "It is wrong every where and for anyone to believe anything upon insufficient evidence."[27] Clifford said that the death of God was a pre-requisite for the coming of the Kingdom of Man.[28] In 1874, in his presidential address to the British Association in Belfast, Tyndall's address was "nothing less than an unapologetic defense of the autonomy of science and an aggressive attack on the cultural authority of Christian theologians."[29] For Tyndall, religion added "inward completeness and dignity to man" if it remained within the "region of poetry and emotion" but became "mischievous if it intruded on the region of objective knowledge."[30]

In 1888, the scientific naturalist Grant Allen suggested that contained within Darwin's work must lie "a gospel according to Darwin."[31] The changing worldview is captured poignantly by Lightman: "Darwinism substituted the rise of man for the Christian dogma of the fall of man, and it replaced the notion of a lost paradise in the dim past with a realizable paradise in the nearer future."[32] In 1865 in his Bampton Lectures the English theologian J B Mozley said that miracles were "proof of the truth of revelation."[33] Darwin said that "the more we know of the fixed laws of nature the more incredible do miracles become."[34] By the 1880s revelation was judged not by miracles but "by the character of Christ and his effect upon mankind, by its

24. Wilson, *God's Funeral*, 251–52.

25. Lightman, "The Creed of Science," 449.

26. Livingston, "Natural Science and Theology," 143.

27. Wilson, *God's Funeral*, 253.

28. Wilson, *God's Funeral*, 252.

29. Lightman, "Scientists as Materialists," 199.

30. Lightman, "Scientists as Materialists," 201.

31. Lightman, "The Creed of Science and its Critics," 454.

32. Lightman, "The Creed of Science and its Critics," 454.

33. Chadwick, *The Victorian Church II*, 31.

34. Wilson, *God's Funeral*, 235.

correspondence with the highest moral aspirations of the soul, by the direct apprehension of the divine in so many members of the human race."[35]

Honestly or deceitfully, scientific naturalists portrayed their search for truth through the discipline of the natural science as self-abnegation, self-sacrifice or self-annihilation. In 1887, William Allingham, poet and editor of *Fraser's Magazine*, outlined what he called the "creed of the future." Its articles included ideas "that human beings are basically animals; that only matter existed; that there are neither souls nor heaven; that there were no moral obligations; and that there was no trace of a divine being."[36] A central and unsettling question for the Victorians was, "What does it mean to be human?" Otis writes:

> The rapid development of industrialization, physiology, evolutionary theory, and the mental and social sciences challenged the traditional view of people as uniquely privileged beings created in the divine image. While religion remained a powerful social and ideological force, it became increasingly difficult for educated writers to refer to a soul. Too many other fields offered alternative explanations of human behavior, from muscle reflexes to inherited memories. If nineteenth century physiological psychologists were right, and human thoughts and actions could be explained by the laws of chemistry and physics, it was unclear how people could be distinguished from the machines on which they increasingly depended.[37]

Atheists partly avoided criticism and condemnation by claiming their creed was based on science. The novelist William Hurrell Mallock (1849–1923) was extremely critical of the "whole gospel of atheistic ethics [based on] heroic self-abnegation."[38] For Mallock, while the moral law of atheism claimed to "de-religionize life," in fact religion is "lurking everywhere, even in the notion of self-abnegation."[39] In the 1860s, Huxley had been content to allow scientific naturalism to be adorned with a religious gloss. In the earlier half of the century, scientists frequently made reference to poetry and fiction. Charles Lyell's *Principles of Geology* (1830–1833) was widely read because he presented his evidence for gradual geological change alongside literary references to Milton, Scott and Wordsworth.[40] However,

35. Chadwick, *The Victorian Church II*, 31.
36. Lightman, "The Creed of Science," 457.
37. Otis, *Literature and Science*, xxvi.
38. Lightman, "The Creed of Science," 457.
39. Lightman, "The Creed of Science," 457.
40. Otis, *Literature and Science*, xix.

by 1889 Huxley came to see that the use of a religious gloss exposed scientific naturalism to a "damaging comparison" with "dogmatic Christians."[41] In the same year, Mallock argued that Huxley and others were "cowards for not having the courage to admit that they had a creed, and that it required the denial of God and morality."[42]

Herbert Spencer

Charles Chapman, Principal of Western College, Plymouth, states that evolutionists can be divided into two schools of thought. The first school includes Haeckel, Büchner, Voght, and Strauss, and the second school is that of Herbert Spencer (1820–1903). The first school "postulate matter and mechanical force as constituting all that is . . . [and] that thought is the sole product of molecular motion."[43] By contrast, the second school holds that "at the base of all phenomena, and as the causal explanation of the facts of matter and mind, there lies an Eternal Reality—unknown and unknowable as to its nature, but known in so far as it is the assured source of all phenomenal existence."[44]

In the middle to late Victorian years, periodicals carried debates on the philosophy of mind between idealists and empiricists. Few writers believed that the brain's physiology could replace "the science of mind."[45] Scientific naturalists did not believe that changing the origin of facts changed the facts or values.[46] It seemed that the more scientists of the medical profession explored "the physiological relation of mind . . . the deeper the new science went, the more it confirmed the untenability of materialism."[47] In a very positive review of Laycock's *Mind and Brain* (1860), we read: "Inductive science . . . will never be able to put its finger on that which is before, and above, and beyond all induction, viz., the mind of the human investigator, with all its innate and ineradicable instincts, and the kindred mind of the Divine Creator, with its exhaustible riches of primordial types."[48]

Many writers on the subject of brain and mind held a religious worldview and assumed their readers did also. In his long study in the early 1870s,

41. Lightman, "The Creed of Science," 462.
42. Lightman, "The Creed of Science," 463.
43. Chapman, "Evolution," 174.
44. Chapman, "Evolution," 174.
45. Smith, "Physiology of the Will," 90.
46. Smith, "Physiology of the Will," 91.
47. Smith, "Physiology of the Will," 91.
48. Smith, "Physiology of the Will," 93.

Knowing and Feeling, the psychologist William Smith wrote: "My position as a psychologist is clear . . . It seems that all our lives of thought bring us from the natural to the supernatural, bring us to that Absolute Being and Power on which all nature rests."[49] Smith held that seeking an understanding of the body's capacity for thought was "to approach the problem of creation."[50]

From 1860 to 1896, Spencer published in ten volumes his work *System of Synthetic Philosophy*, which included volumes on biology, ethics, psychology, sociology and religion. For Spencer, "all phenomena were interpreted in a systematic fashion according to the law of evolution."[51] Among scientific naturalists, many believed that their creed "contained a profoundly religious quality."[52] The Irish physicist John Tyndall (1820–1893) said that, "No atheistic reasoning can dislodge religion from the human heart."[53] However, Spencer went much further than Huxley and others. In 1862, in the first volume of his work, Spencer confirmed his belief in the existence of divine being, which he said is the place where science and religion meet. For Spencer, the divine being was the "Unknowable."

By the 1880s, disaffected secularists, including Charles Albert Watts, Richard Bitchell and Samuel Laing referred to themselves as Spencerian agnostics. In 1883, Bitchell published his work *Creed of a Modern Agnostic*, in which he set out "a series of propositions about the manifestations of the unknowable."[54] Four years later, in his work *Agnostic Problem* (1887), Bitchell said that "we not only can worship the Unknowable . . . it is the only proper object of supreme worship."[55] Watts suggested that an Agnostic temple be built in southwestern London. Lightman states that, in part, the religious dimension of the scientific naturalists was intended to give them intellectual credibility and, at the same time, differentiate them from atheists of the lower classes.[56]

For many across Victorian society, the scientific naturalists possessed an arrogance and bigotry similar to that of the worst excesses of religion.[57] In 1887 George Douglas Campbell, the eighth Duke of Argyll, called for a revolt against "that Reign of Terror which had come to be established in the

---

49. Smith, "Physiology of the Will," 94.
50. Smith, "Physiology of the Will," 94.
51. Lightman, "The Creed of Science," 453.
52. Lightman, "The Creed of Science," 453.
53. Lightman, "The Creed of Science," 453.
54. Lightman, "The Creed of Science," 452.
55. Lightman, "The Creed of Science," 454.
56. Lightman, "The Creed of Science," 454.
57. Lightman, "The Creed of Science," 460.

scientific world under the abuse of a great name."[58] While some spoke of a reign of terror, Lightman states that scientific naturalists were succeeding in creating a new creed that was "indispensible to [their efforts] in presenting themselves as the cultural elite best equipped to guide Britain as it was being transformed into a modern, industrial nation. It retained all the advantages of the Anglican creed it was designed to replace; yet it was fully in keeping with the most current science."[59]

Historical Context: Religious Developments

The term "scientific naturalism" was coined by Huxley. Huxley and other scientific naturalists sought to "secularize nature."[60] However, resistance came from within the scientific community, from the geologist Adam Sedgwick and the North British physicists: William Thomson, Professor of Natural Philosophy at Glasgow University, the Scottish Natural Philosophers James Clerk Maxwell and Peter Guthrie Tait and the engineers Fleming Jenkins and Macquorn Rankine. Bearing the impress of Scottish Presbyterianism, the North British physicists viewed the scientific naturalists as "anti-Christian materialists."[61] Among the liberal divines, it was relatively straightforward to "welcome Darwin and the new science generally" because they did not feel that they needed to defend "the literal inspiration of the Bible."[62] Chadwick suggests that theologians were "busier with the consequences of Biblical criticism than the consequences of the natural sciences."[63]

In 1884, one year before Matheson's book on creation and evolution, Henry Drummond (1851–1897) published his book *Natural Law in the Spiritual World*. This was followed ten years later with a second volume, *The Ascent of Man*. Inspired by the work of Dwight L Moody and Ira Sankey, Drummond was "the most popular and influential of the Scottish evangelical theologians."[64] In 1877, he was appointed to a lectureship in natural science at the Free Church College in Glasgow. Six years later, Drummond was appointed professor, a post which he held until his death. *Natural Law in the Spiritual World* "sold a thousand copies a month in Britain a year after its publication. In 1905 the hardback edition continued

58. Lightman, "The Creed of Science," 460.

59. Lightman, "The Creed of Science," 455.

60. Lightman, "The Creed of Science," 451.

61. Lightman, "The Creed of Science," 451.

62 Chadwick, *The Victorian Church II*, 26.

63. Chadwick, *The Victorian Church II*, 30.

64. Livingston, *Religious Thought*, 58.

to sell a thousand copies a year."[65] Drummond argued that the laws of the spiritual world were identical to that of the natural world. In order to defend and promote religious belief, Drummond said that what was required was "a truly scientific theology."[66] In some quarters theology was sufficiently fearful of the challenge of scientific naturalism that it sought to justify itself in the guise of science. Some theologians were fearful of the scientific method and increasingly felt the need to produce what they thought would count as scientific evidence.

In 1875 in their anonymously published *The Unseen Universe*, two Scottish physicists, Balfour Stewart (1828–1887) and Drummond's mentor, P G Tait (1831–1901), promoted the law of continuity. Grove (1867) argued that "we are satisfied that continuity is a law of nature, the true expression of the action of Almighty Power" rather than "special interventions of creative power in changes that are difficult to understand."[67] Stewart and Tait said that, "Divine providence is . . . to be understood in terms of the transference of energy from the invisible to the visible sphere, according to the operation of natural laws."[68] For Drummond "the greatest of the theological laws simply are the Laws of Nature in disguise."[69] Drummond sought "to take off the mask and disclose to a waning skepticism the naturalness of the supernatural."[70] Darwin's *Origin of Species* was perhaps "the most important contribution to the literature of Apologetics which the nineteenth century had produced."[71] In his book *The Greatest Thing in the World* (1880), Drummond stressed the immanence of God: "The old theory that God made the world, made it as an inventor would make a machine, and then stood looking on to see it work, has passed away. God is no longer a remote spectator of the natural world, but immanent in it, pervading matter by His present Spirit, and ordering it by His will. So Christ is immanent in men."[72] Drummond has been described as an amateur in both theology and science, while A. B. Bruce said that Drummond's book *Natural Law in the Spiritual World* "reminded him of a pamphlet titled *Forty Reasons for the Identification of the English People with the Lost Ten Tribes*."[73] It is certainly the case that in order

65. Livingston, *Religious Thought*, 58.

66. Livingston, *Religious Thought*, 59.

67. Livingston, *Religious Thought*, 59.

68. Livingston, *Religious Thought*, 59.

69. Livingston, *Religious Thought*, 60.

70. Livingston, *Religious Thought*, 60.

71. Drummond, *Late Victorian Scotland*, 27.

72. Drummond, *Late Victorian Scotland*, 28–29.

73. Drummond, *Late Victorian Scotland*, 28.

to demonstrate continuity Drummond forced many shallow comparisons. In considering death, Drummond did not differentiate with any credibility the difference between "the impersonal authority of law" which led to the "breakdown of an organism" and "the personal attentiveness of a loving heavenly Father."[74] For Drummond, it mattered little that the God who was present was largely indifferent to suffering. It is worth noting that for all his flaws, Drummond spoke of the Divine "pervading" matter. This is not only a statement of immanence; it hints at a theology of union.

Some leading religious figures argued that science and religion belonged to "disparate spheres of knowledge and truth."[75] A good example would be John Henry Cardinal Newman (1801–1890). For Newman, doctrinal knowledge could not be new because for him the "Divine Voice [had] spoken once for all, and the only question [was] about its meaning."[76] In addressing Divine omnipotence, the theologian ignores the laws of nature as a possible restraint upon God's power, while the scientist is concerned with natural phenomena and puts aside all thought of God's power. The German theologian Albrecht Ritschl (1822–1889) similarly argued that "Christian theology is independent of scientific developments."[77] For Ritschl, "The mind judges sensations and impressions according to the causal relations in an objective (scientific) system of nature. [Equally], the mind receives these sensations according to their worth to the individual. The latter is the source of the mind's knowledge of value."[78] For Ritschl, the latter was the mode of cognition in religion. Both modes offered real and objective knowledge, but knowledge that was categorically different. There was no attempt at reconciliation.

In the same year Drummond published his work *Natural Law in the Spiritual World* Frederick Temple (1821–1902) Bishop of Exeter and later Archbishop of Canterbury, in his Bampton Lectures titled *The Relations between Religion and Science*, sought to reconcile theology with Darwinian naturalism. "The crux of Temple's lectures is the argument that natural theology is strengthened by Darwinism."[79] Temple said that Darwin was concerned with how design was implemented. For Temple, God does not perpetually modify what God has made through special acts of creation. Rather, "there is more divine foresight, there is less divine interposition, and

74. Livingston, *Religious Thought*, 61.

75. Livingston, "Natural Science and Theology," 145.

76. Livingston, "Natural Science and Theology," 146.

77. Livingston, "Natural Science and Theology," 146.

78. Livingston, "Natural Science and Theology," 146.

79. Livingston, *Religious Thought*, 61.

whatever has been taken from the latter has been added to the former."[80] Temple was sure that there was nothing in the new science which could shake the fundamental convictions of religion, namely, the original act of creation and the existence of the human soul. He believed that however far back in time science may go, there would still lie "behind the beginning the original act of creation."[81] Temple famously said that the Creator:

> impressed on certain particles of matter which, either at the beginning or at some point in the history of His creation He endowed with life, such inherent powers that in the ordinary course of time living creatures such as the present were developed. The creative power remains the same in either case; the design with which that creative power was exercised remains the same. He did not make things, we may say; no, but He made them make themselves. And surely this rather adds than withdraws force from the great argument.[82]

Temple maintained that the spiritual faculty of humanity was given "by a direct creative act as soon as the body . . . had been sufficiently developed to receive it."[83]

One notable critic of Temple's theological accommodation of science was Aubrey Lackington Moore (1848–1890), curator of the Botanical Gardens in Oxford. For Moore, Temple and others made two "disastrous errors."[84] Firstly, Moore argued that Temple settled for a form of dualism, in which he created a false antithesis between natural evolution and the supernatural creation of species. Moore preferred to speak of either "supernatural evolution" or "natural creation."[85] In 1883, in his address at a Church Congress in Reading, Moore claimed that theologians were happy to leave science students to their work providing that they were not antitheists. Moore believed that, in accepting such a division as real, that "God's work is partly natural and partly supernatural," was tantamount to recognizing a power other than God.[86] In 1883, Moore said that "for the Christian theologian the facts of nature are the acts of God."[87] For Moore, God is present everywhere. Secondly, Moore argued that Temple, in claiming

---

80. Livingston, *Religious Thought*, 62.

81. Livingston, *Religious Thought*, 62.

82. Livingston, *Religious Thought*, 61–62.

83. Livingston, *Religious Thought*, 62.

84. Livingston, "Natural Science and Theology," 150.

85. Livingston, "Natural Science and Theology," 150.

86. Livingston, *Religious Thought*, 64.

87. Livingston, *Religious Thought*, 64.

that God had impressed God's will on creation "once for all" by "His one original impress," meant that God had withdrawn to let creation evolve it-self.[88] Moore did agree with Temple that Darwin had done theology a good service in defeating the dogma of special creations. Acts of special creation amounted to no more than "a theory of ordinary absence."[89] Darwinism, he said, "as a theory is infinitely more Christian than a theory of 'Special Cre-ations,'" because the former implied "the immanence of God in nature, and the omnipresence of his creative power."[90] As the 1880s progressed, new theologies such as neo-Hegelian philosophy in the Scottish universities and also at Oxford increasingly stressed divine immanence.

In summary, the context in which Matheson was writing was a spec-trum of scientific and religious views. Spanning a century of continuing discussion, Matheson faced challenges of materialism; the accuracy of the biblical narrative in relation to geology; dogmatism on both the religious and scientific sides; calls for a "gospel of Darwin;" claims that scientific in-quiry was as selfless as the highest ethics of religion; and scientific claims that the universe is dependent upon transcendence but an unknowable transcendence.

Matheson on Evolution and Creation

In 1885 Matheson published his work *Can the Old Faith Live With The New? Or The Problem of Evolution and Revelation*. His publication appeared in a century of enormous scientific change and in a decade which saw numerous publications on issues of natural science and religion by scientists, theolo-gians, novelists, poets and editors. Matheson's work is measured in tone and careful in its representation of views different from his own. In his preface, Matheson stated that he will consider the modern doctrine of evolution and its relation to "those doctrines of the Bible which bear on the development of the world."[91] At the outset, Matheson noted the work of Joseph John Murphy in *The Scientific Bases of Faith* (1873) and Henry Drummond in *Natural Law in the Spiritual World* (1884). Matheson does not challenge the credibility of the theory of evolution but asked, if true, what it may mean for religious doctrine and revelation. He understood evolution to mean "the particular mode in which things become what they are."[92] He noted that in the view

88. Livingston, "Natural Science and Theology," 150.
89. Livingston, "Natural Science and Theology," 150.
90. Livingston, *Religious Thought*, 65.
91. Matheson, *The Old Faith Live*, v.
92. Matheson, *The Old Faith Live*, vii.

of many natural evolution leads to religious agnosticism[93] and that the challenge for theology in the late nineteenth century was "to discover some positive ground for the continuance of a belief in that which transcends nature."[94] He said that theology has: "to meet Agnosticism by proving that something can be known beyond the things of experience; or, to speak more correctly, by proving that there is a region beyond the things of experience—a region of whose essential nature we are, indeed, in ignorance, but of whose existence we have the most satisfactory evidence."[95]

Matheson approached Scripture analytically while seeking its inner meaning. There were numerous attempts to interpret the opening chapters of the Book of Genesis in a way that made sense in light of evolution. The geologist William Buckland had earlier taken the view that the first verse of Genesis 1 ("In the beginning God created heaven and earth") represented primal creation, while the second verse ("And the earth was without form and void") was the beginning of natural history after a prolonged period of time.[96] Matheson began by stating that the doctrine of evolution could not have been further from the mind of the author of the Book of Genesis, either to confirm or deny the doctrine. Drawing on the Hegelian method, Matheson cited the progression in religious thought as an example of the principle of evolution: "the slightest scrutiny of human annals makes it apparent that, in every case, the displacement has been effected not by abolition but by transmutation."[97] The doctrine of Buddhism is a transmutation from Brahman (Hinduism); the Buddha was a reformer, not an innovator. Matheson understood Christianity as a progression and evolution from Judaism. The illustration chosen by Matheson from Buddhism not only highlights the evolution of theological thought but brings to the fore the importance of inner change within Buddhism. It is a significant choice of example. The Buddha said that "his countrymen . . . might enter into rest in the very heart of the present scene of things, and in the midst of the world of life might obtain the Nirvana of peace. He told them that the true death of the spirit of man was the death of self, the surrender of individual desire, the giving up of the anxious longing for seen and perishable things."[98] Matheson's example explicitly draws on an emphasis central to mysticism, that of death to self, to the world, and inner change. Matheson believed that "the most advanced

93. Matheson, *The Old Faith Live*, v.

94. Matheson, *The Old Faith Live*, 31.

95. Matheson, *The Old Faith Live*, 31.

96. Livingston, *Religious Thought*, 152.

97. Matheson, *The Old Faith Live*, 5.

98. Matheson, *The Old Faith Live*, 6.

evolutionists" would welcome a secure place for the religious consciousness in their system of natural evolution.[99] Religion "is essentially based upon the belief in the existence of something which transcends the world."[100] It is based upon "a Presence behind law, a presence which gives to law at once its existence and its vindication."[101] Without that presence, nature would be the product of "a blind necessity."[102] Matheson understood the supernatural or the miraculous as the power behind nature. In a critical passage to understanding the relationship between science and religion, between the world of nature and the Transcendent, Matheson wrote:

> We call that miraculous which transcends the order of nature; we ought not to limit the word to that which supersedes the order of nature. To supersede the order of nature is to violate it, but to transcend it may be to manifest it. If we believe in the existence of a Power behind nature, then the manifestation of nature itself is a revelation of that which transcends it, because it is a revelation of the existence of that Power which lies at the back of that order which it originates.[103]

For Matheson, belief in the miraculous is essential for religion, but miraculous meant that which transcends nature, not violates it. Following the publication of his work, severe criticism came from "the side of religious conservatism."[104] Many of his critics felt that the distinction he made between transcending a law and violating it was false and that the distinction was intended to mask his disbelief in a Supreme Will.[105] In response, Matheson separated the Will of God from the character of God. He acknowledged that the Will of God is an ultimate fact in relation to the universe, but God's will is not ultimate in relation to God's Self. Matheson said, "We believe that the Divine will has something behind it—a Divine Nature, or, which is the same thing, a law of Divine being."[106]

In the Lord's Prayer, Christians pray the petition, "Thy Will be done in earth as it is in heaven." Matheson asked his critics, "Who is 'Thy' in this prayer?" Is the God of the Lord's Prayer "a Molloch . . . a crushing power . . . a being whose sole desire is the aggrandizement of himself?" Or do we

99. Matheson, *The Old Faith Live*, 16.

100. Matheson, *The Old Faith Live*, 21.

101. Matheson, *The Old Faith Live*, 21–22.

102. Matheson, *The Old Faith Live*, 22.

103. Matheson, *The Old Faith Live*, 22.

104. Matheson, "Christianity And Evolution," 2.

105. Matheson, "Christianity And Evolution," 4.

106. Matheson, "Christianity And Evolution," 5.

pray to One who is "already in possession of a law of life which impels Him to do good?"[107] He wrote:

> If the will of God be only an expression of the nature of God, and if the nature of God be but another phrase of the law of His being, it follows inevitably that the universe ultimately rests, not upon the mandates of an arbitrary will, but upon the basis of a steadfast, fixed, invariable law—so steadfast and invariable as to justify the application of the word: 'Heaven and earth may pass away, but my words shall not pass away.'[108]

Belief in a violation of law, in other words, a violation contrary to God's being, was not reverence for the Divine but an assertion of atheism.[109] Instead of revelation through special acts, through the actions of an arbitrary will, Matheson saw the whole of life as revelation, as a manifestation of the Divine. For example, "the human is a miracle in the light of the animal, because it reveals a law that transcends the sensational life, and is able to criticize that sensation."[110] For Matheson, God is seen in and through nature, through the laws of nature. In the *Epistle to the Hebrews*, we read, "By faith we understand that the worlds were prepared by the word of God, so that what is seen was made from things that are not visible" (11:1). The essence of the religious faculty is the "power to discover that there is something which transcends nature—that the very existence of a visible order presupposes the existence of something which is not visible."[111] The writer of the Epistle found "evidence for the supernatural in the order of nature itself; it is through the things that are seen that he reaches his conviction of the existence of that which is not seen."[112] The miraculous is not a violation of the law of nature but "a manifestation that the law proceeds from something behind it—a revelation that it is not self-constituted, but constituted by a Divine Power."[113] As a theologian within the mystical tradition, Matheson saw God in all things rather than appearing in special or isolated acts. The Spirit that filled creation filled Matheson's soul.

Matheson wrote of the Power behind nature. Nature is a manifestation of that presence; nature and the laws of nature are a revelation of the Divine. In 1890/91 Caird delivered the first twelve of his Gifford Lectures. Caird

107. Matheson, "Christianity And Evolution," 6.
108. Matheson, "Christianity And Evolution," 6–7.
109. Matheson, "Christianity And Evolution," 7.
110. Matheson, "Christianity And Evolution," 25.
111. Matheson, *The Old Faith Live*, 24.
112. Matheson, *The Old Faith Live*, 25.
113. Matheson, *The Old Faith Live*, 27.

began by articulating the relationship between natural and revealed religion. Caird said that it did not matter whether we heard "a voice from heaven, from the lips of an inspired prophet, by sacred tradition . . . *or* by the observation of nature, by the study of history, by the teaching and influence of other minds, by the moral and spiritual results of our own experience and reflection."[114] Caird said that through the "office of revelation" humanity is instructed on the nature of life in this life and not instructed on "some transcendental order of things" or "something that pertains to the superhuman, supernatural sphere."[115] The purpose of revealed religion is to enable us to "penetrate to the moral and spiritual meaning of the world in which we are."[116] Both Caird and Matheson trusted human reason as a means of discerning and encountering the Sacred. However, Matheson went further. In the language of a mystic, he said that faith is "to see the supernatural in everything."[117] Matheson's language is intense: "To faith . . . all things alike are to be revelations of the supernatural; every event is in this sense to be startling, every sight in this sense miraculous. The object of faith is to [see] the supernatural in the natural, or rather behind the natural."[118] For Matheson, encounter with the Divine is startling: every event and sight is illumined with God. Matheson sensed the miraculous; it was a direct experience.

Like Caird, Matheson argued that the theologian cannot take refuge in the mysterious. While there was an element of mystery in religion a religion which is entirely mysterious—with an object of religion which is entirely unknown—is absurd. The Agnostic, said Matheson, would argue that taking refuge in a sense of mystery is no more than an escape into a fancy.[119] Yet, properly understood, the miraculous is "just the deepest experience of our lives."[120] Again, we hear Matheson encounter God directly; intimately and all-consuming.

Existence of the Universe

Matheson argued that there are only three options which potentially account for the existence of the universe. Firstly, that the duration of the universe is eternal; secondly, that the present system is a product of chance;

114. Caird, *Fundamental Ideas of Christianity*, 6.

115. Caird, *Fundamental Ideas of Christianity*, 7.

116. Caird, *Fundamental Ideas of Christianity*, 7.

117. Matheson, *The Old Faith Live*, 28.

118. Matheson, *The Old Faith Live*, 28.

119. Matheson, *The Old Faith Live*, 31.

120. Matheson, *The Old Faith Live*, 34.

and, thirdly, that the first principle of the universe is a Divine Intelligence. "It is the doctrine of evolution that there never has been an absolute beginning."[121] Matheson argued that the first option is not credible because it assumes that the physical, dependent universe, a universe which is incapable of self-existence, is "suspended on nothing . . . or that a series of consequents exists without any antecedent."[122] For Matheson, the second option is equally problematic. Huxley himself admitted that "if spontaneous generation ever happened, it must have occurred under conditions which no longer exist."[123] Matheson stated: "The belief that life at one time arose spontaneously from dead matter is itself the belief that dead matter at one time possessed a power which it does not now possess . . . It is the acceptance of a doctrine which is confessedly contrary to all scientific [evolutionary] experience . . ."[124] The third option, that "the visible order of things [is] the result of a spiritual and creative intelligence," involved no violation of the law of nature; "it is only a miracle of transcendence."[125] Some argued that if God has no cause, then why cannot the universe have no cause? Differentiating between existence and change, Matheson stated that "the principle is not that every existence must have a cause, but that every change must have a cause."[126] He stated: "It is because this world exhibits to us only a succession of changes that we are driven to infer the existence of a power underlying these changes."[127] Having briefly examined the three options which purport to account for the existence of the universe, Matheson argued that only faith, belief in a Divine Intelligence, made sense because it was the only option in which "there is a place for [evolutionary] nature itself."[128] The natural is bounded by the supernatural and "beyond the sphere of experiment and understanding there lies a region of the supersensuous and the mystical."[129] For Matheson, as with Caird, humanity is able to perceive the possibility of infinitude because it is aware that this world is finite: "every object in the world is finite or limited—is bounded or marked off from other things by a certain definite form."[130] Infinitude is an

121. Matheson, *The Old Faith Live*, 36.

122. Matheson, *The Old Faith Live*, 39.

123. Matheson, *The Old Faith Live*, 41.

124. Matheson, *The Old Faith Live*, 41–42.

125. Matheson, *The Old Faith Live*, 43.

126. Matheson, *The Old Faith Live*, 45.

127. Matheson, *The Old Faith Live*, 46.

128. Matheson, *The Old Faith Live*, 48.

129. Matheson, *The Old Faith Live*, 49.

130. Matheson, *The Old Faith Live*, 62.

attribute of the Divine, not the Divine essence. God is different from time, space and matter not by infinitude, but the Divine nature.[131]

Union

Matheson asked, "Can humanity know God?" In Genesis we read, "Let us make man in our own image" (1: 26), Matheson stated humanity can only know God "by having a kindred nature to God."[132] A theology of union lies at the heart of his work: "The necessary postulate to any knowledge of God whatever is the belief that some mode of the Divine nature is in union with some phase of the human nature."[133] For Matheson, all religions are incarnational: the "doctrine of the incarnation openly or implicitly pervades the whole circle of sacred thought."[134] It is an emphasis of mysticism to see the Sacred in all things, in Christianity and in other world faiths. Matheson acknowledged the doctrine of incarnation in the worship of Brahman, the creed of the Polytheist, the philosophy of Plato and in ancient Judaism. Incarnation "is necessary to the belief of the Theist; it is the life and soul of the Christian." Incarnation, the doctrine of union, is at the centre of Matheson's faith. In eloquent terms, he described the process of creation which he said comes from the poetic imagination of the scientist. The scientist "starts from the conception of a vast nebulous mass of heated matter, slowly revolving round its own axis, and gradually cooling down. Within this heated nebulous mass he conceives to have been originally embraced all the forces of the physical universe."[135] At this earliest stage, life was latent, not non-existent. Matheson drew on the work of Spencer to make his point about the immanence of God. Spencer's "Inscrutable Force or Power" is "The ultimate uniting principle of all other forces and powers, is a principle which itself transcends every material process of nature. It is not a result of physical forces, but a cause of physical forces; it unites them not simply by combining, but mainly by underlying them."[136] During the 1870s, "the periodical literature on science was replete with a language of 'force', 'energy' and 'will', which conjured up a feeling for correspondence between the life and purposes of self and the eternal embedded in nature."[137] Richard Simpson argued that

---

131. Matheson, *The Old Faith Live*, 68.
132. Matheson, *The Old Faith Live*, 72.
133. Matheson, *The Old Faith Live*, 74.
134. Matheson, *The Old Faith Live*, 74.
135. Matheson, *The Old Faith Live*, 84–85.
136. Matheson, *The Old Faith Live*, 86–87.
137. Smith, "Physiology of the Will," 97.

human life would be "meaningless without belief in a spiritual world, without something beyond material civilization."[138]

For Matheson, more than rooted in "a region of mystery," the universe exists in "a region of mystery."[139] The Inscrutable Force, the Transcendent, the Mystery envelopes the whole of creation. Of material things, he said: "Their reality lies in that Existence which they manifest—an Existence which transcends them even while it supports and manifests them—a Power whose being is to them inscrutable even while in it they live and have their being."[140] Matheson stressed the doctrine of Spencer: "Force" is the "deepest essence" of the universe, an essence which is "incapable of change." It is always and everywhere: "the lowliest and the loftiest processes of nature equally manifest its power."[141] Driving home his sense of oneness with the Transcendent, his sense that the Sacred saturates the entire cosmos and every living thing, even thought itself, Matheson wrote: "In each tremor of a nerve, in each wearing of a tissue, in each motion of a limb, in each perception of an organ, we find ourselves perpetually in the presence of a Power which we do not comprehend, but which yet comprehends us and encloses our entire being."[142] Spencer's "God," though he would deny it, is the God of Christian theism: He is a Presence not outside of the world but in the world . . . He is every moment the cause of all existence, the reality of all being, and the source of all movement; the world only lives because He lives."[143] Chapman said that "Job could easily have adopted the term 'the Inscrutable' to indicate his idea of the unsearchableness of the mysterious source of all things."[144] In contrast to Gnosticism, the belief that the individual must escape from self, from this world, the doctrine of evolution means that God is "discerned in nature."[145] The Transcendent is present to the whole of creation equally. What differentiates humanity is that humanity alone is aware of the limits of creation.[146] Humanity knows the Transcendent because "that which transcends nature is already existent within [humanity]."[147] Throughout his book, Matheson cited Spencer

138. Smith, "Physiology of the Will," 97.
139. Matheson, *The Old Faith Live*, 88.
140. Matheson, *The Old Faith Live*, 88.
141. Matheson, *The Old Faith Live*, 89.
142. Matheson, *The Old Faith Live*, 90.
143. Matheson, *The Old Faith Live*, 91.
144. Chapman, "Evolution," 179.
145. Matheson, *The Old Faith Live*, 94.
146. Matheson, *The Old Faith Live*, 98.
147. Matheson, *The Old Faith Live*, 100.

precisely because Spencer espoused the reality of the Transcendent, albeit that Spencer did not intend the God of Christianity.

The Book of Genesis

Matheson sought to harmonize the doctrines of evolution and creation. He sought a re-interpretation of the creation narratives, one that could be read sympathetically alongside the doctrine of evolution. Unlike Drummond, whose interpretation of Scripture was often thought to be forced, Matheson maintained scriptural integrity and intellectual credibility. This is evident in his interpretation of the opening chapter of the Book of Genesis. The account of creation in Genesis is "the most majestic description of creative power ever given by the pen of man."[148] Given the Hebraic tradition of the author of Genesis, Matheson suggested that one might have expected God's immense power to be the central characteristic of the story, so that the whole of creation would be made in six seconds, not six days. The fact that the author extended creation through evenings and mornings "is a proof that there must have been in his mind some sense of scientific congruity."[149]

Matheson said that the Hebraic formula, "God said" is intended to show both the power of God and that there is "no second cause."[150] In Scripture, God speaks to humanity through agents. In communing with "the human, He had to make the winds His messengers, and the flaming fires His ministers."[151] Matheson wrote: "To meet the face of man, to conduct the events of history, the Eternal had to veil His presence—had to clothe Himself in the garments of time—had to speak in the language of men—had to employ the agency of material things."[152] Matheson maintained the integrity of nature, the law of nature, but also preserved the hiddenness of God.

In Genesis, we read that "a wind from God swept over the face of the deep" (Genesis 1:2). For Matheson, the wind or Spirit is suggestive of the inscrutable Force described by Spencer: that "movement should have preceded the existence of light is not a natural supposition, not a supposition in accordance with the appearance of things."[153] Matheson noted "that light owes its origin neither to the sun nor to any other luminary, but to those movements or vibrations of ether which are necessary to the

148. Matheson, *The Old Faith Live*, 108.

149. Matheson, *The Old Faith Live*, 110.

150. Matheson, *The Old Faith Live*, 112.

151. Matheson, *The Old Faith Live*, 113.

152. Matheson, *The Old Faith Live*, 113.

153. Matheson, *The Old Faith Live*, 116.

existence of all suns and of all luminaries."[154] Unlike Spencer, the author of Genesis is "not afraid to define the agency which creates that power as a spiritual intelligence manifesting the attributes of personality and revealing the prerogatives of will."[155]

Following the work of the Scottish geologist Hugh Miller, Matheson noted that the account of creation in Genesis is of what could be seen and that, in fact, was "the order of Geology."[156] Matheson speculated whether the "earlier marine creation is not obliquely glanced at in the remarkable statement that the Spirit or breath of God moved upon the face of the waters."[157] He wrote: "The breathing of God is a Hebrew symbol for the impartation of life; and so far as grammar is concerned, the natural reading of the passage would be, that one of the earliest manifestations of the Divine Force was the production of life in the depths of the ocean."[158] Matheson offered a careful reading of Scripture, noting each detail, mindful of Hebraic meaning and imaginatively suggesting interpretations that may be implied.

More than marine life, Matheson argued that the text may also suggest material agency in the creation of the world. Genesis 1:11 reads, "And God said, 'Let the earth bring forth . . .'" For Matheson, because it was the earth which will bring forth, this represented the physical basis of life.[159] Similarly, in the creation of humanity, humanity's physical origin is cited in Genesis 2:7, "And the Lord God formed man from the dust of the ground."[160] It is the same earth which brings forth or gives birth to the plant, animal and human beings. This, noted Matheson, is in "anticipative harmony with the philosophy of Herbert Spencer."[161] We are from the same source. For Matheson, Spencer is "a Darwinian plus a transcendentalist" because Spencer is committed to belief in both evolution and an inscrutable Force.[162] If the inscrutable Force is present equally to the whole of creation, how then is humanity to be differentiated from the animals, plants and the rest of creation? Matheson answered that humanity is higher than the animal because there is more of God in us. There is "a higher manifestation of the power of that central life

154. Matheson, The Old Faith Live, 117.

155. Matheson, The Old Faith Live, 118.

156. Matheson, The Old Faith Live, 186.

157. Matheson, The Old Faith Live, 186.

158. Matheson, The Old Faith Live, 187.

159. Matheson, The Old Faith Live, 188.

160. Matheson, The Old Faith Live, 189.

161. Matheson, The Old Faith Live, 190.

162. Matheson, The Old Faith Live, 191.

which constitutes the being of all other lives."[163] Humanity receives the breath
of God, which is "the highest symbol by which to describe [God's] creative
power."[164] In receipt of the Divine breath, humanity becomes "an intelligent
actor and a possible fellow-worker with God."[165] In possession of the Divine breath, we become God-bearers, made in the image of the Divine Life.
Matheson noted that the Hebrew word used of God's breath in Genesis 2:7 is
different from that of Genesis 1: 2, but he believed that this is no more than
"Hebrew reverence" for God.[166] Breathing into humanity does not constitute
a special act of creation or in any way detract from the doctrine of evolution
because the "breath of life which constitutes the height of the new creation is
itself but an impartation of that original Divine breath which moved at first
over the unconscious elements of chaos."[167]

For Matheson, the biblical account of Genesis may hint at the missing
link between the animal and humanity. He noted that the creation of humanity in Genesis 2 is not one act, but two. Humanity is first formed from
the dust of the earth and it is later that God breathes life into the nostrils
of humanity, a living soul. Matheson wrote: "For all the writer of Genesis
says to the contrary, there may have intervened between these acts a long
period of ages, an interval as wide as that which we imagine to have divided
the transitional developments of the preceding creative days."[168] Matheson's
imagination is nowhere better found than in a later meditation on the story
of Adam and Eve (Genesis 2:21–23).[169] This is a story which, traditionally
understood, may be viewed as the epitome of patriarchy. However, Matheson alleviated that interpretation, at least to some extent. He began by
asking, "Where did this scene occur?" Matheson understood the writer to
mean that the entire event is a dream. Adam is placed into "a deep sleep;"
it is "a vision of the night." Here, as elsewhere, Matheson stressed that a
moment of spiritual encounter and insight occurs in the darkness, in the
stillness of meditation. In the vision, Adam saw the rib and watched it "take
form and grow." The more closely he watched it, the more he saw "a shape
of great beauty:" "it was the very woman who had been by his side from the
beginning, but whom he had hitherto despised." It was in his dream that
Adam came to realize that Eve was bone of his bone and flesh of his flesh.

163. Matheson, *The Old Faith Live*, 193.
164. Matheson, *The Old Faith Live*, 193.
165. Matheson, *The Old Faith Live*, 194.
166. Matheson, *The Old Faith Live*, 194.
167. Matheson, *The Old Faith Live*, 195.
168. Matheson, *The Old Faith Live*, 196.
169. Matheson, *Leaves for Quiet Hours*, 39.

Matheson wrote: "It is not . . . an account of woman's creation. It is rather the first record of her marriage—the earliest assertion of her equality with man. This is not the day of her birth; it is the day of her nuptials—the hour when man recognized her to be a part of his own life and a sharer of his own fortunes."[170] Matheson had cleverly brought together the creation of humanity in the differing accounts of Genesis 1 and 2. In prayer, Matheson said that God trained the human heart "by its dreams as much as by its actions."[171] In the dream, Adam saw Eve as his equal.

While Matheson's insight is illuminating, there is no record that he argued for greater equality for women in late Victorian society. Matheson used his insight into the story of Eve's marriage to consecrate the domestic life. The vision had "wreathed our domestic altar . . . hallowed our family tree [and] enthroned motherhood."[172] For Matheson, as was the case in his own experience, women served family and society in the home, not in public service. Caird had publicly supported the higher education of girls. While it seems likely that Matheson would have been sympathetic, there is no record of Matheson adding his voice to that call. At times, mystical perspective is criticized for its failure to engage with the concerns of the secular world: while he spoke of service to others, Matheson did not publicly enter into the wider political discussion. The perception that mysticism is self-contained and careless of the world's needs has to be balanced with the spiritual maturation inherent in mysticism: in entering more deeply into God, the mystic is freed from the lure of the world. The mystic's detachment from the world does not preclude active concern for others. On the contrary, the more sensitized the mystic becomes to the presence, love and suffering of God, the more the mystic is present to the suffering of others.

In his book *Can the Old Faith Live with the New?*, Matheson's interpretation of Genesis binds together the doctrines of creation and evolution. Crucially, both Spencer's doctrine of evolution and the Bible point to the inscrutable Force as the source of all existence. As he progressed his argument through successive chapters, Matheson increasingly drew the conclusion that far from being a denial of Christian faith, the doctrine of evolution is a vindication of it.

In the 1880s, besides Matheson, there were many ministers and academics commenting on the relation of the Book of Genesis and the doctrine of evolution, including Chapman, Drummond and A F Muir. In 1887 the Revd Professor Charles Chapman followed the lead of Spencer and Matheson

---

170. Matheson, *Leaves for Quiet Hours*, 39.

171. Matheson, *Leaves for Quiet Hours*, 39.

172. Matheson, *Leaves for Quiet Hours*, 40.

to stress the immanence of God. Mindful of the potential for misunderstanding the Bible and, in particular, the Old Testament, Chapman said that when the ancients spoke of God "sending hail and frost and of watering the earth, they are as far from thinking, after the example of the savage, of the arbitrary action of a Being outside of things as is Mr. Spencer; they are only using bold language to set forth their idea of the presence and action everywhere and in everything of the Eternal Power. They believed in the immanence in Nature of the only Efficient Cause."[173]

In 1877 the monthly periodical, *The Nineteenth Century*, was founded by Sir James Knowles, formerly editor of the *Contemporary Review*. Many of the earliest contributors to the periodical were members of the Metaphysical Society, a gathering which drew from across the theological and scientific spectrum. In 1886, the year after Matheson's work was published, writing in *The Nineteen Century* Henry Drummond said that scientific theory formed no part of the Book of Genesis. For Drummond, the ancient text dated from the childhood of the world. On one level, Drummond is correct to say that the ancient writer of the narratives did not have evolutionary theory in mind. However, his dismissal of the text, as if it were written by a child or, at the very least is childish, is a failure to analyze the potential depths of Scripture.

In 1887, in a publication of which Matheson was the lead contributor, the Revd A F Muir applied the theory of evolution to the whole of Scripture. While Muir acknowledged that there was disagreement on many aspects of evolution, nevertheless together with the majority of scientists, he noted that a large proportion of Christian theologians "distinctly formulated and explicitly adopted" the doctrine.[174] In broad terms, Muir traced the evolutionary development and progress of theology in the Old and New Testaments. The names used of God begin with Elohim and Jahveh and end with Our Father, Spirit and Love. Sacrifice evolved from its beginning in Genesis to the Book of Hebrews; Law moved from Deuteronomy to Romans; atonement advanced from "the rude Adamic altar" to "the final spiritual oblation of the Cross."[175] Muir stated that there are "scattered up and down Holy Scripture hints of ultimate aims and ends which connect in sublime evolutionary order the fragmentary, discordant experiences of the race in regard to pain, sin, evil, separation, schism and death."[176] In the hands of the apostle Paul, resurrection is portrayed as "a change—a passage or transition from the natural to

---

173. Chapman, "Evolution," 182.
174. Muir, "Has Evolution a Claim," 250.
175. Muir, "Has Evolution a Claim," 275.
176. Muir, "Has Evolution a Claim," 275.

the spiritual in which identity, personal continuity, is not destroyed but only sublimated." For Muir, evolution was "in the air."[177]

Union between God and humanity may also be found in Matheson's interpretation of the relationship between the two Adams, the First and Second Adam. Matheson's argument was that, prior to the Fall (tradition-ally understood), humanity in the Garden was not fully human and, as a consequence, morally innocent. Following Hegel, Matheson understood the Fall to be an evolutionary step forward: it represents the moment when hu-manity evolved to the point that it became a moral decision-maker. The end point for humanity is life in union with God, which we see in the Second Adam. The Second Adam is the one who deliberately chooses union with the Divine. Incarnation is a process, not an event and, as such, takes time. The characteristic which defines the Second Adam is a life of selflessness: it is by means of sacrifice that we overcome the presence of sin and enter into a life of holiness or union with the Eternal.

In the book of Genesis we read, "The LORD God commanded the man, 'You may freely eat of every tree of the garden; but of the tree of the knowledge of good and evil you shall not eat, for in the day that you eat of it you shall die'" (2:16–17). Matheson argued that humanity's original state in the Garden of Eden was not that of a perfect being, but of a perfectly in-nocent being. Living in the Garden was humanity's least powerful state: "it is man without scientific knowledge, without philosophic thought, without reflective reason, without the strength of virtue."[178] In the Garden human-ity was "material Man," that is, humanity comprising vegetal and animal nature,[179] and before the emergence of consciousness and the possibility of free choice. It is the possibility of choice, of making a deliberate decision no longer driven by animal instinct, which means that humanity enters a new sphere, the moral sphere: "the man is become as one of us, to know good and evil."[180] It is from this new sphere, "the sphere of intellectual evolution,"[181] that "the earliest discoveries in science and in art" emerge.[182] In the gar-den, when humanity was in its innocent state, morality was impossible.[183] "The power to choose was in itself a step in the direction of evolutionary

177. Muir, "Has Evolution a Claim," 250.

178. Matheson, *The Old Faith Live*, 201.

179. Matheson, *The Old Faith Live*, 211.

180. Matheson, *The Old Faith Live*, 202.

181. Matheson, *The Old Faith Live*, 202.

182. Matheson, *The Old Faith Live*, 202.

183. Matheson, *The Old Faith Live*, 203.

progress."[184] It is the evolutionary moment of self-consciousness. Matheson stated that, following the so-called Fall, an evolutionary development occurred: "an evolution in which the goal is no longer the perfection of the structure but the maturity of consciousness."[185]

For Matheson, the Fall was not a fall, but a rise. In contrast to Augustine, Matheson said: "The primitive innocence of man was broken by the mere fact of this choice, but we cannot agree with Augustine that in view of the writer of Genesis the choice was the beginning of his fall. In itself it was a rise, and might have resulted in the transition from innocence into conscious virtue."[186] In his Gifford Lectures, Caird said that while gaining knowledge of good and evil is often portrayed as a degeneration or regression, he said that it was an advance: "Ye shall be as gods, knowing good and evil." Caird argued that the popular understanding of the perfect humanity dwelling in the Garden of Eden possessing "an original and pristine perfection" is "irrational and untenable."[187]

For Matheson, had humanity chosen a life of holiness instead of a life of sin, humanity would have attained holiness and entered into union with God. The possibility of choice was not itself the Fall of humanity. Humanity's moral fall was not because of the evolutionary emergence of choice, not because of the new possibility of moral decision-making, but because humanity instead of choosing "the higher and spiritual world" succumbed to "the solicitations of the animal world."[188] For Matheson, humanity's fall was no surprise because the history of evolution is one of "alternate advance and regress."[189] He summed up his position: "The one compensating feature of the fall was the fact that the destruction of man's innocence did actually introduce him into an intellectual world—a world in which the distinction of good and evil were no longer concealed by a life of spontaneity, but where the spontaneous had given way to the conscious, and the conscious had become the source of a deliberate choice."[190]

In Genesis 2:17 we read that death entered the world because of humanity's fall, because of sin. Matheson stated that, on the face of it, this cannot be the case because, from an evolutionary point of view, death existed in the world long before the emergence of the human species: "the presence of

184. Matheson, *The Old Faith Live*, 205.

185. Matheson, *The Old Faith Live*, 220.

186. Matheson, *The Old Faith Live*, 204.

187. Caird, *Fundamental Ideas of Christianity*, vol. 1, 172.

188. Matheson, *The Old Faith Live*, 205.

189. Matheson, *The Old Faith Live*, 205.

190. Matheson, *The Old Faith Live*, 220.

death was inseparable from the very beginning of life."[191] Geological research revealed that, thousands of years before the emergence of the human species, "generations of living creatures came and passed away, and that they passed away by . . . the method of death."[192] Matheson distinguished between two kinds of death: material death and spiritual death. Material death, he said, was death that belonged to "the nature of the original creation because the original creation was material."[193] By contrast, spiritual death came with the presence of sin. Matheson argued that, according to the doctrine of the Bible, death comes into the world because of the presence of sin. He defined sin as "the absence of holiness."[194] The possibility of holiness was precluded by the presence of sin. Having distinguished two kinds of death, Matheson was able to show that the account of creation in the Book of Genesis is not at odds with the doctrine of evolution. Matheson was working towards establishing that the purpose and climax of creation is incarnation, the union of the human and the Divine. He had found within Scripture the evolutionary emergence of self-consciousness with the possibility of a life of holiness freely chosen and shown that physical death is not the result of sin.

Matheson asked how can it be that, in a universe in which death pervades all matter, we can speak of immortality? For Matheson, immortality is possible for humanity because of "the impartation of an immortal Principle already existing in the universe."[195] Matheson held very closely to the Spencerian principle of primal Force. Humanity becomes immortal because it possesses the immortality of God. Spencer defended the belief that, despite the perishable nature of all forms of life,[196] there is nonetheless a Power "everywhere persistent;" a Power which is immortal. Matheson said that, "To make a creature immortal, it must be filled with the life of God."[197] In gaining immortality, humanity is not in receipt of something new, a new creation, but receives the breath of the Divine life.[198] For Matheson, immortality of the soul rests on nothing other than "union with the life of God."[199] It is only in union with the Divine that humanity can rise to the higher and spiritual world. Before the Fall and rise of humanity, in the garden during humanity's

---

191. Matheson, *The Old Faith Live,* 207.
192. Matheson, *The Old Faith Live,* 207.
193. Matheson, *The Old Faith Live,* 211.
194. Matheson, *The Old Faith Live,* 208.
195. Matheson, *The Old Faith Live,* 213.
196. Matheson, *The Old Faith Live,* 214.
197. Matheson, *The Old Faith Live,* 214.
198. Matheson, *The Old Faith Live,* 216.
199. Matheson, *The Old Faith Live,* 216.

early evolutionary state of innocence, humanity unconsciously possessed "the seed of immortality."[200] For Matheson, conscious and deliberate union with the Divine comes in the Second Adam, who is "to be perfect through suffering, and mightiest in the hour of his tribulation."[201]

For Matheson, creation follows "a benevolent plan,"[202] a "higher teleology,"[203] in which the pinnacle of creation is Divine union with self-conscious humanity and the process by which union is reached is sacrifice. The existence of human consciousness, of the human will, is proof of the existence of a Divine or intelligent Will. For Matheson, the existence of human will in a material universe in which the prevailing characteristic is instinct and the absence of volition is a proof that the primal Force of which Spencer speaks is an intelligent Will. While some argue that the universe has no need of design and that natural law is sufficient to account for all phenomena, Matheson followed Spencer who stated that "the prime agent of all evolution is force and . . . that the only force with which we are conversant is will."[204] Matheson wrote: "If we say that the primal Force of the universe is itself an intelligent Will, we shall thereby have explained the existence of the sense of freedom within us; we shall have discovered in the process of evolution an agent sufficient to account for the fact that such a peculiar manifestation has been evolved from nature."[205] Matheson argued that from the days of animal innocence in the Garden, from the time in evolutionary history in which humanity did not possess the power of moral decision-making, the emergence of self-consciousness, of human will, not only opens up the possibility of a freely chosen life lived in union with the Divine but the fact that human will emerged at all in a material universe is a proof that the primal Force of Spencer is an intelligent Will. Humanity takes on immortality when it is united with the life of the Immortal.

Within the doctrine of creation the benevolent plan of the Divine is not merely the evolutionary emergence of a creature with the capacity to freely respond to God, a human soul, but "the raising of the human soul into a species of equality with the Divine life, 'that we all maybe one.'"[206] Following the Hegelian method, Matheson argued that in creation "the

---

200. Matheson, *The Old Faith Live,* 217.

201. Matheson, *The Old Faith Live,* 221.

202. Matheson, *The Old Faith Live,* 223.

203. Matheson, *The Old Faith Live,* 225.

204. Matheson, *The Old Faith Live,* 234.

205. Matheson, *The Old Faith Live,* 234.

206. Matheson, *The Old Faith Live,* 236.

finishing touch in time was the first element in thought."[207] When the Spirit of God moved over the face of the deep, "it was travailing with the birth of the human soul."[208] In the narrative of Genesis, God is able to declare that each of the six days of creation was very good because God saw them "in the light of that seventh morning when He finds rest in communion with the human spirit."[209] The process of evolution is survival of the fittest, where the fittest is not necessarily the strongest. Evolution is a struggle of life striving to free itself from death. Matheson believed that the goal of evolution is "the production of immortality, the bringing forth of something which shall resist the original tendency to die."[210] The defining characteristic of evolution throughout its entire history is that of sacrifice.[211] Entirely in keeping with all the evidence of evolution, union with the Divine is only possible through sacrifice.

Kenosis

Sacrifice is present throughout creation in the world of matter, including the animal world, in the involuntary surrender made by compulsion or instinct. In humanity, the sacrificial spirit "becomes for the first time a deliberate and voluntary act."[212] Sacrifice lies at the very heart of the nature of reality: the Lamb is slain from the foundation of the world. For Matheson, humanity has the ability to choose the path of sacrifice and to surrender personal joy.[213] With the birth of self-consciousness, the emergence of personal care and the freedom to choose, Matheson saw an "evolution of sorrow"[214] in which humanity evolves from spontaneity to a life of sacrifice. Sacrifice (or suffering) lies at the center of both the doctrine of creation and the doctrine of evolution[215] and is most marked in creatures of "the higher type."[216] The perfect human being is the one who epitomizes the life of sacrifice: "the perfect man must be a man of sorrows."[217]

207. Matheson, *The Old Faith Live,* 237.
208. Matheson, *The Old Faith Live,* 238.
209. Matheson, *The Old Faith Live,* 236.
210. Matheson, *The Old Faith Live,* 242.
211. Matheson, *The Old Faith Live,* 244.
212. Matheson, *The Old Faith Live,* 245.
213. Matheson, *The Old Faith Live,* 245.
214. Matheson, *The Old Faith Live,* 247.
215. Matheson, *The Old Faith Live,* 249–50.
216. Matheson, *The Old Faith Live,* 250.
217. Matheson, *The Old Faith Live,* 251.

Caird too looked to the Man of Sorrows: "The whole life of the Man of Sorrows—His earthly lowliness and meanness, His weakness, grief, and sorrows, His loneliness and forsakenness, His drinking of the cup to the dregs, yea, in His very crucifixion and death—must be to us the disclosure of an ineffable joy triumphing over sorrow, of a divine bliss in sacrifice, which is the last, highest revelation of the nature of God."[218] The spiritual life and the life of the Spirit meant self-surrender, the yielding of a human self-consciousness to the divine consciousness, of spirit to Spirit; it is here that unity and communion occur. Caird said: "The perfect life of humanity can never be reached till our separate individual life is surrendered to the universal and infinite life, and by dying to self we begin to live in the eternal life of God."[219]

Matheson argued that incarnation, that is, union of the human and the Divine, is the essence of every religion. In common with others,[220] Matheson believed that incarnation gives us the best insight we can gain into the character and nature of God. It has been argued that the doctrine of Incarnation is irreconcilable with the doctrine of evolution because, traditionally understood, the former requires a miracle or special act of God, while such an intervention is not possible in the latter. Matheson maintained that incarnation is the union of the immortal with the mortal, of the self-conscious spirit with the Spirit of the Divine. With Spencer in mind, Matheson wrote: "If a union between God and man has ever occurred in history, it can only have occurred through the agency of that Power which the most advanced representative of modern science has placed at the basis of the law of evolution."[221] The primal Force has been in the universe progressively; the benevolent design of Intelligent Will has been "emptying out more and more of its own being in order to manifest more and more of its highest glory."[222] Through evolution, the Divine has been working towards the Second Adam. For Matheson, the writer of the Book of Genesis looked forward to the time when God would penetrate the heart, soul and consciousness of humanity. The writer longed for the moment when moral action would spring from humanity, from the "irresistible impulse" of the Divine life dwelling within the human soul; God would be humanity's "deepest life."[223]

---

218. Caird, *Fundamental Ideas of Christianity*, vol. 2, 146.

219. Caird, *Fundamental Ideas of Christianity*, vol. 2, 161–62.

220. Evans, *Kenotic Christology*, 192.

221. Matheson, *The Old Faith Live*, 259.

222. Matheson, *The Old Faith Live*, 261.

223. Matheson, *The Old Faith Live*, 254.

When this moment arrived, it would be "the age of holiness."[224] Matheson said that Christ is "the union of heart with heart, the blending of spirit with spirit, the meeting of the human with the Divine."[225]

It is through a life of sacrifice, even death on a cross, that the Second Adam is united with the life of the Divine. Like incarnation, for Matheson, the resurrection of Christ required no special miracle. The inscrutable Force, the immortal Power upon which the entire universe is dependent, is the source of the incarnation and the resurrection. Matheson wrote: "The animation of dead matter by the Spirit of life is no unprecedented occurrence in the history of evolution . . . Every evolutionist will admit that it occurred once, in that day when the first germ-cell began to live."[226] Science believes that by the power of the inscrutable Force life can come from dead matter and, in defending the resurrection, this is the claim of Christianity. Matheson did not suggest in any way how resurrection may occur; he simply asserted that it was no different from the process of incarnation. He was making a broad statement of faith rather than philosophically exploring what is meant by resurrection in an evolutionary universe.

Union with God for humanity means to embark on a life of holiness. The Spirit of life is the source of holiness. For Matheson, incarnation is an evolutionary process. Through time, by the deliberate decision of the worshipper, the Spirit takes the individual out of individualism; "the pure spirit weaves for itself a pure environment."[227] Paul is for Matheson the archetypal example of what it means to wrestle with the Spirit in overcoming the world and seeking harmony with the Divine. Of Paul, Matheson wrote:

> "O wretched man that I am, who shall deliver me from this body of death?" "There is a law in my members warning against the law of my mind;" "the flesh lusteth against the spirit, and the spirit against the flesh; the evil that I would not, that I do, and the good that I would, that I do not."—these are amongst the utterances that come from the days of his high spiritual culture. His sense of sin seems to increase in proportion to his advance in holiness, and his feeling of distance from the goal becomes more pronounced and painful in proportion as the goal itself is neared.[228]

For Matheson, the struggle is "an ascent" because "the increasing sense of sin is the increasing power of holiness, and the increasing power of holiness

---

224. Matheson, *The Old Faith Live*, 254.

225. Matheson, *The Old Faith Live*, 256.

226. Matheson, *The Old Faith Live*, 275.

227. Matheson, *The Old Faith Live*, 282.

228. Matheson, *The Old Faith Live*, 294.

is the enlarged diffusion of the Spirit of life."[229] By increasing our sense of holiness, the Spirit of life leads us out of self into community, into the Body of Christ. Alone we are "incomplete and meaningless fragments" while our unity with others brings "our completeness and our significance . . . in the membership of the organic body."[230] The Spirit also leads us into religion, that is, moves the soul towards God, to humanity's deepest life.[231]

Divine Communion and Immortality of the Soul

As he brought his work on evolution to a close, Matheson returned to questions of oneness with the Sacred and the possibility of the immortality of the soul. Immanence, the presence of the Transcendent in and through creation, leads to union of the human and divine. Matheson had earlier said that incarnation is the key doctrine of every religion. While many Christian writers in discussing incarnation would focus principally on Jesus, the Second Person of the Trinity, Matheson made no reference to the God-Human of the ancient creeds. In this section I shall discuss the prevailing points of Matheson's understanding of Divine Communion, the immortality of the soul and their relationship with the doctrine of evolution.

Matheson asked if the doctrine of evolution would reduce the sense of Divine communion to "a delusion and a dream?"[232] He had already established that far from being a barrier to Christian belief, the doctrine of evolution places God at the center of creation, the "main factor" in the entire process.[233] Spencer's theory of the inscrutable Force places humanity in the presence of the transcendental Power that lies at the basis of the universe, is itself a belief in the perpetual necessity of that presence.[234] Humanity finds itself in "the immediate presence of the great First Cause."[235]

Prayer, Matheson said, is the desire to be in the presence of the Eternal:

> The deepest want in every true prayer is the want of God. What a devout man seeks in his petitions is, first and foremost, a communion of his own heart with the Divine nature. It is not too much to say that to such a man the act of prayer is itself a greater

229. Matheson, *The Old Faith Live*, 295.

230. Matheson, *The Old Faith Live*, 301.

231. Matheson, *The Old Faith Live*, 301.

232. Matheson, *The Old Faith Live*, 308.

233. Matheson, *The Old Faith Live*, 311.

234. Matheson, *The Old Faith Live*, 312.

235. Matheson, *The Old Faith Live*, 312.

motive than its results, for he looks upon the act of prayer as itself giving him the highest boon he can receive—the actual fellowship of his soul with the life of the Divine Spirit.[236]

The central purpose of prayer is to unite the soul of the worshipper with Eternal Reality. Union with the Divine was Matheson's practice and experience of prayer. He wrote:

> We pray, "Enlighten our eyes!" but often we can only get our inner eye enlightened by having the outer eye shaded. Is the soul never to get moments for repose—for meditation, self-reflection! Is it never to have an hour all to itself—and hour when its doors are shut, when its windows are covered, when its outside voices are hushed, when it is untouched by the heat of the day! God says, "Yes, it *shall* have such moments;" and He prepares a place for it in the wilderness. He stops me midway in the race. He lays His hand upon me, and I fall. He bears me into the silence, into the solitude. He puts the multitude all out, and locks the door. He closes the shutters of the casement. He interrupts the music in the street; He forbids the dancing in the hall. He says, "Your nerves are weary with excitement; in this desert place you shall rest awhile."[237]

In prayer, Matheson noted three elements: the human suppliant, the Divine respondent, and the Divine prompter. It is the Divine prompter who leads the worshipper in prayer in order that the worshipper may pray for the Divine Will. According to Paul, there is a Power "which suggests to the human soul that which it ought to offer."[238] Such a prayer is not a "violation of the law of nature, or, which is the same thing, an infringement of the will of God—'the Spirit itself helpeth our infirmity.'"[239] Prayer is not an attempt to manipulate or change the Divine Will but is a means of revealing it: "the impulse to pray is a process of illumination or prophecy, a revelation to the heart beforehand of the purpose of God."[240]

Matheson stated that the "ultimate desire prescribed for all Christian prayer is the desire of harmony, with the ultimate law, 'not as I will, but as Thou wilt.'"[241] He cites the Lord's Prayer as the supreme example of the Christian worshipper desiring union with God, alignment with the will of God, and

---

236. Matheson, *The Old Faith Live*, 312.
237. Matheson, *Rests by the River*, 120.
238. Matheson, *The Old Faith Live*, 323.
239. Matheson, *The Old Faith Live*, 324.
240. Matheson, *The Old Faith Live*, 325.
241. Matheson, *The Old Faith Live*, 326.

no violation of the law of nature. Matheson said of the petition, "Thy will be done on earth as in heaven," that "the will of God maybe done on earth is 'an order which clearly shows that the limits of Christian prayer are ever circumscribed by the possibilities of existing law. The law of nature is here identical with the will of God, and to desire emancipation from the law of nature is held equivalent to desiring a violation of the will of God."[242]

In the Gospel of John, when Jesus invites His disciples to pray, "Ask what ye will and it shall be done unto you," is not "unlimited freedom in the range of prayer" but "a circumscription of that range."[243] The true worshipper prays solely for the will of God; God's will is at one with the law of nature. Matheson stated that, if we can accept that the inscrutable Force of Spencer is "a conscious Personality," then "all the rest of the way will be scientifically smooth and easy."[244] Matheson's repeated appeal is for union with God.

For Matheson, it is a natural progression from discussing communion with the Divine to turn to the immortality of the soul. During the second half of the nineteenth century, there was public doubt about the possibility of life beyond this life. In 1849 Tennyson completed his poem *In Memoriam* in memory of the death of his friend and religious mentor, Arthur Henry Hallam, who died of a cerebral hemorrhage. Tennyson asked:

> Are God and Nature then at strife,
>
> That Nature lends such evil dreams?
>
> So careful of the type she seems,
>
> So careless of the single life.

> 'So careful of the type?' But no,
>
> From scarped cliff and quarried stone,
>
> She cries, 'A thousand types are gone:
>
> I care for nothing, all shall go.'

For Tennyson, humanity like the dinosaurs, "the dragons of the prime," can become extinct and part of the fossil archive. In similar manner, in *Garden of the Proserpine* Swinburne declares "that dead men rise up never" and that the Lord God, like other gods, "is dead." In 1887, the Revd W. F. Adeney asked how can humanity make a claim of immortality? He said,

---

242. Matheson, *The Old Faith Live*, 326.

243. Matheson, *The Old Faith Live*, 327.

244. Matheson, *The Old Faith Live*, 336.

"Death is the fate of all our animal relatives; and death is our fate."[245] Adeney asked at what point does a human being become immortal? "Can we predicate an immortal life to an untimely abortion? If not, then at what stage of the foetal growth does the immortal nature appear? Is it reasonable to suppose that the ovum is immortal?"[246]

In his Gifford Lectures, Caird faced some of the potential obstacles to belief in immortality, such as the apparent immense waste of life. Matheson did not address such searching questions directly. He began discussing immortality by arguing that, following the theory of Spencer, that of Inscrutable Power, "the principle of immortality is already in the universe, that is exists now as a law of nature."[247] Too hastily, "on grounds of the Baconian principle," do we assume that there is no place in the physical sciences for life eternal.[248] Matheson stated that the breath of life which was breathed into humanity was not new life, but the Force present from the beginning of the universe. For Matheson, we know that there is something within us which transcends the limits of nature.[249] We have a consciousness or identity which transcends the body. In the very fabric of the human body, Matheson saw immortality: "[Our] sense of personal identity exists in opposition to the facts. There was not a particle in this body in existence twenty years ago; the organism which [we] now possess is not the organism which [we] then possessed. But the strange thing is, that in the midst of this complete transmutation, this virtual death, there should remain an unbroken sense of identity."[250] Bishop Butler faced the question of the immortality of animals. Given that the Inscrutable Force is present to the whole of life, including animals, Butler concluded that there was nothing in evolution which would preclude their immortality. Matheson noted this but departs from it without comment. Adeney admitted that we simply do not know if animals are capable of surviving death.[251]

In his later work, *Searchings in the Silence*, Matheson charged humanity with the heavy responsibility of our care for animals. Humanity's dominion over the animal world is given to the "one made in the image of God, the God who is love."[252] Matheson said: "Dominion is a very solemn

245. Adeney, "Immortality," 112–113.

246. Adeney, "Immortality," 115.

247. Matheson, *The Old Faith Live*, 339.

248. Matheson, *The Old Faith Live*, 340.

249. Matheson, *The Old Faith Live*, 357.

250. Matheson, *The Old Faith Live*, 354.

251. Adeney, "Immortality," 122.

252. Matheson, *Searchings in the Silence*, 215.

thing; it may oppress, crush, destroy . . . Ye who torture the beast of the field, have you considered the ground of your authority? If you have not a tender heart, you have no right to reign; you are a usurper."[253] Filled with the love of which he spoke, with a sense of union and oneness with creation, including the animals, in prayer Matheson wrote: "My Father, fill me with love for things beneath me . . . Give me tenderness that is born of reverence. Teach me to revere the creation that is under me. Was not its life a stream from Thy life? Is not its life a mystery to me even now? . . . Let me uncover my head before the mystery."[254] Matheson said that the worship of animals that we find in ancient cultures may be due to an acknowledgment that there was modes of inspiration and avenues of knowledge beyond the dreams of human philosophies.[255] In prayer, he wrote: "Let me enter into sympathy with their hunger, their thirst, their weariness, their cold, their frequent homelessness. Let me give their wants a place in my prayers. Let me remember them in the struggles of the forest. Let me remember them in the neglect of the city."[256] While some may criticize his prayer as being sentimental, in fact it reveals the extent and depth to which Matheson saw and felt as God does. The prayer reveals a sensitivity of the soul within all living things and the Spirit within all creation. In meditation, Matheson was one with the presence and suffering of God.

Caird said that it is humanity's self-consciousness, our personal identity, which makes us "akin to that Intelligence which is infinite and eternal."[257] Humanity's ability to observe and understand the nature of matter, "events in their co-existence and succession," raises humanity above creation, lifting us out of time and into eternity.[258] We are superior to change and death because our "immortal stillness is unaffected and unperturbed by the fluctuation and evanescence that conditions all finite things."[259]

Matheson concluded his discussion on the immortality of the soul by defining immortality as being identical with "the indwelling of the Divine Spirit in the soul."[260] Eternity is now. Humanity has come from the First Cause and is sustained by the Transcendent. Matheson declared that the indwelling Spirit is more than mere immanence: "[Immortality] is not

253. Matheson, *Searchings in the Silence*, 216.

254. Matheson, *Searchings in the Silence*, 216.

255. Matheson, *Searchings in the Silence*, 217.

256. Matheson, *Searchings in the Silence*, 217.

257. Caird, *Fundamental Ideas of Christianity*, vol. 2, 258.

258. Caird, *Fundamental Ideas of Christianity*, vol. 2, 258.

259. Caird, *Fundamental Ideas of Christianity*, vol. 2, 260.

260. Matheson, *The Old Faith Live*, 375.

something which is *to be* reached by the indwelling of that Spirit; it is itself the life of the Spirit, and is reached in the first and faintest experience of that life."[261] Immorality is not for the future; it is now. There is nothing in the doctrine of immortality which contradicts the law of nature because creation comes from the Eternal. The Eternal is everywhere and in every-thing. In the New Testament, immortality is nothing less than "the life of the Eternal, the personal presence of that primal Force which lies at the basis of all things."[262] Humanity's immortality means to share in the life of God: "Because I live, ye shall live also."[263] It was Matheson's belief that God lives within us, that we are God-bearers, that we are at one with the Eternal and always will be. Matheson's choice of language, its eloquence, clarity and passion reveal that the indwelling Spirit was a present, at times, overwhelming reality for him.

261. Matheson, *The Old Faith Live*, 375.
262. Matheson, *The Old Faith Live*, 376.
263. Matheson, *The Old Faith Live*, 376.

4

Union

UNION WITH GOD, HUMANITY, and all things is central to Mathesonian theology. In *Natural Elements of Revealed Theology* (Baird Lecture) and *Studies of the Portrait of Christ*, Matheson repeatedly returned to the theme of union, a relationship of oneness between humanity and God. The concept of union with God is readily found within mysticism and is a characteristic of Hegelian mysticism. In this chapter I shall discuss some relevant historical background about biblical interpretation in the mid-to-late nineteenth century which will provide a contrast and context for Matheson's work. I shall discuss sermons preached by Caird and others in order to demonstrate the extent to which Matheson was a man of his generation, one of many whose theology was that of union.

Biblical Interpretation in the Mid-to-Late Nineteenth Century

From the mid-nineteenth century to the late twentieth century, the historical critical method of interpreting the Bible was dominant within academic study. Historical critical method asks when and by whom the books of the Bible were written, and who were the intended recipients of the written work? Historical critics asked, "what 'really' happened—as opposed to what the (far from impartial) writers of those books believed (or wanted their readers to believe) had happened."[1] There was an acknowledgement that the books as we have them are composite in nature and made up from separate sources, originals which we do not have. In 1860, in *Essays and Reviews*, seven essays were published on church matters, six of them by clergy in the Church of England. Drawing on the work of Bunsen, Williams said that the Pentateuch was "not entirely written by Moses," that Isaiah, Zechariah and

1. Barton, "Historical Critical Approaches," 11.

Daniel had more than one author, and that Old Testament prophecies traditionally attributed to Christ (such as Isaiah 7:14) were to be read in their historical contexts.[2] Goodwin said that the science of Genesis 1 was the science
of its time and could not be reconciled with nineteenth century scientific
understanding, while Jowett said that the Bible must be interpreted "like
any other book."[3] Two years later, the Anglican Bishop of Natal, Colenso,
"a formidable and fearless Old Testament critic" questioned "the historicity
of the narrative of the exodus and wilderness wanderings in Exodus and
Numbers."[4] In his critical approach to the story of the exodus, Colenso
exposed the fallible nature of the story, if read literally: "Several passages
gave the numbers of those leaving Egypt as 600,000 males aged twenty and
upward. Colenso calculated that this would mean a total of roughly 2.5 million Israelites together with 2 million sheep and oxen. This was a remarkable
increase in population from the seventy souls who went down to Egypt with
Jacob (Genesis 46:27), and the company would have taken quite a long time
to cross the Red Sea."[5] Colenso's criticism was significant not because it was
new, but because it was expressed by a bishop. In a similar manner to that of
Jowett, in his lectures, *The History of the Jewish Church* (1863–1876), A. P.
Stanley sought to demonstrate that while the Bible ought to be read like any
other book, this in itself was not a danger to faith.

Historical criticism understands history "in the straightforward sense
of the term,"[6] and while Matheson from time to time notes events in the life
of Jesus in such a manner, this is not his primary interest. At the center of the
historical critical method is the belief that scholars can achieve objectivity in
their reading and analyzing of Scripture, a value-neutral pursuit which today
is discredited or, at the very least, in need of qualification.[7] In one sense, the
historical critical method has its roots in the Enlightenment but, in another
sense, reading the Bible critically and independent of the authorized teaching
of the Church is a legacy of the Protestant Reformation. Barton notes: "Faced
with an ecclesiastical interpretation of this or that text, the biblical critic does
not automatically accept that the magisterium of the Church guarantees that
the meaning proposed is the true one, but reserves the right to apply rational
principles of criticism."[8] By the 1850s, there was a growing recognition that

2. Rogerson, "Bible & Theology," 463.

3. Rogerson, "Bible & Theology," 463.

4. Rogerson, "Bible & Theology," 464.

5. Rogerson, "Bible & Theology," 464.

6. Barton, *Companion to Biblical Interpretation*, 11.

7. Barton, *Companion to Biblical Interpretation*, 12–13.

8. Barton, *Companion to Biblical Interpretation*, 16.

the Bible was "organic" in nature and that within it there was "a principle of progression."[9] More than that, with the advent of what we might recognize as the "novel," the Bible was no longer being read as "a single omniscient dogmatic voice" but rather as a "dialogue, or even a heteroglossia (babel of voices), with a plurality of competing voices."[10] Writers such as Austen, Eliot, Dickens, Thackeray, and Trollope illustrate the paradox and complexity of the Bible's position in the nineteenth century: "At the very moment when it was seemingly losing both historical and even moral authority with biblical scholars and philosophers, it was permeating as never before the literature and imaginative thought of the time."[11]

Matheson was more interested in the immediate interaction of the text with the reader/worshipper than laying stress on what may be gleaned from source analysis. The Scottish theologian, Robert Flint, who held chairs at St Andrews and later Edinburgh, was very doubtful about higher criticism; he advised his students that "it is not the work of the Christian minister to discuss in the pulpit, and before people who cannot possibly judge of them with adequate knowledge, the hypotheses debated in the schools of biblical criticism."[12] It is clear in Matheson's meditations on Scripture that he was involved in the text and in no sense detached from his interpretation of it. Rather than taking Scripture apart, Matheson sought to bring it alive through the vividness with which he retold biblical stories or re-imagined biblical characters. Published in 1863, Renan's book *La Vie de Jesus* approached the story of Jesus using literary methodology with which Matheson would have been sympathetic. Stripped of the supernatural and the miraculous, Renan offered "an immediate and imaginative response to the Jesus of the Gospels."[13] Schweitzer wrote:

> Renan's work marked an epoch, not for the Catholic world only, but for general literature . . . He offered his readers a Jesus who was alive, whom he, with his artistic imagination, had met under the blue heaven of Galilee, and whose lineaments his inspired pencil had seized. Men's attention was arrested, and they thought to see Jesus, because Renan had the skill to make them see the blue skies, seas of waving corn, distant mountains, gleaming lilies, in a landscape with the Lake of Gennesarat for

9. Prickett, "Bible and Literary Interpretation," 403.

10. Prickett, "Bible and Literary Interpretation," 404.

11. Prickett, "Bible and Literary Interpretation," 407.

12. McKay, *Kirk and the Kingdom*, 35.

13. Jasper, "Literary Readings of the Bible," 24.

its centre, and hear with him in the whispering of the reeds the eternal melody of the Sermon on the Mount.[14]

It was this intense involvement with the pictures painted by Scripture which Matheson sought to convey to his reader and listener. The power of his preaching and prayers lay in the extent to which worshipers felt themselves to be alongside Jesus. Historical critics may not take seriously enough the over-arching framework of the literary method, which attaches considerable value to "the imaginative and poetic" as well as that of more limited rational inquiry.[15] D. H. Lawrence said of his vocation, "I always feel as if I should be naked for the fire of Almighty God to go through me—and it's rather an awful feeling."[16] The intensity with which Matheson wrote, not least in his pursuit of union with God, betrayed his soul's nakedness. Through literary methodology, Matheson "encounters with a new imme-diacy their power and mystery [and,] like all great texts of literature, they are seen as both historical and contemporary, as living within history."[17] In his *Confessions of an Inquiring Spirit*, Coleridge said that "in the Bible there is more that finds me than I have experienced in all other books put together."[18] The literary method "concentrates attention upon the mo-ment of reading rather than the moment of the text's origin as of primary importance."[19] Critics of the literary method argue that it relativizes the text and thereby robs it of its status and lasting value. While the histori-cal method cannot be abandoned altogether, at the present time there is continuing pressure to move towards "text-immanent" interpretations,[20] a methodology much nearer to Matheson's own. Matheson's involvement in the text reveals his sense of union with the Divine.

Caird's Sermon on Union with God

Matheson was a student of Caird, when Caird held the Chair of Divinity at the University of Glasgow in the 1860s. After his crisis of faith Macmil-lan said that it was Caird's Hegelian theology which helped Matheson re-build his faith. In this section, I shall cite work by Caird and others which

14. Jasper, "Literary Readings of the Bible," 24.

15. Jasper, "Literary Readings of the Bible," 25.

16. Jasper, "Literary Readings of the Bible," 25.

17. Jasper, "Literary Readings of the Bible," 27.

18. Jasper, "Literary Readings of the Bible," 30.

19. Jasper, "Literary Readings of the Bible," 27.

20. Barton, "Historical-Critical Approaches," 9.

demonstrates the strong similarity in thought, if not direct intellectual dependence, between Matheson, Caird and other contemporaries.

In 1880, Caird edited a collection of sermons, *Scotch Sermons*, written by ministers in the Church of Scotland, of which two were Caird's own. In his preface, Caird said that the sermons represented "a style of teaching, which increasingly prevails amongst the clergy of the Scottish Church."[21] He went further adding, "It is the work of those whose hope for the future lies, not in alterations of ecclesiastical organization, but in a profounder apprehension of the essential ideas of Christianity."[22] The collection is an important piece of work: not only does it indicate the sort of theology being preached by Caird and many like-minded clergymen during the time of Matheson's ministry, but it is significant because of the unwelcome reaction to it—at least from some quarters. One of the contributors, William Leckie McFarlan of Lenzie, became the subject of a case at the General Assembly the following year. His accusers argued that McFarlan held views which were "plainly contrary to the fundamental doctrines contained in the Standards of the Church" and, equally, he had failed to affirm "the divinity and mediatorship of Jesus Christ" as being fundamental to the faith.[23] McFarlan "made his peace" with his accusers and the matter rested there.[24]

Caird was criticized for "pantheism and universalism" and failing to recognize "the fall of man or of his need for redemption."[25] One critic said that, between them, the contributors had "repudiated every article of the Apostles' Creed,"[26] while another said that it was "shameful" that such men should remain in the ministry.[27] In the first of his sermons, "Corporate Immortality," Caird stressed the immediacy of God, that God is "not more present anywhere else than on this earth of ours . . . God is here, above, beneath, around us" and that the only change that can take place is our receptivity to God.[28] Of eternity, Caird wrote: "Its light and power are latent everywhere, waiting for human souls to welcome it, ready to break through the transparent veil of earthly things, and to suffuse with its ineffable radiance the common life of man."[29]

21. Anonymous, *Scotch Sermons*, v.

22. Anonymous, *Scotch Sermons*, v.

23. Drummond, *Late Victorian Scotland*, 242.

24. Drummond, *Late Victorian Scotland*, 243.

25. Drummond, *Late Victorian Scotland*, 241.

26. Drummond, *Late Victorian Scotland*, 241.

27. Drummond, *Late Victorian Scotland*, 242.

28. Caird, "Corporate Immortality," 15.

29. Caird, "Corporate Immortality," 16.

In his second sermon, "Union with God," Caird said that Christ declared that there are "Divine elements, Divine possibilities, in the common nature of man" and that, while the consciousness of Jesus was in "absolute union with the consciousness of God,"[30] humanity too may become "partakers of a Divine nature."[31] The realization of humanity as humanity, reaching its highest and fullest potential, is possible when humanity wholly identifies with the nature of God. We have the potential to be as Jesus was, and no less. Using a technique which Matheson himself adopted, Caird has Jesus say: "To enter into such identification with the very nature of Deity that your thoughts, like mine, shall be God's thoughts, your will and actions, like mine, a Divine will, a Divine activity—to become thus one with God as I am, is not to transcend but to realize your true nature as men."[32] Our identification with God is not an external relationship, one between two separate, distinct and independent bodies but rather "a oneness or union with God, of which [God's] own indivisible personality is the type."[33] In our union with God, in our thought and will, we are no longer "divisible from the Divine."[34] Caird was accused of pantheism but in his sermon he had carefully defined pantheism as a theology which overwhelms individuality and robs humanity of its independence and moral responsibility. Our "spiritual individuality" and moral responsibility were gifts "which even Omnipotence cannot invade."[35] Caird defined his thought as "Christian pantheism," which today we would call *panentheism*. Caird said that Jesus points us to: "a oneness with God so absolute that we may be said to be *in* God and God *in* us, that our spiritual being shall be no more separate from God's own than Christ's own, and yet in which, so far from being infringed or sacrificed, our nature as men shall reach its highest perfection."[36] Caird's use of the word "in" highlights both humanity's separateness from God and our nearness to God. In this life, through a friend or lover, our happiness is greater when it is experienced in and through the life, well-being and happiness of another.[37] Titles for God, such as Governor, Judge, or Supreme Ruler, tend to diminish or crush our spiritual nature, freedom,

30. Caird, "Union with God," 20.
31. Caird, "Union with God," 21.
32. Caird, "Union with God," 21.
33. Caird, "Union with God," 22.
34. Caird, "Union with God," 22.
35. Caird, "Union with God," 23.
36. Caird, "Union with God," 24.
37. Caird, "Union with God," 30.

and individuality.[38] For Caird, while acknowledging that "in the best of us" our union with God is only "intermittent and imperfect,"[39] nevertheless Christianity's greatest idea is that the realization of humanity's spiritual nature is found when we are at one with the Divine, when "the very mind and will of God is no longer distinguishable from our own . . . [when] to think God's thoughts shall be to think our own thoughts, and to do God's will shall be only another name for doing our own."[40]

In his sermon "New Birth" delivered before the University of Glasgow, Caird said that the union between God and humanity is of the highest order:

> I believe that if we could reach a spiritual state in which the divine mastery of the mind, heart, will of man were so absolute that we should no longer think our own thoughts or desire own ends or do our own will, but have our whole spiritual being suffused, permeated, inseparably blended with the spur and life of the Eternal—that then, instead of the leveling down of our spiritual life to nature, there would be reached the highest conceivable pitch of spiritual elevation, that liberation, expansion, perfection which is involved in being sharers of the infinite life of Him in whose image we were made.[41]

This is the theology to which Matheson avidly listened in class and found in Caird's published works.

Blindness

Macmillan claimed that Matheson's blindness was the making of the man. It is possible that living in darkness intensified Matheson's experience of God, helped him step into the Gospel stories, that they became part of his consciousness, and gave him a sense of closeness to Jesus. John Hull, professor of religious education, who became blind at age forty-eight, said "Sighted people live in the world. The blind person lives in consciousness."[42]

In the Victorian period, while many regarded blindness as "one of our greatest calamities," others "were determined to see advantages, even privileges, as attaching to the handicap."[43] In her book, *The Victorians and the*

38. Caird, "Union with God," 32.

39. Caird, "Union with God," 34.

40. Caird, "Union with God," 32.

41. Caird, *University Sermons*, 79.

42. Hull, *Touching the Rock*, 153.

43. Flint, *The Visual Imagination*, 64–65.

Visual Imagination, Flint comments on the painting *The Blind Girl* (1854–1856) by John Everett Millais. Flint notes that the blind girl "reminds the spectator of the importance of a higher, inward vision . . . The dominance of the material and visible world is called into question."[44] In *The Blind Girl*, Millais has included a double rainbow, which may be read as a symbol of God's covenant of mercy. Like light, the rainbow was understood as a sign of the power of God; it is an image to which Matheson used frequently. Flint said that *The Blind Girl* can be understood "as alluding to the promise held out by God of inner, rather than external, illumination . . . Calvin had argued that physical blindness was spiritually valuable because it forces one to listen to the voice of God."[45]

In 1860, the author of an article on "The Blind" in the *National Review*, cited philosophers who put out their eyes in order to concentrate their attention on the abstractions on which they were engaged. The author claimed that "Vividness of sensation, and clearness of perception, exist always in an inverse relation."[46] Dinah Mulock Craik wrote that Milton was perhaps able "all the more through that visual darkness, to see clear into the very heaven of heavens."[47] While lamenting being excluded from the world of sight, Milton wrote:

> Presented with a universal blank
>
> Of nature's works . . . So much the rather thou celestial Light
>
> Shine inward, and the mind through all her powers
>
> Irradiate, there plant eyes, all mist from thence
>
> Purge and disperse, that I may see and tell
>
> Of things invisible to mortal sight.[48]

In *Blindness and the Blind* (1872), Levy wrote of Milton:

> As a sighted man, he would not have possessed the powers of concentration necessary to enable him to produce the inimitable "Paradise Lost" and "Paradise Regained." In a word, Milton would never have been what he was unless he has possessed the advantages arising from the possession of sight, and also those which spring from blindness, and it must be generally admitted

---

44. Flint, *The Visual Imagination*, 66.

45. Flint, *The Visual Imagination*, 76.

46. Flint, *The Visual Imagination*, 78.

47. Flint, *The Visual Imagination*, 78.

48. Flint, *The Visual Imagination*, 78.

that the world has only seen one other author at all equal to
Milton, viz., Homer; and he, too, was without sight.[49]

In 1857, Christopher Wordsworth, canon of Westminster, said that seeing
things invisible was "a higher and nobler faculty."[50] Pusey said, "We are
most in peril of deepest, intensest, absolute blindness, when we imagine
ourselves encompassed, arrayed, penetrated with light. One might say
boldly, since He teaches us, that the completest darkness is where there is
the fullest light."[51] In 1856, in her poem *Aurora Leigh*, Elizabeth Barrett
Browning made the central character, Romney Leigh, blind. She said, "He
has to be blinded . . . to be made to see."[52]

Hull spoke of intensified experience or encounter with God facilitated
by his blindness. While Hull did not want to be blind, he came to accept it as
a gift from God. God filled his darkness. He wrote of the pure knowledge of
God which he appreciated through darkness. Referring to conception, Hull
said that he was made "in secret" and was "still being made in the secrets
of blindness, but all secrets are open to God."[53] For Hull, the joy of waking
each day was not the morning itself—it could not be the daylight—but the
presence of loved ones and of God. It is significant that Hull mentions the
presence of God: God's presence seems very real and immanent to him. We
hear Hull's intimacy and communion with God in his reflection on waking: "So although I experience the paradoxes of rediscovering sight in the
unconscious life of dreams and of losing my sight once again every time I
wake up, the paradoxes are transcended in communion with the One who
knows me, whether I wake or sleep, for I am still with him."[54] Hull is immediately conscious of the Divine in his daily experience of waking up. Hull
came to understand his blindness as part of who he was. Hull's personal
wholeness he understood to be part of a universal wholeness. This is what
he understood "communion with God to mean."[55]

Hull discovered new depth to his faith and new insight into God in the
accident of blindness. Hull's intense awareness of God's presence is experienced while attending Mass in Notre Dame Cathedral in Montreal. As Hull
received the broken bread of the Mass, he understood his brokenness—his
blindness—to be of the same kind as the bread. Of the bread, he said, "This

49. Flint, *The Visual Imagination*, 80.

50. Flint, *The Visual Imagination*, 81.

51. Flint, *The Visual Imagination*, 81.

52. Flint, *The Visual Imagination*, 86.

53. Hull, *Touching the Rock*, 61.

54. Hull, *Touching the Rock*, 61.

55. Hull, *Touching the Rock*, 145.

also is broken, and it breaks those who eat it. As long as I have his bread within me and his cloak around me, I will live in him, and he in me."[56] Hull's awareness of the Divine is clearly expressed: he had a sense of union with God; God in all things and all things in God. This is the awareness of the Sacred we discover in the mystics and Matheson. Hull stressed that he lived in God and God lived in him. Similarly, Matheson returned to passages of Scripture which stress Christ within.

The Baird Lectures

In 1881, Matheson delivered The Baird Lectures. Under the terms of the Baird Trust, the lecturer is invited to deliver no fewer than "six lectures on any subject of Theology, Christians Evidences, Christian Work, the Christian Missions, Church Government, and the Church Organizations."[57] Matheson chose to explore the relationship between natural and revealed theology. His purpose was to "look at Christianity as a completed whole" and describe its underlying unity.[58] In his opening lecture, Matheson described revealed religion, properly understood, as working in and through natural religion and the point at which the human soul encounters revelation, the supernatural, is the point at which the supernatural becomes the natural. In his second, third and fourth lectures, he answered the three questions which arise out of religious thought in the pre-Christian world: "What is God?" "What is God's relationship to humanity?" and "Is God's glory consistent with the existence of moral evil?" Matheson's Baird lectures are brought to a close with a consideration of the immortality of the soul. There is a considerable degree of agreement between Matheson's Baird Lecture and Caird's (later) Gifford Lectures in 1890–1891, and 1896.

In this section, I shall argue that Matheson's theology is shaped by his sense of union and that this informs his understanding of atonement. Matheson set himself the task of ascertaining "to what extent the doctrines of revealed religion have a basis in the natural instincts of the human mind."[59] Drawing on an analogy from evolution, Matheson argued that the force behind the germ-cell which propels it forward within conditions and limits is no different from the relationship between the supernatural and the natural. In this analogy, we have "found a common meeting place for the idea of a gradual evolution and the older thought of an immediate,

56. Hull, *Touching the Rock*, 182.
57. Matheson, *Revealed Theology*, iii.
58. Matheson, *Revealed Theology*, v.
59. Matheson, *Revealed Theology*, 1.

direct creation."[60] The relationship of revealed theology to that of natural theology, of the power of the supernatural to that of nature, of that between creation and evolution, is the same question which the apostle Paul faced in his discussion of law and grace: can humanity develop into righteousness by natural means or does humanity require "the creative influence of a new and higher life?"[61]

For Paul, grace is the supernatural and it is offered to "transform the sense of mystery into an intuitive knowledge."[62] Matheson said that Paul "holds with the Ultramontanists that there is a life higher than nature; but he holds at the same time with the Rationalists, that no life can enter the human soul which does not act through its natural powers."[63] The peace of God, which is beyond understanding, is a moment of union in which the supernatural touches the Earth and is wholly part of this world. God's peace "enters into union with the natural laws of our mental constitution, becomes the guardian of our heart and of our mind; it ceases to be supernatural to that soul within which it dwells."[64] The crucial point of revelation is that the veil is drawn back: "Revelation is not mystery; it is the mystery made manifest . . . The human spirit recognizes the vision not as a new vision, but as that for which unconsciously it has been waiting all along."[65]

Matheson sought to contain revelation within the limits of the created world: God's supernatural revelation can only act in and through nature and the natural powers of the human mind. This same point is made by Caird in which he argued that the content of revelation is not an instruction for some transcendental order, some world other than our own; rather, revelation enables us "to penetrate to the moral and spiritual meaning of the world in which we live, and to the teaching which, could we only read it aright, it yields to our minds."[66] Within Matheson's theology of union, revealed theology subsumes natural theology, depriving it of its separateness.[67] For Paul, the supernatural is experienced in and through the natural. Citing Paul, Matheson wrote: "'By Him all things consist' are the words in which he expresses his sense of the glory of Christ's place in history. 'Consist' literally means 'stand together.' Paul says that in Christ the world stands together,

60. Matheson, *Revealed Theology*, 4.

61. Matheson, *Revealed Theology*, 5.

62. Matheson, *Revealed Theology*, 6.

63. Matheson, *Revealed Theology*, 6.

64. Matheson, *Revealed Theology*, 7.

65. Matheson, *Revealed Theology*, 9.

66. Caird, *Fundamental Ideas of Christianity*, vol.1, 7.

67. Matheson, *Revealed Theology*, 25.

that apart from Christ the world is reduced to fragments; He is the bond that unites the lives of men, and the central truth that reconciles the systems of men."[68] Like Hegel and Caird, Matheson believed that religious thought in the world prior to Christianity was, in large measure, a preparation for the emergence of Christianity. Through its doctrines of Incarnation, atonement and immortality of the soul, Christianity has redeemed the systems of the past and has opened "a universal temple."[69] In satisfying the needs of each system, Christianity has "reconciled the claims of all."[70] Christ is the point of union for revealed and natural theology, for the power of the supernatural and nature and He is the point of union of other world faiths; Christ has answered the theological questions raised by other faiths.

In the Baird lectures, the first of Matheson's questions arises from the pre-Christian world: "What is God?" While some, such as Paley and Hume, argue that early humanity would have sought God in the external world Matheson said that, by contrast, "primitive man" would have looked within: "the force he behold . . . was the life-force of its being."[71] Early humanity's starting point was nature, the "great parent," a mystery which humanity would have feared, held in awe and worshiped.[72] As Caird did in his Gifford Lectures, Matheson briefly traced the theological development of Brahmanism in India and the mythology of Greece. In Brahmanism, humanity is reduced in stature because of its powerlessness in the face of nature while, in Greek thought, humanity, arriving at the importance of self-consciousness, the "desire of personal independence" became the primary "impulse of . . . life."[73] For the Greek, "the mystery of nature faded before the mystery of mind."[74] It was in Greece that the "spirit of man revealed its power to furnish a contribution to the human thought of God."[75]

Plato did not look to the external world to find God but sought the Divine in "supersensuous thought . . . upon a universe which was unseen and eternal; God was thought."[76] Matheson wrote of Plato's theology: "It was to transplant the soul into a world of abstract contemplation, where the reign of sense would end and the reign of spirit would begin, where

68. Matheson, *Revealed Theology*, 27.

69. Matheson, *Revealed Theology*, 28–29.

70. Matheson, *Revealed Theology*, 29.

71. Matheson, *Revealed Theology*, 31.

72. Matheson, *Revealed Theology*, 33.

73. Matheson, *Revealed Theology*, 37.

74. Matheson, *Revealed Theology*, 38.

75. Matheson, *Revealed Theology*, 39.

76. Matheson, *Revealed Theology*, 39–40.

reason would be undisturbed by the motives of the outer man, and where the will would be unswayed by the temptations of the earthly life."[77] For Matheson, it was the lovelessness of the Platonic system, the isolation of the soul, which left humanity spiritually craving for something to which it could relate and understand. Human contact with the Divine is necessary for "any perfect system of religion"[78] and it was the abstract, other-worldliness of Platonism which gave rise to mythologies that incorporated human qualities in the gods. Against the Deist, Matheson said, "The needs of human nature have in all ages proved too strong to suffer any widespread providence of so sweeping a religious negation."[79] God as Trinity satisfies the desire of Brahmanism to account of the fecundity of Fatherhood, the originating power of nature and, at the same time, the need for human connection with the Divine sought in popular mythology: "[The Spirit of God] revealed in the human soul possibilities of infinite greatness, yet He revealed these possibilities not in a region of abstract speculation, but in the common walks and aims of everyday life."[80]

Matheson stated that there are three possible models in understanding humanity's relationship with God: firstly, Deism, as a power beyond humanity; secondly, Theism, as a ruler, a king, over humanity; and, thirdly, the one to which he is working, Pantheism, as "the essence pervading man."[81] The God of Deism is a power beyond the world which has no interest in the world's history or human life. Deists did not deny the existence of superior beings but they were incapable of "mingling in earthly affairs."[82] The God of Theism, of divine supremacy, was a God over the world:[83] "He is the King, and we are the subjects."[84] The Theistic God is the God of Judaism, who brings order, government and law to the disorder, misgovernment and lawlessness of human life.[85] Nothing can happen in life, not even the most terrible things, without Judaism asking, "Shall evil be in a city, and the Lord hath not done it?"[86] For Matheson, while Brahmanism made the Divine indistinguishable from humanity, and the Deist removed God from human experience and

77. Matheson, *Revealed Theology*, 40.
78. Matheson, *Revealed Theology*, 43.
79. Matheson, *Revealed Theology*, 65.
80. Matheson, *Revealed Theology*, 53.
81. Matheson, *Revealed Theology*, 60.
82. Matheson, *Revealed Theology*, 62.
83. Matheson, *Revealed Theology*, 61.
84. Matheson, *Revealed Theology*, 65.
85. Matheson, *Revealed Theology*, 67.
86. Matheson, *Revealed Theology*, 68.

concern altogether, the God of Judaism connected with humanity not by "the divine life, but the divine command."[87]

Matheson's choice of language is indicative of his sympathy towards Hegelian mysticism. In opening his comments on what he first called Pantheism, Matheson spoke of God as essence. God is not to be conceived as "the power beyond the soul, nor as the power over the soul, but as the power of the soul—the great comprehensive life in which the life of humanity lives and moves and has its being."[88] Frequently turning to the Epistle to the Hebrews, Matheson stated that the ability of the Divine to be touched by human infirmities is not a weakness but rather an indication of strength,[89] in order that Divine transcendence suggests sympathy and "sympathetic nearness" suggests transcendence.[90] For Matheson, humanity finds God within the soul.

At every stage, Matheson was carefully working towards a greater theology of union. Like Caird, he described Christ's relationship to the Church as that of membership, with Christ as the head. Christ and the Church are to be understood as one organism in which the suffering of the members was felt equally by the head. There is no place here for God as king, somehow separate and detached from the actual experience of suffering. "What is distinctive about Christianity is the possibility of God participating in human weakness and suffering."[91] Not only does the Trinity through the Son connect with humanity, "for the first time in the history of religion, we are able to say, 'Heaven and Earth are met together.'"[92] In Christ, the human consciousness of God attains its highest point of fullness.[93]

At the Last Supper, Jesus spoke of humanity's union with God. The sharing of the elements, the consumption of bread and wine by the disciples is to be understood as an act of union between them and Jesus. In that moment, in digesting the bread and wine which Jesus handed to them, they become one with Him, one Body, flesh of His flesh, blood of His blood. Symbolically, spiritually, it is the moment of supreme union. The Son of Man is glorified at the moment and so too God within Him. Of the scene in the Upper Room, Matheson wrote: "He tells them that their relation to Him is henceforth that of the branches to the vine, that they have no life apart

---

87. Matheson, *Revealed Theology*, 70.

88. Matheson, *Revealed Theology*, 61.

89. Matheson, *Revealed Theology*, 64.

90. Matheson, *Revealed Theology*, 74.

91. Matheson, *Revealed Theology*, 77.

92. Matheson, *Revealed Theology*, 78.

93. Matheson, *Revealed Theology*, 84.

from Him, that He has no life unshared by them; He no longer asks them to come to Him, He entreats them to abide in Him."[94]

Union and the Apostle

Writing in 1897, some sixteen years after the Baird Lectures were delivered, Matheson saw in the work of Paul an over-riding theology of union. In his book, the *Spiritual Development of St Paul*, Matheson sought to write "an inner biography"[95] of the apostle. His attention was on the inner life and he regarded as secondary a history of the missions and adventures undertaken by the apostle as well as interpretations of Paul's letters by Calvin and others. Matheson had no desire to add to the debate about grace and law, of Episcopacy and Presbyterianism or even of predestination and free will.[96] Matheson regarded himself as "the historian of the inner life."[97]

Matheson did not use the Book of Acts to portray Paul because that would be an "eyewitness" account; instead he sought "the secrets of [Paul's] inner life by listening to [the apostle's] inward communings."[98] Matheson proposed a different sort of analysis, one he felt not every commentator would be able to give. The spiritual journey of Paul spanned sixteen years from First Thessalonians to Second Timothy. While scholarship was casting doubt on the authorship of some of the epistles, Matheson accounted for the differences by the growth and development within the inner life of the apostle.[99] Matheson drew attention to the period of absence from sight which followed immediately after Paul's Damascene conversion. He said that, following Paul's dramatic moment of illumination "by the fire of heaven," Paul's life is eclipsed by silence and he is "lost for a time amid the shadows."[100] Darkness is the ground from which Paul's spiritual life springs.

For Matheson, the life of the Christian is a transformation into the image of Christ: "the follower of Christ is transformed into the same image from glory to glory."[101] Paul's core message is Christ within us: "No man can read Paul's epistles without being impressed on every page with the predominance of this thought. The key-note of his whole teaching is 'Christ in

94. Matheson, *Revealed Theology*, 86–87.

95. Matheson, *Spiritual Development*, 1.

96. Matheson, *Spiritual Development*, vi.

97. Matheson, *Spiritual Development*, 2.

98. Matheson, *Spiritual Development*, 20.

99. Matheson, *Spiritual Development*, 8–9.

100. Matheson, *Spiritual Development*, 22–23.

101. Matheson, *Spiritual Development*, 6.

you.'"[102] In Galatians, Paul wrote, "It pleased God to reveal His Son *in me*."[103] The apostle does not say "to me," but "in me."[104] It is the inner nature of Paul's experience which led the apostle to see that revelation is within:

> He knew that a revelation from without is a contradiction in terms—that no external manifestation, however striking, could possibly reveal God to the soul. He insists upon this fact constantly, pertinaciously, at times even polemically. He says elsewhere, "God, who commanded the light to shine out of darkness, hath shined in our hearts, to give the light of the knowledge of the glory in the face of Jesus Christ." (2 Corinthians 6:6)[105]

The "deepest essence of heaven" can never be represented by "sight and sound."[106] Paul had been set apart to "his specially apostolic work" by an "act of priestly consecration . . . performed in his inner spirit by a hand and by a voice impalpable to the earthly sense."[107] For Paul, "the objects of sight are really objects which prevent sight . . . They are the curtains of another world . . . They are the shadows which intervene between the eye and a higher and holier light."[108] Crucially, the outer eye must be blinded if we are to see the image of God.[109] All things must be crucified if we are to have a "vision of a higher world."[110] Only at the moment when the outer world was suppressed in Paul did the apostle begin to see. In Paul's case, in that moment on the road to Damascus, the outer world was extinguished in him by a time of "black darkness."[111] It is impossible to read Matheson on Paul's blindness and how critical it was for the growth and development of the apostle's inner journey, without thinking of Matheson's experience both of his physical blindness and also his period of atheism; that spiritual darkness at the beginning of his public ministry in Innellan. Matheson wrote: "Doubtless it was this sense of revelation by desolation that prompted Paul to see in his own experience an analogy to the creative work of Genesis, and to say that, in giving to him the knowledge of His glory, God

---

102. Matheson, *Spiritual Development*, 7.

103. Galatians 1: 15—16

104. Matheson, *Spiritual Development*, 47–48.

105. Matheson, *Spiritual Development*, 48.

106. Matheson, *Spiritual Development*, 48.

107. Matheson, *Spiritual Development*, 116.

108. Matheson, *Spiritual Development*, 58.

109. Matheson, *Spiritual Development*, 58.

110. Matheson, *Spiritual Development*, 58.

111. Matheson, *Spiritual Development*, 60.

had "commanded the light to shine out of darkness."[112] Paul's retreat in Arabia was a time when he found the Divine in the transmutation of "his own dark deeds."[113] The primary concern for Paul was the inner life, the struggle within the soul. Paul discovered that Christianity was a power which gave him strength in the face of his own weakness, "the ability to support with unmurmuring love the weight of a bitter thorn."[114] Paul came to realize that it was through his suffering that he was united with Christ. Paul understood himself to be at one with God:

> He felt that, instead of needing to wait for the advent of heaven and earth, he himself had already made his advent from earth into heaven. He had been translated without seeing death. He had been borne aloft into the third heaven. He had been carried up into the very bosom of the Master and made to lie upon His breast. He had been allowed to anticipate the second advent, to enter here on earth into the fellowship, the communion, the citizenship of the life everlasting.[115]

While it is unlikely that Matheson was aware of the Celtic tradition, within Celtic Christianity there is a story that the Beloved Disciple in leaning against Jesus at the Last Supper heard the heartbeat of God.[116] Matheson's rendering of Paul's encounter with Christ portrays closeness, a most intimate relationship. Paul emancipates himself from "the cares of the present world by a process of spiritual asceticism."[117] Paul came to see that the vision or hope he expressed of heaven in Thessalonians was something that he came to experience by the time of his later works, Romans, First and Second Corinthians and Galatians: "the four later epistles is the asceticism of a man who believes himself to have already entered into heaven and to have left the present world actually behind."[118] After Galatians, Paul's life is "permeated with a new consciousness . . . the sense of being actually and at this moment in union with Christ."[119]

For Matheson, Paul's understanding of the resurrection similarly stresses union with the eternal now. Matheson interpreted the analogy of the seed in First Corinthians 15 as the apostle's teaching about the

112. Matheson, *Spiritual Development*, 61.
113. Matheson, *Spiritual Development*, 86.
114. Matheson, *Spiritual Development*, 163.
115. Matheson, *Spiritual Development*, 163.
116. Newell, *A New Harmony*, xi.
117. Matheson, *Spiritual Development*, 164.
118. Matheson, *Spiritual Development*, 164.
119. Matheson, *Spiritual Development*, 170.

resurrection, not the body. Paul is describing the "gradations through which the resurrection passes."[120] The spirit, whose journey begins planted in the earth, climbs the ladder of the resurrection in order to reach the heavens: "The birth of the risen life was not in the world above but in the world below."[121] Again Matheson used the imagery of darkness: "The hour in which the Divine life first enters into the heart of man is precisely that hour in which the heart of man is in its deepest and darkest gloom."[122] It was Paul's sense of spiritual elevation which shaped his understanding of revelation. Revelation is in the soul but, more importantly, it is not the annulling of humanity's thoughts by the thoughts of God: "it is the lifting up of a creature to a spiritual level with the Creator."[123] In order to understand the love of God, one must already have caught a "beatific vision of the Divine life."[124] Only those who understand God can be recipients of the life of God. Of *Romans*, Matheson wrote, "The spirit of Christ had become his own spirit, the life of Christ his own life."[125] Without passing through death, Paul is bold to say that he has "entered already into the promised land, has become a partaker already of that beatific glory."[126]

Matheson's understanding of the Last Supper and Holy Communion is remarkably open and sympathetic to the intent lying behind the theologies of different traditions within Christianity. Matheson said that both Roman Catholics and Protestants were straining to express that the spiritual can dwell in the material: "Every Christian believes in something equally miraculous, and miraculous, moreover, in a somewhat similar direction. The Catholic recognizes the truth of transubstantiation, the belief that the Divine Spirit can transmute itself into material elements; the Protestant, without accepting a transmutation, equally coincides in the conclusion that the Divine Spirit can manifest itself in these material elements."[127] The point is that there is union between the spiritual and the material, between God in the sacrament and God in the soul of the worshipper. There came a point in the inner life of Paul that he was no longer satisfied with being a Christian or being reconciled through Christ's sacrificial blood. Paul wanted more: he desired union. He wanted to be "a sharer in the life

---

120. Matheson, *Spiritual Development*, 171.

121. Matheson, *Spiritual Development*, 171.

122. Matheson, *Spiritual Development*, 174.

123. Matheson, *Spiritual Development*, 177.

124. Matheson, *Spiritual Development*, 179.

125. Matheson, *Spiritual Development*, 182.

126. Matheson, *Spiritual Development*, 184.

127. Matheson, *Spiritual Development*, 110.

of Christ, a partaker of His image, a member of His body."[128] The concept of sacrificial blood or reconciliation was not enough: "he must himself be inoculated with that blood, must himself be sent forth to fulfill the ministry of reconciliation."[129] For Matheson, this is the intimacy of lying on the breast of Jesus. He saw in Paul an intense desire for the closest possible union with God in Christ. Given that Matheson wrote with such energy on this matter it is reasonable to conclude that that desire is biographical: it reveals something of his own ambition.

Studies of the Portrait of Christ

In 1899 and 1900 Matheson published in two volumes his semi-devotional book, *Studies of the Portrait of Christ*. The portrait of Christ was "the united impression produced upon the heart" by the Gospels.[130] Matheson's approach was literary rather than that of historical criticism. Matheson read Scripture with the heart; he sought a portrait, not a forensic analysis; an emotional engagement with the story's development and its characters, their insights, strengths and flaws, not a detached or doctrinal perspective. Like Orthodox Christians gazing into an icon, Matheson gazed into a portrait of Jesus, a masterpiece painted in his mind, full of colour, texture and depth. Described as an "imaginative work of genius," his purpose was to "sing a song" not "write an essay." [131] Commenting on the first volume, one reviewer went so far as to say that Matheson's studies "form the freshest contribution to the literature of the subject which has appeared since Seeley's *Ecce Homo*."[132] The second volume followed a year later and, again, it was celebrated for its genius. One reviewer wrote:

> It is impossible in the space available at our disposal to describe how Dr. Matheson groups and interprets the incidents, and develops the inward significance of the drama. We can say, however, that though the materials have been worked over by countless writers, we do not remember anyone who has handled them with so much imaginative power and originality. Scholastics will no doubt often question his exegesis. It is, however, always

128. Matheson, *Spiritual Development*, 186.
129. Matheson, *Spiritual Development*, 186.
130. Matheson, *The Portrait of Christ*, vol. 2, vi.
131. *The Glasgow Herald*, Thursday 26 October, 1899.
132. *The Glasgow Herald*, Thursday 26 October, 1899.

brilliant and suggestive, and generally more convincing than the laboured expositions of ordinary commentators.[133]

The second reviewer drew attention to the "inward significance" which Matheson imaginatively elicited from the text. Matheson believed that the Bible was not only inspired of God but that it has "left the largest margin to the imagination of man."[134] Throughout the two volumes, Matheson laid stress on the inner life and, in particular, a sense of union or oneness with God. Matheson's encounter with Christ was in "the heart."[135] The Kingdom of God is not something external, outside of the self, but "an influence from within,"[136] "an inward Kingdom . . . a Kingdom from within."[137] The inward influence of the Kingdom was, in large measure, "the sacrificial spirit," and anything that might be achieved in the world outside was in proportion to one's selfless nature.[138] The theme of the Sermon on the Mount was "the power of the internal;"[139] salvation was not "an external thing," an "outward inheritance."[140]

In his portrait Matheson's stated purpose was to "trace the spiritual development, not of the life, but of the work, of Jesus exhibited in the Gospel narrative."[141] Approaching the narrative with "the eye of the heart" Matheson sought to capture the spiritual immediacy of the Gospels. The blessedness of the poor lay in the fact that they are "born from above—theirs is the Kingdom of heaven."[142] Similarly, Christ's endurance in facing the cross lay in the fact that He was focused on "the joy set before Him."[143] The joy within Christ was the "spirit of peace," the "rest within," a "mental calm;"[144] He had "treasures of the heart in the storm."[145] Matheson gazed into the face of Jesus, into the Divine, in a manner of a lover: "Thy face gives new meaning

133. *The Glasgow Herald*, Friday 9 November, 1900.

134. Matheson, *The Portrait of Christ*, vol. 2, 88–89.

135. Matheson, *The Portrait of Christ*, vol. 2, vi.

136. Matheson, *The Portrait of Christ*, vol. 2, 1.

137. Matheson, *The Portrait of Christ*, vol. 2, 2.

138. Matheson, *The Portrait of Christ*, vol. 2, 2.

139. Matheson, *The Portrait of Christ*, vol. 2, 5.

140. Matheson, *The Portrait of Christ*, vol. 2, 3.

141. Matheson, *The Portrait of Christ*, vol. 1, Preface.

142. Matheson, *The Portrait of Christ*, vol. 1, 6.

143. Matheson, *The Portrait of Christ*, vol. 1, 8.

144. Matheson, *The Portrait of Christ*, vol. 1, 9–10.

145. Matheson, *The Portrait of Christ*, vol. 1, 13.

to the instincts of my soul."[146] Matheson's phrasing and pace of prose was intense: he was caught up in his subject.

In his interpretation of demoniacal possession, Matheson suggests that each of us is divided and within every human being there rages a struggle between two lives, "the lower a conqueror, the higher a slave."[147] Jesus' instruction was to the soul, the inner self.[148] This is the wrestling with the ego, the overcoming of the shallower self. The ancients "were mistaken in believing that the impeding foe was a foreigner; [in fact], he was [within], one of their own household."[149] In prayer, in language reminiscent of Donne's *Holy Sonnets*, Matheson drew upon the metaphor of possession:

> Possess my soul, O Christ! I feel that something must possess me. My heart cannot be its own master; it must be ruled either from above or from below . . . Come into my soul, O Christ! Come, and restrain the advance of the lower man . . . Come, and make me Thy captive evermore. Put Thy fetters on me—Thy golden fetters which make free. Put Thy mark on me—Thy mark of ownership which ennobles . . . I shall own no other master when I am possessed by Thee.[150]

In addition to Matheson's craving for union, his wrestling with the ego, and his call of self-forgetfulness, he appreciated the silence of God. Acknowledging that silence allows humanity space for free choice,[151] the silence of God is at "the very heart of the gospel history."[152] It is "one of the privileges of the follower of Jesus."[153] In prayer, Matheson said: "Remind me that Thy education of my soul demands hours of silence. Remind me that if I would grow to the perfect stature the help must not be all on Thy side—that there must be moments in which I shall feel myself alone."[154]

In prayer, at times, Matheson's language is tender, even intimate: "Marvelous to me are these words of Thine, O Jesus—marvelous even at the end of so many days."[155] Matheson was sensitive to all that Jesus may be suffering and his use of the term, "O Jesus," is phrased almost as that

146. Matheson, *The Portrait of Christ*, vol. 1, 14.
147. Matheson, *The Portrait of Christ*, vol. 1, 165.
148. Matheson, *The Portrait of Christ*, vol. 1, 188.
149. Matheson, *The Portrait of Christ*, vol. 1, 168.
150. Matheson, *The Portrait of Christ*, vol. 1, 172.
151. Matheson, *The Portrait of Christ*, vol. 1, 183.
152. Matheson, *The Portrait of Christ*, vol. 1, 182.
153. Matheson, *The Portrait of Christ*, vol. 1, 183.
154. Matheson, *The Portrait of Christ*, vol. 1, 183.
155. Matheson, *The Portrait of Christ*, vol. 1, 208.

of a lover; he felt the "calm repose" of Christ.[156] Christ's words came to Matheson in a mystical experience, "from the height, from the mountain summit."[157] Matheson stressed the words of Jesus, "Blessed are the poor in spirit; theirs is the Kingdom of heaven." He stressed the word "is:" "It was not a world to come; it was here now . . ."[158]

Caught up in the intensity of prayer, Matheson was lifted into God. The union of Christ and the Father Matheson felt within his soul; the breathing of Jesus is one with his own breath. Of Jesus, he wrote: "Thou hadst no need of faith. There was a mountain view, a Pisgah view. Others believed in Thee; but Thou wert not a believer; Thou wert a seer. There was no messenger between Thee and Thy Father. There was not trust but experience. Thou wert breathing the perfumes of Paradise . . . Thou beholding the unveiled face of the Father."[159]

From intense awareness of God, Matheson acknowledged that spiritual growth is often preceded by spiritual crisis. Drawing upon the Gospel narrative of Jesus asleep in the boat in the midst of a storm, he said that, like the disciples, it is our experience of helplessness which can lead us to God. Of the disciples, he wrote: "[Their] cry was the real object of the voyage. It is the storm itself, not the stilling of the storm, that constitutes the significance of this narrative . . . The storm woke in the hearts of these men echoes that never died. It taught them their need—not as Galileans, not as Jews, not even as Christian, but as human creatures . . ." [160] Like Jacob wrestling with the angel, the storm taught the disciples their weakness. It was their brokenness, their need of God, which was their point of encounter with God. Vulnerability connects humanity, one with another.[161] In prayer, Matheson steps out on the water; his ego is shattered: "Therefore, O Christ, I bless Thee for the storm. I thank Thee for the moment of loneliness which I called the sleep of Thy power. It seemed to me as if I had the waters all to myself, as if there were none to help me. In that hour my pride died, to rise no more; I felt how poor a thing I was without Thee."[162]

The reassurance that Jesus offered His disciples in facing the metaphorical storms was to remind them of their special place in creation and that

156. Matheson, *The Portrait of Christ*, vol. 1, 208.
157. Matheson, *The Portrait of Christ*, vol. 1, 208.
158. Matheson, *The Portrait of Christ*, vol. 1, 209.
159. Matheson, *The Portrait of Christ*, vol. 1, 209.
160. Matheson, *The Portrait of Christ*, vol. 1, 219–20.
161. Matheson, *The Portrait of Christ*, vol. 1, 220.
162. Matheson, *The Portrait of Christ*, vol. 1, 220–21.

the greatest part of the human being is "the region of the soul."[163] Jesus said that dying to self in life is more difficult than death. Jesus said that He would confess before His Father those who, in this life, confess Him before others. It was a call to white martyrdom, to "take up the cross and follow:" the sacrifice of will required to confess Christ in this life was greater than that demanded of a sacrifice of the body.[164] Dying to self, self-forgetfulness, the overcoming of the ego, was the defining character of Christ's life. Citing Paul, Matheson wrote: "One of His disciples says of Him that "He bare our sins in His own body on to the tree"—not merely "on the tree" as our version has it, he means that the life was, with Him, itself true martyrdom."[165] In other words, the self-sacrifice was in Christ, in His life. The sacrifice He made in death was a continuation of His life. His life was a "living surrender."[166]

Jesus called the Father, "Lord of heaven and earth" because it revealed the Father's universality. In speaking to the child in human beings Jesus was speaking to the "universal faculty."[167] In prayer, the human heart is to beat in response to "the Heart of the universe."[168] In the liturgy of Teilhard de Chardin, the Jesuit priest wrote of God as the "Heart of the world's heart . . . Heart of Jesus, heart of evolution, unite me to yourself."[169] Matheson's understanding of union with the Divine is nowhere better illustrated than in his theology of the Sacrament of Holy Communion. Reflection on the Sacrament is found also in his Baird Lectures and biography of Paul. For Matheson, there are two significant communions: the feeding of the 5000 and the Last Supper. In the first, Jesus sought to be at one with humanity, to descend into humanity and, in the second, Jesus sought to be at one with humanity, to draw humanity up to Him: "The symbol of the one was the breaking of the bread in the desert; the symbol of the other was that broken body which Jesus said should draw all men unto Himself."[170] When Jesus fed the 5000, He offered them "rest unto your souls:" "He tells us in effect that the secret of His own rest came from within."[171] In sharing the bread and wine, Jesus "conceived for them the interest of a blood-relationship."[172]

163. Matheson, *The Portrait of Christ*, vol. 1, 243.

164. Matheson, *The Portrait of Christ*, vol. 1, 244–45.

165. Matheson, *The Portrait of Christ*, vol. 1, 245.

166. Matheson, *The Portrait of Christ*, vol. 1, 313.

167. Matheson, *The Portrait of Christ*, vol. 1, 281.

168. Matheson, *The Portrait of Christ*, vol. 1, 283.

169. King, *Christ in All Things*, 62.

170. Matheson, *The Portrait of Christ*, vol. 1, 285.

171. Matheson, *The Portrait of Christ*, vol. 1, 290.

172. Matheson, *The Portrait of Christ*, vol. 1, 291.

He proposed to impart rest, "not from without, but from within."[173] Matheson prayed for "indoor rest," for rest found within the soul: "all things will speak peace if my spirit is calm."[174]

Jesus' teaching was often expressed through parables and, at times, the meaning of the parables was not immediately clear to the listener; the parables need to be explained. Matheson believed that, as a teaching technique, parables evoke wonder, inquiry and, at the same, represent the hiddenness of the Divine. "The parables cause the multitude to exclaim 'Behind the veil! Behind the veil!'"[175] In drawing from everyday life and pointing to things that are unexplained or hidden, Jesus revealed "the presence of the unseen."[176] Citing Wordsworth, Matheson wrote: "It is a moment of glorious revelation when a man can see mystery in common things, when he can say, 'I see, and yet I do not understand.' It is what Wordsworth calls a 'presence that disturbs'; but it is glorious."[177] It is in God's absence or hiddenness that we encounter God. It is in "obscure moments," "ever with clouds" and, like Paul, the "blinding of the natural eye" in which God is revealed: "Tell me that I have learned the silence by hearing Thy step, that I have learned the darkness through the rising of the dawn. So shall my hour of inquiry be an hour of deep solemnity, so, when the clouds have gathered, shall I say, 'Behind the veil! Behind the veil!'"[178]

In his interpretation of Jesus walking on the water, in the midst of the storm, Matheson said that what is most striking was not that Jesus walks on water but that He walks alone. Matheson "hears" the "solitary grief" of Christ.[179] Matheson craved to go with Jesus: "May I go with Thee? Bid me that I come to Thee on the waters!"[180] Matheson repeated the call; he was moved not by Christ's majesty but His loneliness: "It is Thy loneliness. Thou art all alone. Bid me come to Thee, O Lord!"[181] Utterly present to Jesus, Matheson felt Christ's loneliness. Christ's loneliness may have touched Matheson's own isolation. He hopes that Jesus will satisfy his longing and perhaps, to some extent, he can satisfy that of Christ. At a deeper level, we are hearing the spiritual restlessness of which Augustine spoke, which finds

173. Matheson, *The Portrait of Christ*, vol. 1, 293.

174. Matheson, *The Portrait of Christ*, vol. 1, 297.

175. Matheson, *The Portrait of Christ*, vol. 1, 303.

176. Matheson, *The Portrait of Christ*, vol. 1, 304.

177. Matheson, *The Portrait of Christ*, vol. 1, 305–6.

178. Matheson, *The Portrait of Christ*, vol. 1, 310.

179. Matheson, *The Portrait of Christ*, vol. 1, 322.

180. Matheson, *The Portrait of Christ*, vol. 1, 324–25.

181. Matheson, *The Portrait of Christ*, vol. 1, 325.

its rest in Christ. We can imagine Matheson lying at night in the manse at Innellan, with the stillness of the village and only the waves to be heard: "Through the dark waters of the night, through the cold singings of the wave, through the vast spaces of solitude, I will follow and find Thee. I have bid Thee come to me on the land; bid me come to Thee on the waters. Thou hast answered my prayer, and I will respond to Thine."[182]

In all his writings, doctrinal discussion was peripheral and, Matheson said, it was incidental to Christ's Sermon on the Mount. The central point of the Sermon was that "heavenly bread is better than earthly bread; the things of the spirit are more valuable than the things of the flesh."[183] Lasting happiness comes when we are "fed within. Life's outward privileges can only relieve symptoms; they do not cure the actual unrest."[184] New life is to be found in "inner bread."[185] This is the bread of the Lord's Prayer that "sustains your steps in weariness, it will keep your feet from falling, it will prevent your heart from sinking; it will raise you up even at the death hour."[186]

Christ's retreat to the mountain top was "to drink of His favourite spring—communion with the Father."[187] On the Mount of Transfiguration, Jesus "stands right below the vaulted sky and communes face to face with the Father."[188] Matheson drew the reader into that sacred moment: "As He stands there, as we stand there, we have a strange spectacle—a radiance all from within. There is no increase of light in the gallery. There is no added sunbeam pouring through the panes . . . We are left in no doubt that the cause is inward—'As He prayed, the fashion of His countenance was altered.' Here, as ever, His glory is from within."[189] There was no miracle: the light of transfiguration came from "the beauty of His own soul."[190] The reader is encouraged to enter the scene: "You must put yourself in the place of Jesus . . . you must stand on the Mount with Him."[191] Matheson desired nothing more than to be one of Christ's chosen disciples, for the entire experience to be repeated in him: "I dare ask, I do ask, to be taken up beforehand to

182. Matheson, *The Portrait of Christ*, vol. 1, 325–26.

183. Matheson, *The Portrait of Christ*, vol. 2, 6.

184. Matheson, *The Portrait of Christ*, vol. 2, 6.

185. Matheson, *The Portrait of Christ*, vol. 2, 6.

186. Matheson, *The Portrait of Christ*, vol. 2, 8.

187. Matheson, *The Portrait of Christ*, vol. 2, 61.

188. Matheson, *The Portrait of Christ*, vol. 2, 62.

189. Matheson, *The Portrait of Christ*, vol. 2, 62.

190. Matheson, *The Portrait of Christ*, vol. 2, 62.

191. Matheson, *The Portrait of Christ*, vol. 1, 64.

the mount with Thee."[192] On the Mount of Olives, it is Christ's experience on the Mount of Transfiguration that filled His soul: "All night He spends in imbibing this joy. He returns in the morning and resumes His labours in the temple."[193] Present with Christ, Matheson was drawn to the darkness, the solitude, the aloneness of Jesus, not only because it spoke of his own sense of the mystical but, perhaps, it was the way in which the story and personality of Jesus most spoke to him. Matheson was a man who, while surrounded by assistants and an attentive sister, lived in darkness, solitude and the pain of loneliness. For Matheson, Jesus was a spiritual and emotional comfort: their relationship was an intense one. As in his meditation on John 8, even in judgement, Matheson imagined himself alone with Christ: "I would have no lamp to search my soul but the flaming lamp of heaven. I shall only be judged in righteousness when I am alone with Thee."[194] With immense feeling as if the experience were his own, Matheson said that Jesus was in sympathy with the "heart of God;" Jesus "felt it throbbing."[195] Jesus heard God "calling in the night."[196] In both volumes, each chapter is closed with prayer, some of which seem autobiographical in tone. Having noted the disappointment and dismay in Jesus because the world had been so unresponsive to the Father, in prayer, Matheson revealed his own suffering, albeit without being specific about the cause: "I know what it is to see the fading of an ideal dream; there have been to me far deeper bereavements. Therefore, I am glad that across even that river of trouble there is a bridge to Thee."[197]

Within the mystical tradition, if not the experience of faith more widely, it is sometimes the experience of darkness, bereavement and suffering which leads to a deeper and more spiritual understanding of faith and Scripture. Often the experience of human brokenness leads to new spiritual life. Christ saw heaven in this life. The parables of Jesus had one refrain, "Earth not sufficient without heaven."[198] In the Parable of the Prodigal Son, having left home, the brother spent "his substance in riotous living [and] Earth can do no more for him"[199] while, in the Parable of the Unjust Steward, it is in his moment of gain that the steward called out for

192. Matheson, *The Portrait of Christ*, vol. 2, 71.

193. Matheson, *The Portrait of Christ*, vol. 2, 94.

194. Matheson, *The Portrait of Christ*, vol. 2, 102.

195. Matheson, *The Portrait of Christ*, vol. 2, 11.

196. Matheson, *The Portrait of Christ*, vol. 2, 42.

197. Matheson, *The Portrait of Christ*, vol. 2, 13.

198. Matheson, *The Portrait of Christ*, vol. 2, 142.

199. Matheson, *The Portrait of Christ*, vol. 2, 142.

"everlasting habitations."[200] The beggar at the rich man's gate is promised a "rest in the Paradise of God."[201]

Union and Atonement

Matheson framed atonement in terms of union: love is at the heart of God; it is God's defining nature.[202] Oneness with God is achieved through our union with Christ which, in turn, means uniting ourselves with the character of Christ, namely, selflessness. Christ's death is not an atoning death, save in the extent to which He lived a selfless life, a life in which He sought closer union with God and with humanity. Matheson considered three forms of sacrifice, which he understood cumulatively: thanksgiving, propitiation and expiation. These different dimensions arise because of human need and have evolved through history.

Matheson said that thanksgiving arises from humanity's perception of insignificance and powerlessness in the face of nature's power. Humanity developed a desire to offer thanks for life itself by giving up something of its own. This early concept of sacrifice had little to do with sin: "It does not seem to us that the consciousness of sin was necessary to the birth of sacrifice."[203] Propitiation is, in some sense, an attempt to placate the anger of the gods for offenses caused. When sacrifice "averted the vindictive blow, it has reached its goal."[204] The most mature dimension to sacrifice is expiation: this is more than forgiveness, more than any external remission of a penalty, but reconciliation and union with the Divine:

> Propitiation is not enough; the burden of wrong is not lifted merely by averting a blow. You want a crucifixion of the moral past. You ask to be put in a position which you occupied before the deed, to be able to feel that the deed was never done by you, that your hands are free from it, that your heart is pure from it, that your life is untouched by it; this, and nothing less than this will pacify your wounded conscience.[205]

200. Matheson, *The Portrait of Christ*, vol. 2, 143.

201. Matheson, *The Portrait of Christ*, vol. 2, 143.

202. Matheson, *Revealed Theology*, 59.

203. Matheson, *Revealed Theology*, 114.

204. Matheson, *Revealed Theology*, 116.

205. Matheson, *Revealed Theology*, 118.

It is when we, through expiation, become a new creature that we experience "a larger life, a purer life," a diviner life."[206] Union with the Divine makes forgiveness and reconciliation possible:

"If a divine life would enfold my personality, it must enfold all that my personality contains—my disorder, my liability to divine enmity, my penalty of death. It must take up the impurity of my nature into its own pure nature, it must bear my sin and all that is involved in my sin, it must become partaker of my actual human experience."[207] For Matheson, it is because Christ is organically connected to His Church as the head of the body, at one with humanity, that forgiveness and reconciliation are achieved. As the head of an organism, Christ absorbs the sin and death of the body: "The moment we have given ascent to the doctrine of mystical union, we have given ascent to the doctrine that a pure head has been attached to an impure body."[208] For Matheson, atonement is full and all-embracing: "Give Him your past, and He will give you His past, His present, and His future. Give Him your corruption, and even while it bears Him down to death, there will issue from His divine headship a stream of incorruptible life which shall make you incorruptible.[209] God came so close to humanity that God made humanity's experience God's own, had "entered into so intimate a union with the sons of men, that the moral burdens of the race became potentially His burdens."[210] Our union with the head of the body, with Christ, means that the members receive the divine life from the head. The testimony of the apostle, "I die daily," is comprehensive: "the spirit of sacrifice had become the law of his being."[211] The inward spiritual struggle is an emotional experience which, in one sense, is open to scientific investigation but, while such experience runs throughout history, "only spiritualized men can study religion as it is manifested in the individual soul."[212]

Within his theology of union, Matheson includes "humanitarianism." In his meditation on the Transfiguration, Matheson said that Jesus did not go to Jerusalem with the single purpose to die but rather, in death, to unite Himself with the whole of humanity. Despite humanity's many and varied differences, humanity is one in that all die. In death, Jesus joined Himself with all people of all races and time. His death, then, may

206. Matheson, *Revealed Theology*, 120.
207. Matheson, *Revealed Theology*, 121.
208. Matheson, *Revealed Theology*, 123.
209. Matheson, *Revealed Theology*, 122.
210. Matheson, *Revealed Theology*, 125.
211. Matheson, *Revealed Theology*, 128.
212. Matheson, *Revealed Theology*, 131.

be said to be a humanitarian act because it united Him with humanity in a way that no other act could. The "second exodus" of the Transfiguration was "the vision of humanitarianism."[213] Aligned to the expansive understanding which Matheson had of the gospel, he believed that only such broad-mindedness could cope with intolerance or narrowness. In prayer, he asked: "Teach me that the summer of broad-mindedness is the power to tolerate intolerance! I call myself a catholic mind; and I deem the proof of it to be that there is one thing I have no sympathy with—narrowness."[214] Matheson understood atonement as union. It begins with Jesus' sympathy for the suffering of God: He sought to "compensate the heart of God."[215] Christ asked Himself, "Can I do anything to atone—through myself, through others?"[216] His desire was to surrender Himself.[217] In his reflection on Christ's ascension, Matheson said that it was sacrifice to God that led Jesus to Jerusalem and Calvary, not Calvary and death that led Him to Jerusalem: Jesus' purpose was ascension, ultimate union, not death.[218] It distressed Christ that He would reach the climax of His sacrifice at the very moment of the world's worst deed. He shrank from death because "it seemed to impede His expiation—because His crucifixion would multiply the world's sin."[219] In the Garden of Gethsemane, the pain suffered by Jesus was "the dread of an interference with His work of expiation."[220] Drawing from the Book of Hebrews, Jesus' death was "a contradiction to His work of atonement."[221] Christ sought union, not death.

It was at Caesarea Philippi that Jesus first understood His death to be "a perfect point of union with humanity."[222] Death is "the common ground for the meeting of all humanity."[223] In facing his own death, Jesus was uniting Himself with "universal Man": "When He bowed His soul to the thought of death, His interest ceased to be national; it became cosmopolitan. He experienced a sympathy which made the world His country. Death

213. Matheson, *The Portrait of Christ*, vol. 2, 76.

214. Matheson, *The Portrait of Christ*, vol. 2, 86.

215. Matheson, *The Portrait of Christ*, vol. 2, 11.

216. Matheson, *The Portrait of Christ*, vol. 2, 11.

217. Matheson, *The Portrait of Christ*, vol. 2, 12.

218. Matheson, *The Portrait of Christ*, vol. 2, 31.

219. Matheson, *The Portrait of Christ*, vol. 2, 40.

220. Matheson, *The Portrait of Christ*, vol. 2, 242.

221. Matheson, *The Portrait of Christ*, vol. 2, 41.

222. Matheson, *The Portrait of Christ*, vol. 2, 47.

223. Matheson, *The Portrait of Christ*, vol. 2, 48.

is not the only thing universal to man, but it is that universal thing which most unites the world."[224]

In his reflection on the Parable of the Good Shepherd, the first taught by Jesus "under the shadow of death,"[225] Matheson stressed that "death was not dear to Him."[226] Death is the wolf, "a power in the way of the sheep;" a good shepherd "is to lead the sheep even though death does lie in the path."[227] For the sake of the universal gospel, for the benefit of humanity and not solely His own people, Jesus was prepared to face death: it is "the only path on which the sheep can breathe; their one hope of life is there."[228] At the Last Supper, the words of Jesus which mark the breaking of the bread and the pouring of the wine are, said Matheson, to be understood in the present tense: "To my mind, Jesus speaks in the present because His expiation was in the present. He was not waiting for death to begin His work."[229] Jesus' death, the giving up of flesh and blood, is not the atonement: "From dawn to dark He had been surrendering Himself to His Father, yielding up flesh and blood by a sacrifice of the will. From dawn to dark He had been giving His life to God, seeking to atone for a world's lovelessness."[230] At Supper, Jesus' focus was on the fuller communion He would have with the disciples in His Father's Kingdom; it was not His death. He went to prepare another upper room for them, one in which they will enjoy "permanent communion."[231] For Matheson, the stress was to be laid on Jesus' looking to His ascension, His union with the Father, and not on His death. This is why He said to His disciples: "If it were not so, I would have told you. I would have made this a farewell. I would not have asked you to keep a feast in remembrance of me if I did not know that I should be alive . . . But I shall be alive . . . My spirit shall be with you."[232] The peace promised by Jesus can come "in the presence of the cloud;"[233] it is "contemporaneous with pain."[234] Christ's inner life, His sense of union with the Father, gave Him strength even as He fell under the weight of the cross:

224. Matheson, *The Portrait of Christ*, vol. 2, 49.

225. Matheson, *The Portrait of Christ*, vol. 2, 123.

226. Matheson, *The Portrait of Christ*, vol. 2, 124.

227. Matheson, *The Portrait of Christ*, vol. 2, 124.

228. Matheson, *The Portrait of Christ*, vol. 2, 124.

229. Matheson, *The Portrait of Christ*, vol. 2, 226.

230. Matheson, *The Portrait of Christ*, vol. 2, 227.

231. Matheson, *The Portrait of Christ*, vol. 2, 228.

232. Matheson, *The Portrait of Christ*, vol. 2, 229.

233. Matheson, *The Portrait of Christ*, vol. 2, 229.

234. Matheson, *The Portrait of Christ*, vol. 2, 232.

"The cross of humanity is still carried in His heart."[235] The expiation which Christ offered was not pain, but an act of will: "There can be no expiation in mere physical pain . . . Expiation demands an act of will. However complete be the surrender, it must be a conscious surrender, a voluntary surrender. The expiating work of Jesus, whether in life or in death, is not the fact that He lay passive in the hand of the Father; it is His determination to lie passive."[236] The bruises which Christ endured did not please God: "It is not the agony, but the acquiescence, that expiates the sin of the world."[237] "The expiatory sacrifice of Jesus was finished on Calvary. Easter Morning added nothing to its completeness. So far as the surrender of Jesus is concerned, Calvary is a climax; greater love hath no man than this!"[238]

Matheson's theology of union is found throughout his work spanning the length of his entire ministry. The most important feature of mystical theology is the mystic's sense of union with the Divine and with all things. We can confidently say that we find this in Matheson.

235. Matheson, *The Portrait of Christ*, vol. 2, 286.
236. Matheson, *The Portrait of Christ*, vol. 2, 301.
237. Matheson, *The Portrait of Christ*, vol. 2, 320–21.
238. Matheson, *The Portrait of Christ*, vol. 2, 328.

5

Inner Life, Silence, and Immortality

Introduction

IN THIS CHAPTER I shall discuss Matheson's focus on the inner life, the importance to him of silence and solitude and the immortality of the soul. I shall discuss in detail his meditations in *Moments on the Mount* (1884), *Times of Retirement* (1901), and *Messages of Hope* (1908) with occasional references to *Voices of the Spirit* (1892), *Searchings in the Silence* (1895), and *Leaves for Quiet Hours* (1904). I have chosen these publications because they are representative of Matheson's thought over the course of his literary career. At the height of his popularity, praise for his work was readily forthcoming:

> As a poetical expositor of Biblical themes, Dr Matheson is unsurpassed. His "Enoch the Immortal," "Abraham the Cosmopolitan," "Isaac the Domesticated," and others in his gallery of statues, serve as lay figures for an investiture of thought, philosophic, religious, original, of which all must acknowledge the charm.[1]

And,

> We doubt whether there is now in print a more beautiful and suggestive series of biographical studies of the familiar heroes of Old Testament times.[2]

Matheson regularly chose to write what he described as biography. His approach was similar to that of his own minister in his youth, William Pulsford. Matheson believed that moments of devotion were not to be devoid of thought or empty of content: "the wings on which the spirit soars must

1. Matheson, *Leaves for Quiet Hours*, 1.
2. Matheson, *Leaves for Quiet Hours*, 1.

always be wings of thought."[3] In his meditations, Matheson sought to follow "the different phases of the spiritual life" and to walk beside the stream of Scripture, and follow its path.[4] Above all, he desired to "track [the] influences of the Divine Spirit."[5] It is typical of Matheson to use non-anthropomorphic language of the Deity, such as "Divine Spirit," "Spirit Divine," "Spirit of Holiness" and "Spirit of Truth." Matheson's interpretation is largely metaphorical. His purpose in writing was not intended for intellectual assent but a deeper journey into the heart.

Macquarrie said that, within the mystical tradition of Christianity, the act of prayer involves "letting oneself be mastered, immersed in a power and wisdom transcending one's own."[6] Hartley argued that mystical writers lay stress on the spiritual: the mystics are the "guardians" of "the spirituality of true religion."[7] In common with Origen and Keble, Matheson did not read Scripture "like a piece of information."[8] James said that mysticism unleashed energy and saintliness in the life of the mystic: we find these qualities in Matheson's writing.[9] Matheson repeatedly, almost monotonously, returned to the spiritual life, the inward life, in his interpretation of Scripture. His selection of Scripture passages for his meditations allows him to focus on the life of the soul.

Alone, he "never felt himself to be alone . . ."[10] Matheson's daily routine was marked by prayer, study, praise, solitude and silence. He welcomed his desert experiences; from his private hours of quietness emerged his sense of God's Presence. Having endured a spiritual crisis, Matheson spiritually matured and he came to see the unity of all things: religion and science, faith and reason and God's mercy in joy and suffering. Similarly, Matheson's secretary at St Bernard's, William Smith, wrote of Matheson's "talismanic medium, his calumet of peace." Each evening Matheson restricted an hour of meditation without interruption; he described it as "an hour of communion."[11]

Regularly travelling to Argyll, Matheson would have been familiar with the ferry crossing, the movement of the waves and the freshness of the

3. Matheson, *Voices of the Spirit*, 1.

4. Matheson, *Voices of the Spirit*, 1.

5. Matheson, *Voices of the Spirit*, 1.

6. Macquarrie, *Two Worlds are One*, 25.

7. Schmidt, *Journal of American Academy*, 281.

8. Macquarrie, *Two Worlds are One*, 222.

9. James, *Varieties of Religious Experience*, 231.

10. Macmillan, *Life of George Matheson*, 242.

11. Macmillan, *Life of George Matheson*, 303.

wind on his face and through his hair. Without the noise pollution of cars, he will have been aware of the waves and the wind each day of his life in Innellan. At night, with the absolute stillness of the village and in the manse, the swell of the sea it seems was a sacrament to him; a means of grace and a medium through which he became intensely, intimately aware of the Presence of God, a presence filling all things and at one with his own soul. Night was the best setting for prayer: "Prayer could only come with the night, with the need. It is incompatible with full fruition. It needs the shadow to make its starlight, the silence to make its music, the want to make its cry. It is the bow set in the cloud, and it could be set in no other thing."[12] In the isolation of his study or bedroom, Matheson experienced either incredible personal torment, perhaps due to loneliness and the inability to read or entertain himself or, at another level, a spiritual hunger which he felt most keenly in his evening meditations. He understood his personal suffering to be his doorway into the Divine. In his poem *The Other*, the Welsh poet R. S. Thomas captures vividly the spiritual experience similar to that expressed by Matheson. In stillness, aloneness, and the darkness of night, Thomas writes of "that other being who is awake."

Matheson wrote of wrestling with his "night-angel."[13] He placed himself in the story of Jacob wrestling at night in the darkness with the angel at Peniel. While the "vows of the night" and the "songs of the night" were lost with the arrival of morning, Matheson prayed that he would retain his night-angel. It was in the night that he lost his sense of importance and realized "what an awful thing it is to be a human soul."[14] He ceased to be "a solitary man—an island of life in the darkness" and was able to "cling to the visible garment of the outer universe. I become one of the vast multitude. I lose my separate conscience, and, along with it, my separate struggle."[15]

In a meditation on Genesis 1:1a, "The Spirit of God moved upon the face of the waters," Matheson noted that before God said, "Let there be light," God said, "Let there be Spirit." He wrote, "It was the key note of all His voices to the human soul."[16] Matheson stressed that God's starting place—the Spirit—was the joy of the soul; God's Spirit had "its seat within."[17] What we are "depends on the Spirit."[18] For Matheson, the Spirit

12. Matheson, *Leaves for Quiet Hours*, 16.

13. Matheson, *Searchings in the Silence*, 111.

14. Matheson, *Searchings in the Silence*, 111.

15. Matheson, *Searchings in the Silence*, 111.

16. Matheson, *Voices of the Spirit*, 2.

17. Matheson, *Voices of the Spirit*, 2.

18. Matheson, *Voices of the Spirit*, 2.

is in all things and all things are in the Spirit. In prayer, he said, "I am forgetting that without Thee the light would not charm, the grass would not grow, the bird would not sing . . . Come and give to the light its charm, to the herb its greenness, to the bird its song."[19] Despite his blindness of many years, Matheson regularly and vividly incorporates color into his imagery. It is difficult to know to what extent Matheson had an accurate visual memory of the natural world, including light, grass or greenness. The blind theologian John Hull said that over time concepts such as place, space, appearance became "by degrees, with the advance into blindness, completely empty of meaning."[20] If that is true for Hull who enjoyed 48 years of sight, how much more would that be true of Matheson who not only lost his sight at the age of eighteen but, through his childhood and adolescent years, had suffered poor eyesight? If Matheson's memory of these things was poor or non-existent, his precision and eloquence in using such imagery was always apt and potent. Matheson's use of vivid imagery serves to illustrate the extent to which the Spirit is woven through the whole of creation: the Divine gives life its charm, the grass its growth, the herb its color and the bird its song. The whole of creation, its beauty, goodness and richness, is alive with the Divine Spirit. For Matheson, "eternity includes the present hour."[21] Writing over seventy years later, the French philosopher and paleontologist, Teilhard de Chardin wrote of the universe on fire with the presence of the Spirit: every touch is the touch of God. In a passage with a Christological focus, de Chardin said of God's omnipresence:

> His power animated all energy. His mastering life ate into every other life, to assimilate it to himself . . . Since first, Lord, you said, "*Hoc est corpus meum*," not only the bread on the altar, but (to some degree) everything in the universe that nourishes the soul for the life of the Spirit and Grace, has become *yours* and has become divine . . . it is divinized, divinizing, and diviniz-able. Every presence makes me feel that you are near me; every touch is the touch of your hand; every necessity transmits to me a pulsation of your will. And so true is this, that everything around me . . . has become for me . . . in some way, the substance of your heart: Jesus![22]

For Matheson, the more we absorb ourselves into the Spirit of Jesus, the more we will see the seemingly secular world is not a separate sphere

19. Matheson, *Voices of the Spirit*, 2.
20. Hull, *Touching the Rock*, xi.
21. Matheson, *Voices of the Spirit*, 3.
22. de Chardin, *In Time of War*, 146–147.

from the world of the church and worship. Christians will begin to see and understand that the world is one of the many mansions of the Father's house. In similar sentiment to de Chardin, the world is: "a room within the temple. It is a place of worship. It is an altar of sacrifice. It is a scene of prayer. It is a school of humility. It is a spot for revelation. It is a possible meeting-place with God."[23] For Matheson, the peace of God was not a matter to be experienced only in death but was "something to live by."[24] It was in his moments of deepest devotion that Matheson found "fresh glimpses of hidden things."[25] It was in his meditations, his moments of silence and solitude, that his imagination was most fertile. He believed in the "consecration of the natural:" "uncover your head in the temple of the commonplace! Bow down to the harmony God weaves out of trivial things!"[26] God saturated everything. For Matheson, Eden is an image, a place or reality which was "flooded with the Divine presence!"[27] However, the loss of Eden brought a new possibility of encounter with the Eternal, namely, prayer:

> In the land of swamps and marshes I have found something I could not meet in Eden—the gate of prayer . . . My Christ is gone into a far country, and I stretch my hands to Him. Yet there is a beauty in the stretching of the hands, the calling upon Thy name—His name . . . It is something to see Thee when Thou art passing by; but to cry for Thee when Thou art past has music all its own. It is love in absence . . . It is the refusal of my soul to be weaned from Thee by distance or disaster . . . I thank Thee that the loss of Eden has brought the hour of prayer.[28]

Inner Life

A central characteristic of the mystical tradition of Christianity (and other religions) is self-examination of the inner life. In this section I shall discuss Matheson's mystical reflections on the Transfiguration, the Old Testament characters of Enoch and Isaac, the Parable of the Prodigal Son, Job, the story of Abraham and the binding of Isaac, Jacob, and Cleopas on the Road to Emmaus. Mystics understand the spiritual journey as an inner journey:

23. Matheson, *Times of Retirement*, 147.

24. Matheson, *Voices of the Spirit*, 3.

25. Matheson, *Leaves for Quiet Hours*, 1.

26. Matheson, *Leaves for Quiet Hours*, 2.

27. Matheson, *Leaves for Quiet Hours*, 15.

28. Matheson, *Leaves for Quiet Hours*, 16.

it is a journey into union or oneness with the Divine and an overcoming of the ego. For Matheson, the prize of the spiritual life is "union and communion with God."[29] Our very hunger for God is only possible because God is already within us.[30] In his prayers and meditations, Matheson was concerned with the soul, his soul. Citing the words of Paul, Matheson asked, "Can a thing be revealed *to* me which has not been revealed *in* me?"[31] Following Peter's confession of Jesus as the Christ, Matheson quoted the words of Jesus: "Flesh and blood hath not revealed it unto thee."[32] "The voice of conscience is not uttered by anything within the world."[33] The soul was a place of comfort for him; it was his larger world. He prayed: "Inspire this consciousness with that thought which transcends all the channels of the natural sense. Unseal the inner eye, unstop the spiritual ear, that the symmetries and the harmonies of all worlds may be revealed . . . I shall see the King in His beauty when His beauty shall be revealed in me."[34] Humanity is to wait on God and there find refreshment and renewal. He bids his soul, "Be still": "In God thy past shall be cancelled and thou shalt be free . . . Thy years of remorse shall be no more . . . The dark deeds shall be undone, the hard words unspoken, the lost chances restored, the golden dreams revived in the life of God."[35] In a meditation on the Transfiguration, Matheson imagined himself on the same spiritual journey as that of the disciples. Only when he lies "prostrate in the struggle to be holy" does Matheson understand what it means to keep his conscience clear.[36] Above all, he sought to see Christ and Christ only. In prayer, he addressed the Son of Man: "I would meet Thee in life's cloud alike as in its sunshine; I would feel that in Thy presence the night were even as the day. I would allow no tabernacle to be build beside Thee . . . I would feel my need of Thy presence more and more."[37] In a passage reminiscent of his reflection on Psalm 139, Matheson did not fear the darkness or times of suffering but found the Divine in them: "I would be nearer to Thee every day, every hour, every moment, for it is only in being near to Thee that I shall learn how far off I am following

29. Matheson, *Moments on the Mount*, 272.

30. Matheson, *Heart Chords; My Aspirations*, 30.

31. Matheson, *Moments on the Mount*, 52. Matheson cites Galatians 1:16: "To reveal His Son in me."

32. Matheson, *Moments on the Mount*, 53. Matheson is referring to the confession of Peter (Matthew 16:17) Matheson repeats this point in *Messages of Hope*, 78.

33. Matheson, *Messages of Hope*, 15.

34. Matheson, *Moments on the Mount*, 54.

35. Matheson, *Heart Chords; My Aspirations*, 34–35.

36. Matheson, *Moments on the Mount*, 254.

37. Matheson, *Moments on the Mount*, 255.

Thee, how infinitely thou transcendest me. When I have beheld the summit of the mount I shall find none there but Thee."[38]

Hull offered a very similar reflection on the same Psalm:

> Just as blindness has the effect of obliterating the distinctions, so the divine omniscience transcends them. Because I am never in the light, it is equally true that I am never in the darkness. I have no fear of the darkness because I know nothing else. So it is with God . . . In [a] sense, it is true that if darkness is as light, then light is as darkness. The older translation of the Authorized Version brings out the point more vividly: "Darkness and light are both alike to thee . . . God does not overwhelm the darkness by his light; he represents that pure knowledge to which both light and darkness in their different ways point.[39]

In his reflections on both Enoch and Isaac, Matheson said that their defining quality was not the outward drama of their lives but all that was unfolding inward. Enoch was the greatest figure of that old world, yet his life was the shortest. Matheson considered Enoch to be greater than the others because Enoch's "life was more inward . . . more hidden."[40] Enoch lived his life in the soul: "His life was hid with God, because in its essence it was the life of God—love. It was too inward a life to make an impression on the world; its walk was divine, and therefore it was deemed a lowly walk, a thing to be forgotten . . . but Enoch, by his walk with God, is alive for evermore."[41] Answers to prayers are not seen by the eye or heard by the ear; history does not record them. The only place where prayer is answered is "in the silent depths of the soul."[42] Our journey in life is an opportunity for education: to learn to walk with God. God is a mother inviting her child to walk for the first time. "She stands at a seeming distance and says, 'Come.' She stands at a seeming distance, but all the time the intervening space is bridged by the arms of love."[43] God's desire is that we make our way to Christ and our journey is "a walk with God."[44]

Matheson described Isaac as "the man of meditation" whose life in the eyes of the world was uneventful.[45] The events of Isaac's life lie not on the

---

38. Matheson, *Moments on the Mount*, 255.

39. Hull, *Touching the Rock*, 60.

40. Matheson, *Moments on the Mount*, 16.

41. Matheson, *Moments on the Mount*, 16–17.

42. Matheson, *Moments on the Mount*, 207.

43. Matheson, *Moments on the Mount*, 194.

44. Matheson, *Moments on the Mount*, 195.

45. Matheson, *Moments on the Mount*, 268.

surface of history but in the depths of the heart: "Isaac's calm was the calm of inanity; it was the calm of conquered storm."[46] Through prayer, Matheson invited his readers to meditation:

> My soul, God has a time for thee to work and a time for thee to meditate. Would it not be well for thee to come up betimes into the secret place and rest awhile? The burden and heat of the day are hard to bear, and impossible to bear without the strength of the Spirit . . . Enter for one blessed hour into the secret of His pavilion, and He will send thee a flash of light that will keep thee all day. Thy work for man shall be glorious when thou hast meditated on the mount of God.[47]

Matheson saw that same pervading Spirit, the spirit of calm, in the life of the elder son in the Parable of the Prodigal Son. In the life of the elder son, Matheson felt not only the presence of the Spirit but the peace that the Spirit's presence brings. The elder son enjoyed the breath of God "in him every moment, every hour, every day."[48] Matheson bids his own soul never to undervalue this sense of peace. Peace—the breath and presence of God— is to be treasured over passing excitements: "To breathe the breath of God as a natural atmosphere—that is the highest blessing, and the highest tribute of Infinite Love is this: 'Son, thou art ever with me, and all that I have is thine.'"[49] Peace is spoken only to the heart: it is a secret known only to those who fear Him.[50] It is a peace which passes understanding. Matheson prayed that he would experience the marvel of God's presence within:

> Let me know what it is to have the incomprehensible rest,
>
> the stillness that cannot be stirred though the earth be
>
> removed and the mountains cast into the depths of the sea.
>
> Let me experience the Divine sleep in the midst of the waves—
>
> the sleep that Thou promisest to Thy beloved;
>
> so shall I learn what it is to possess the secret of the Lord.[51]

Listening to the waves on the shore at Innellan, in meditation, Matheson placed himself out on the water in the boat with Jesus. He felt the peace of Jesus, the Divine sleep, in the midst of the storm. He sought to possess

46. Matheson, *Moments on the Mount*, 268.

47. Matheson, *Moments on the Mount*, 269–70.

48. Matheson, *Moments on the Mount*, 116.

49. Matheson, *Moments on the Mount*, 117.

50. Matheson, *Moments on the Mount*, 196.

51. Matheson, *Moments on the Mount*, 198.

that peace not only in meditation but also in the suffering and fears of his own life. He once referred to the peace of Jesus as spiritual chloroform.[52] While physical chloroform renders us unconscious, spiritual chloroform creates a new consciousness within us. God's chloroform is for our death:

> He does not bid us shut our eyes; He bids us lift our eyes.
>
> He does not send us to sleep; He wakes us to a new impulse.
>
> He does not still our fear of lethargy; He stills it by excitement—
>
> by the sight of a coming joy.[53]

In prayer, Matheson asked that he not grow old in body until he had "taken the Child-Christ" into his soul.[54] For death, he prayed for the Divine anesthetic, a freedom from care which comes from the love of God.[55] In his moment of death, Matheson's family spoke of the peace and calm that shone from his face. The message he preached throughout his ministry, that we have the breath of God within us, immortality of the soul, filled his final moments. Matheson knew he had nothing to fear. In the final meditation of his posthumous publication, Matheson found the storms of life to be a true source of God's presence and blessing. He wrote:

> I bless God that He strengthened me to bear my thorns, for I am indebted to my thorns more than to my roses. It is the briars that have braced me. It is the storms that have steadied me. It is the nights that have dowered me. It is the losses that have leavened me. It is the heart-aches that have humanized me. It is the misadventures that have made me manly . . . I have learned the glory of obedience by the things which I have suffered.[56]

The challenge and suffering of this life are, at times, the doorways into the Divine. For Matheson, they come as messengers or manifestations of the Eternal. Though suffering is not to be sought, Matheson regularly affirmed God's presence in suffering. This is potentially a difficult pastoral message, with which not every sufferer would agree in the moment or in the future, but it is one Matheson strongly affirmed.

It is in the soul, in imaginative meditation, that Matheson intensely craved union with Jesus, a union which Matheson knew no spiritual or physical trial could ultimately overcome. In his reflection on the ascending

52. Matheson, *Messages of Hope*, 267.

53. Matheson, *Messages of Hope*, 267.

54. Matheson, *Messages of Hope*, 268.

55. Matheson, *Messages of Hope*, 268.

56. Matheson, *Messages of Hope*, 292–293.

and descending angels upon the Son of Man (John 1: 51), Matheson addressed Jesus:

> On the steps of Thy human life let my soul climb to God. Let me ascend from earth to heaven on the ladder of Thy human growth. Let me become a child with Thy child-life, a young man with Thy youth, a full-grown man with Thy maturity. Let me rise step by step with Thee—from Thy Bethlehem to Thy Nazareth, from Thy Nazareth to Thy Temptation, from Thy temptation to Thy Calvary, from Thy Calvary to Thine Olivet . . . Let me climb at last into the inheritance of Thy calm joy—into that peace which a cross itself cannot ruffle.[57]

Matheson sought not only to climb into the calm joy which the presence of Jesus gives but he desired to see the face of God. In the Old Testament, Job is told that when he has the favor of God he will be able to lift up his face to God. Matheson said that in Eastern lands only an exclusive few people were permitted to stand in the presence of the king, "to gaze into the face of royalty."[58] In contrast to Eastern custom, Matheson said that our destiny is to share the joy of communion with God and experience the rapture of fellowship with God.[59] This is our birthright: "to this end camest thou into the world, that thou mightest have communion with thy God."[60] Like the sea reflecting an over-hanging moon, the Father desires nothing more than for humanity to reflect His light. "When thou shalt lift up thy face to Him, He shall see His image in thy bosom."[61] The desire for every deeper union led Matheson to seek the face of God.

Matheson said that "when the cares and sorrows of life fall upon" him he had "no choice but to remember" God.[62] It was not through "any pressure from without, but by impulse from within."[63] In his reflection on Psalm 39:3, "While I was musing the fire burned," Matheson desired to muse more in order that the fire would burn more in his soul.[64] Though his life was shaped by his study, preaching, writing and meditation, he said that he would feel the fire more intensely if he had more enthusiasm. His seeming

---

57. Matheson, *Heart Chords; My Aspirations*, 40–41.

58. Matheson, *Moments on the Mount*, 277–278.

59. Matheson, *Moments on the Mount*, 278.

60. Matheson, *Moments on the Mount*, 279.

61. Matheson, *Moments on the Mount*, 280.

62. Matheson, *Heart Chords; My Aspirations*, 64.

63. Matheson, *Heart Chords; My Aspirations*, 65.

64. Matheson, *Heart Chords; My Aspirations*, 68.

lack of enthusiasm he attributed to "so little meditation."[65] To his soul, he said, "Thou wouldst be better fitted for the world if thou wert less worldly."[66] The power which changes the world is the fire within the soul:

> Is there no secret pavilion into which thou canst go to warm thyself? Is there no Holy of Holies where thou canst catch a glow of impulse that will make thee strong? Remember, all things that have stirred the world have come from within! Is it not written of the Son of Man that "as He prayed the fashion of His countenance was altered?" Yes; it was from His prayer that His transfigured glory came . . . It was when He was musing that the fire burned![67]

In his reflection on the story of Isaac, Matheson spoke of the secret of God's pavilion: "Enter for one blessed hour into the secret of His pavilion." Matheson bids the soul to enter God's secret pavilion, to reach up into "the heights of contemplation" catching the "breezes of heaven;" he calls his readers to prayer.[68] Pavilion perhaps suggests a place of refreshment as well as being a building set in a garden. A garden may suggest Eden, a place where lovers meet. It is a place of shelter and happiness. Matheson said, "Thy prayers shall be luminous; they will light thy face like the face of Moses when he wist not that it shone . . . when thou hast prayed in Elijah's solitude thou shalt have Elijah's chariot of fire."[69] Matheson said that, on the night before Jesus died, the prayer of Jesus was that the power of God's love would be in the hearts of His disciples (John 17:26).[70] The desire of Jesus was not that His disciples be loved *by* God but that they would have God's love within them:

> To love with God's love; to love with God's love in its moment of utmost intensity; to love with the love wherewith He beholds that Son who is the brightness of His own Glory: greater height than this can no man aspire to gain! I am told to aim at the Infinite in that which is the center of His infinitude—His LOVE! I am bidden to feel with His heart; to vibrate with His pulse; to glow with His warmth![71]

---

65. Matheson, *Heart Chords; My Aspirations*, 68.

66. Matheson, *Heart Chords; My Aspirations*, 68.

67. Matheson, *Heart Chords; My Aspirations,* 68–69.

68. Matheson, *Heart Chords; My Aspirations*, 69.

69. Matheson, *Heart Chords; My Aspirations*, 69.

70. Matheson, *Heart Chords; My Aspirations*, 76.

71. Matheson, *Heart Chords; My Aspirations,* 77–78.

It is sight of God's beauty which lets the heart be born again. In order to love the kingdom of God "you must *see* the kingdom of God."[72] What is seen is not reached by reason or proved by testimony but Matheson asked, "Hast thou seen His beauty?"[73] Physical beauty can be of no comfort in sorrow but beauty within, that is, the resurrection life is what sustains: "the holiest Sabbath rest will be nothing to thee if thou hast not rest within."[74] It is the Spirit which created the soul, the Spirit which was the first act in creation, which gives peace within. Only the Spirit can "calm the sea of the heart . . . The power that would heal my sorrows must begin not with my sight but with my soul!"[75] It is the Spirit within that can make death a joy.[76] It is only because we already have the Spirit of God within us that to meet God is a joy.[77] For Matheson, God saturates the whole of life. Life is not divided into sacred and secular. When we leave our prayers and meditations, we should not think that we have left the house of God:

> God's house shall to thee be everywhere, and thine own house shall be a part of it. When thou enterest into thy home thou shalt feel that thou art going into a temple, a place of Divine worship, an atmosphere of holy service. Thou shalt feel that all the duties of this place are consecrated, that it is none other than the house of God and one of the gates of heaven. Thou shalt feel that every one of its duties is an act of high communion. If thou art breaking thy bread to the family circle thou art fulfilling one form of the command: "this do in remembrance of me . . . Be it thine to make thy house *His* house. Be it thine to consecrate each word and look and deed in the social life of home."[78]

Matheson said that faith is needed not only for religious matters, but for the whole of life.[79] He repeated this same sentiment years later: "The climax of moral goodness is goodness in the domestic circle."[80]

In an original interpretation of the story of Abraham and Isaac (Genesis 22:7), Matheson wrote of the fire within the soul. In that ancient drama Isaac said, "Behold the fire and the wood, but where is the lamb for a burnt

72. Matheson, *Heart Chords; My Aspirations,* 81.

73. Matheson, *Heart Chords; My Aspirations,* 82.

74. Matheson, *Heart Chords; My Aspirations,* 94.

75. Matheson, *Heart Chords; My Aspirations,* 103–4.

76. Matheson, *Heart Chords; My Aspirations,* 104.

77. Matheson, *Heart Chords; My Aspirations,* 111.

78. Matheson, *Heart Chords; My Aspirations,* 115–116.

79. Matheson, *Heart Chords; My Aspirations,* 116.

80. Matheson, *Times of Retirement,* 174.

offering?" Rather than read this verse literally or acknowledge any sense of mortal danger and moral tragedy, Matheson spoke of the fire in the heart of Isaac. He said that "the fire in the heart was accepted as a *substitute* for something in the hand."[81] Matheson said that Isaac "had nothing to give but himself—his will, his inward fire; there was no lamb. Yet God accepted him *without* the lamb . . . God accepted the inward combustion, the fire in the soul, the seal in the spirit, the intention of the heart. The lamb was only slain in imagination; but the imagination was counted a reality; the offering was deemed complete."[82]

A fertile imagination is a central feature of Matheson's engagement with Scripture. He said that the lamb which God sees is "the lamb of the heart;" the sacrifice is within.[83] Matheson said, "I hear thee speak of the difference between the imaginary and the real. But to thy Father the most real thing about thee *is* thine imagining."[84] It may be that because Matheson was limited to his inner world he came to understand that for all of us the inner world is the most real; the world of mind is the only world for humanity. Equally, as an idealist, he believed that mind precedes matter and that as humans we are creatures of the mind. In response to the question "What is man?" Matheson replied, "He is a creature of the imagination."[85] Matheson's interpretation is more than an avoidance of the textual or doctrinal complexities in a difficult passage of Scripture; it is an excellent example of him seeing and feeling the Spirit within Scripture and in his own soul. Basking in the light of God, Matheson said we find our freedom.[86] In surrendering his life to God, Isaac was one with God on the summit of Mount Moriah.[87]

In his work *A Dish of Orts*, Matheson's contemporary George Macdonald held imagination to be of the highest value to humanity. It is imagination which is the root of human creativity. Macdonald wrote: "The imagination of man is made in the image of the imagination of God. Everything of man must have been of God first; and it will help much towards our understanding of the imagination and its functions in man if we first succeed in regarding aright the imagination of God, in which the imagination of man lives and moves and has its being."[88] For Macdonald, humanity is "but a thought

81. Matheson, *Times of Retirement*, 187.

82. Matheson, *Times of Retirement*, 188.

83. Matheson, *Times of Retirement*, 188.

84. Matheson, *Times of Retirement*, 188.

85. Matheson, *Times of Retirement*, 197.

86. Matheson, *Times of Retirement*, 191.

87. Matheson, *Times of Retirement*, 192.

88. Macdonald, *A Dish of Orts*, 2.

of God."[89] Following Bacon, Macdonald said that imagination is "the seed of knowledge."[90] For Macdonald, a wise imagination is "the presence of the spirit of God."[91] Matheson too found imagination to be the greatest gift of God, the place in which he encountered the Sacred.

Part of the inner journey is wrestling with the ego. Matheson wrote, "Teach me my nothingness in the hour of my prosperity; tell me in my adversity that I am something to Thee."[92] Overcoming the ego is integral to the life of the soul: "It is not the want of sight that prevents me from seeing my possibilities; it is something between me and the sun; it is the shadow of myself. If I could only get rid of self-contemplation, there would be revealed within me latent heaps of gold."[93] In the story of Jacob wrestling in the night at Peniel, Matheson reflected on the inner struggle of conscience. That struggle is always "in the form of a man."[94] Matheson wrote: "It is my higher self that strives with me—the Christ within. We have all a higher self—a photograph which God took in some pure moment. We have left it behind, but it follows us. It meets us in silent hours. It confronts us with the spectacle of what we might have been. It refuses to let us go until it has blessed us."[95] In prayer, Matheson implored God: "Impute to me the inner Christ, the better self. The groanings of my spirit are the voice of Thy Spirit."[96] It is when we are filled with God that we will be emptied of pride, when we are conscious of God that we are forgetful of self.[97] He said, "In Thy fullness shall I awake to the sense of my nothingness."[98] In his reflection on Psalm 23, Matheson said that prosperity and adversity both lie within the soul: "The sweetness and the bitterness of life are alike within us, and we shall get from the world just what we bring to it."[99] We must overcome our selfishness if we are ever to find a place of spiritual tranquility:

> If thou are at rest all things are thine—the world, life, death, angels, principalities, powers . . . Thou shalt sleep in the ship of life when the storm is raging around thee. Thou shalt spread thy

89. Macdonald, *A Dish of Orts*, 4.

90. Macdonald, *A Dish of Orts*, 15.

91. Macdonald, *A Dish of Orts*, 28.

92. Matheson, *Voices of the Spirit*, 3.

93. Matheson, *Leaves for Quiet Hours*, 3.

94. Matheson, *Searchings in the Silence*, 108.

95. Matheson, *Searchings in the Silence*, 108.

96. Matheson, *Searchings in the Silence*, 109.

97. Matheson, *Moments on the Mount*, 131.

98. Matheson, *Moments on the Mount*, 131–32.

99. Matheson, *Moments on the Mount*, 68.

table in peace in the presence of thine enemies, and shalt fail
to perceive their enmity. Thy calm shall reflect itself . . . All the
days of thy life goodness and mercy shall follow thee when thou
thyself hast been restored.[100]

Matheson said that "thy rainbow," a symbol of God's presence, strength
and mercy, must be "renewed from within."[101] In the Gospel of John, in
the post-Resurrection story of Jesus appearing to the fishermen, the critical difference which made the catch of fish possible was "a new color in
the heart' of the disciples. In the darkness of night, "it was not so much
because Jesus commanded as Jesus was there."[102] Matheson encouraged
his readers to "try again" in life "with Jesus;" the presence of Jesus in the
heart is life-changing.[103]

   In his reflection on Moses entering the tabernacle (Numbers 7:89),
Matheson suggested that Moses heard the voice of God when he entered
the tent because it was in the tent that Moses had for the first time "put
himself in the attitude of hearing."[104] The voice of God had spoken before,
had spoken all along, but the difference was that Moses "woke within"
and heard God's voice for the first time.[105] Matheson wrote of his own
soul crying in the silence of the night but hearing no Divine voice. The
voice of God cannot be heard by "the ear of sense . . . its accents are too
still and small to be caught by the natural ear . . . If thou would hear them
thou must enter the inner tabernacle, thou must open the inner ear."[106] For
Matheson, "Faith is the vision of the soul, the audience-chamber of the
soul."[107] Only in God's secret pavilion may we speak with God and "there
shall break upon thy heart the wondrous revelation that all thy life He has
been speaking with thee."[108]

   In similar manner to that of his reflection on the words of Jesus to
Peter ("Flesh and blood had not revealed it unto thee"), Matheson suggested that in life as we gaze at nature, at the ocean's boundlessness, we
often experience revelation and rapture not from what is seen by the physical eye or heard by the ear but by the sense *within* of the boundlessness

100. Matheson, *Moments on the Mount*, 69.
101. Matheson, *Leaves for Quiet Hours*, 27.
102. Matheson, *Leaves for Quiet Hours*, 27.
103. Matheson, *Leaves for Quiet Hours*, 27.
104. Matheson, *Mounts on the Mount*, 96.
105. Matheson, *Moments on the Mount*, 96.
106. Matheson, *Moments on the Mount*, 97.
107. Matheson, *Moments on the Mount*, 97.
108. Matheson, *Moments on the Mount*, 98.

of the Infinite.[109] The soul is more than "all materialisms."[110] Like Cleopas on the Road to Emmaus, we see the beauty of God "by another eye than sense": "If thy heart has burned as He talked with thee by the way, if thine aspiration has soared as He pointed thee to the mount of God, it can only be because thy heart is already one with His heart . . . Thou couldst not have seen Him as He is if thou hast not been like Him, for the divine alone can recognize the divine."[111] Matheson said that we have no need of miraculous messengers or special visions; no need of intermediaries. With the eye of the heart, God is to be seen in all things: "What need for thee to see special visions, when all sense is one continuous vision—the vision of His divine garment as His presence passes by?"[112] Matheson's vision of God is an inner vision; it is all-consuming. God is to be seen everywhere, in and through all things. For Matheson, "the summing up of the universe is the revelation of harmony."[113] The author of the Book of Revelation, the Seer of Patmos, saw the Lamb of sacrifice and the union that comes through the giving of self.[114] The union Matheson imagined is not one in which the individual is lost in God, in which the personality and uniqueness become an unidentifiable drop in the ocean of God, but rather one in which individuality and personhood are preserved: "He would not have my being to be lost in His, for His being is love, and love demands love."[115] If who we are is lost in God, then "my goal is death indeed."[116] Matheson wrote: "If my personality is to melt into the being of God as a cloud melts into the blaze of sunshine, then, surely, is God not my life but my annihilation."[117]

For Matheson, God is all *in* all. God's life does not obliterate the varieties of being but vibrates through creation in all its diversity, including humanity. When Matheson spoke of losing oneself in the ocean of God's love, he said that "this is only poetically true. Love is an ocean where no man permanently loses himself; he regains himself in richer, nobler form."[118] He preferred to express humanity's relationship with God in terms of immediacy and intimacy with God rather than explicitly with Christ.

109. Matheson, *Moments on the Mount*, 109.
110. Matheson, *Moments on the Mount*, 110.
111. Matheson, *Moments on the Mount*, 110.
112. Matheson, *Moments on the Mount*, 113.
113. Matheson, *Moments on the Mount*, 134.
114. Matheson, *Moments on the Mount*, 135.
115. Matheson, *Moments on the Mount*, 145.
116. Matheson, *Moments on the Mount*, 182.
117. Matheson, *Moments on the Mount*, 182.
118. Matheson, *Moments on the Mount*, 183.

The work for which Matheson is best known today is his hymn, "O Love That Wilt not Let Me Go." It was composed on the evening of 6 June, 1882, at the manse of Innellan. Matheson was alone at the time with the rest of the family away at a wedding in Glasgow. Matheson wrote:

> Something happened to me, which was known only to myself, and which caused me the most severe mental suffering. The hymn was the fruit of that suffering. It was the quickest bit of work I ever did in my life. I had the impression rather of having it dictated to me by some inward voice than of working it out myself. I am quite sure that the whole work was completed in five minutes.[119]

The hymn first appeared in print in the Church of Scotland's magazine, *Life & Work*. Two years later, it was incorporated into the Scottish Hymnal with A L Pearce's tune *St Margaret*. The Hymnal Committee required the change of a line from "I climbed the rainbow in the rain" to "I trace the rainbow through the rain."[120] The hymn powerfully captures Matheson's belief that the joy of God can be found in pain and that our humanity is not only preserved but reaches its richest and fullest expression in the ocean of God's love.

For Matheson, it is God who is to be craved, not God's gifts: "I would have my heart open at all times to receive Thee—at morning, noon, and night; in spring, and summer, and winter . . . Knock and I shall be open unto Thee."[121] In prayer, he said:

> Teach me that Thou art not in one place more than another. Teach me that I cannot flee from Thy presence, that Thou art with me not only in the Bethanies and the Calvaries, but in the common toil of Nazareth, and in the silent solitudes of the wilderness . . . I shall cease to live by the impressions of the hour when every breath of my being comes to me as a gift Divine.[122]

In a reflection on 1 Peter, Matheson said that the apostle had grown in a "Godwardly" direction; Peter had found "a new confidence—no longer in self, but in heaven."[123] Matheson felt that same leading of God in his own life. Even in the sobering hour, in times of suffering, grief and pain, Matheson saw such times as a blessing: "Bless thy Father for the sobering hour."[124]

119. Matheson, *Moments on the Mount*, 181.
120. Matheson, *Moments on the Mount*, 181.
121. Matheson, *Moments on the Mount*, 146.
122. Matheson, *Moments on the Mount*, 150–51.
123. Matheson, *Times of Retirement*, 39.
124. Matheson, *Times of Retirement*, 40.

Christ is experienced "*in* the storm:" "these feet divine shall touch thy human sea, and the marriage bells shall ring, It is I; I and the storm are one."[125] For many people, it is human suffering which most challenges their faith in God. Matheson understood God to be in our suffering and that suffering could be our most meaningful encounter with the Divine. He does not suggest in a trite, superficial or clichéd manner that God will meet us in our suffering. Matheson wrote on suffering with depth, authority and authenticity. At one in his inner life with Jesus, he said, "Thou canst bear a thousand waves if they claim identity with Jesus; the storm will not grate upon thine ear if He says, 'It is I.'"[126] For Matheson, this came from the heart.

By late 1899, Matheson had retired from preaching regularly at St Bernard's Church, Edinburgh. His intention was to devote more time to his writing. Though now more mature with decades of books behind him, Matheson continued to return to the same themes, including encountering and experiencing heaven, the Eternal, in this life. In prayer he wrote, "I could not long for Thee if Thou wert not *in* me; my want is the shadow of Thy sunshine. I am the only creature on earth that is not content with its environment."[127] God's house was "home, sweet home."[128] Drawing on the story of Jacob (Genesis 28), Matheson said that humanity is "made for the ladder of angels" and we ought not to be content with "the pillow of stone."[129] Like the writer of the book of Hebrews (8:5), Matheson said that "the spiritual world is the only real world, and the natural world is the land of shadows."[130] Earth is but a reflection of heaven: the best within us, the best within the soul, is "only the shadow of something more substantial!"[131] He said: "O my soul, thou hast mistaken thy true home; heaven is thy home. Thou art not going to travel at *death*; thou art travelling now. This is thy foreign land."[132] Matheson was filled with God and filled with love. His sense of the Sacred sensitized him to the Divine and to the natural world. At times, he seemed caught up in a mystical vision: "Enthrone in your heart an object of love, and you have renewed the universe. You have given an added note to every bird, a fresh joy to every brook, a fairer tint to every flower. The greater part of this world is painted from within. Its deepest

125. Matheson, *Times of Retirement*, 40.
126. Matheson, *Times of Retirement*, 40.
127. Matheson, *Times of Retirement*, 48.
128. Matheson, *Times of Retirement*, 49.
129. Matheson, *Times of Retirement*, 52.
130. Matheson, *Times of Retirement*, 80.
131. Matheson, *Times of Retirement*, 81.
132. Matheson, *Times of Retirement*, 82.

colors are given to the eye by the heart."[133] In tones of ecstatic vision, he continued: "Today there has come a new thought to my soul; and creation groans no more. The world has caught fire from the joy of my love; the heavens declare its glory; the earth showeth its handiwork."[134] For Matheson, God was as much here in this life as God is in heaven.[135] God is behind us "in memory," before us "in prospect" and beside us "in the pressure of the hand."[136] The pressure of a hand is a particularly poignant metaphor of God for Matheson, whose blindness meant that he knew what it was to rely on a trusting hand to guide and care for him every day; a body by his side and a hand placed in his hand, an arm supporting his arm. While science pointed to the evolution of humanity through the generations, Matheson said that his ancestry extended further back than that: "I have come from a Father in heaven . . . It is because I believe in heredity that I believe in Jesus."[137] He said, "The river may have come from thy fathers; but the fountain of thy life was with God."[138]

In his meditation on Abraham, Lazarus and Dives (Luke 16: 31), Matheson said that the reason why one rising from the dead would not persuade Dives and those like him was because they doubted "the eternity of love."[139] The spirit of love Jesus told His listeners could not be "created from the outside. No opened heaven will give it; no sights of beauty will give it; no scenes of horror will give it; it must exist within."[140] The revelation of heaven does not come from beyond the grave, from one rising from the dead, but rather "the essence of heaven is below, within."[141] The very essence of heaven is love. Of Dives' five brothers, Matheson said: "Wouldst thou tell thy five brothers that they are immortal? Thou needst not send a message from the tomb. Show them the power of love."[142] In an imaginative interpretation of the story of the raising of Lazarus, Matheson made a direct comparison between Lazarus and Judas Iscariot. In the Gospel of John, Jesus first told Lazarus to come out of the tomb but then told others, "Loose him, and let him go!" Matheson's meditation centered on the graveclothes (John 11: 44). He said that, on first sight, the clothes of the risen Lazarus and the dead

133. Matheson, *Times of Retirement*, 92.

134. Matheson, *Times of Retirement*, 94.

135. Matheson, *Times of Retirement*, 115.

136. Matheson, *Times of Retirement*, 115.

137. Matheson, *Times of Retirement*, 117.

138. Matheson, *Times of Retirement*, 118.

139. Matheson, *Times of Retirement*, 122.

140. Matheson, *Times of Retirement*, 123.

141. Matheson, *Times of Retirement*, 123.

142. Matheson, *Times of Retirement*, 124.

Lazarus look no different but, crucially, "the difference is all within."[143] He said that two people meet on one landing of a stair and, though they look to be on the same level, one is going up and the other down, one is a movement towards earth, while the other is "a resurrection movement."[144] On the face of it, Judas may have looked as good as Lazarus but he was "putting *on* his graveclothes; Lazarus was about to take his *off.*"[145] Matheson looked for the spiritual in the Scriptural story, looked continually for the spirit within the soul and saw in the soul our immortality.

For Matheson, the human soul is a far grander thing than all the beauty in nature. Did the wonders of astronomy shake his faith in Christ? He said, "I have always felt that the greatest thing in the world is just an individual soul. I magnify one throb of consciousness above all the united masses of the material creation."[146] The stars in the sky do not compare to "the hopeful heart of a little child."[147] He said, "Thou mayest be an infant crying in the infinite night; yet thine infancy is bigger than the night's infinitude."[148] God has set eternity in the heart.[149] Matheson made this same point in his meditation on Paul's Second Letter to the Corinthians (4:6): "God hath shined in our hearts to give the light of the knowledge of the glory in the face of Jesus Christ." Matheson said that there is "no revelation to the human heart unless that heart is already on the line of the revelation."[150] He repeated Paul's words that God revealed "His Son *in* me" and that the revelation to Peter did not come from flesh and blood.[151] He said, "The sublimity of the night is in my soul."[152] And, again, "Neither sunlight nor moonlight nor starlight can reveal to me the portrait of Christ; only heart-light can."[153]

Matheson's focus on the inner life led him on many occasions to reflect on the struggles faced within. He understood the life of the spirit to be a wrestling with inner demons. He said that we are forbidden to be jealous because jealousy narrows the soul; we are forbidden to be selfish because selfishness locks the soul; and we are commanded to love because "love is

143. Matheson, *Times of Retirement*, 129.

144. Matheson, *Times of Retirement*, 129.

145. Matheson, *Times of Retirement*, 129.

146. Matheson, *Times of Retirement*, 194–195.

147. Matheson, *Times of Retirement*, 195.

148. Matheson, *Times of Retirement*, 196.

149. Matheson, *Times of Retirement*, 257–258.

150. Matheson, *Messages of Hope*, 77.

151. Matheson, *Messages of Hope*, 78.

152. Matheson, *Messages of Hope*, 78.

153. Matheson, *Messages of Hope*, 79.

liberty."[154] In love, "to take captive a heart is to release it."[155] This sentiment is echoed in his hymn, "Make Me a Captive, Lord":

> Make me a captive, Lord,
>
> And then I shall be free.
>
> Force me to render up my sword,
>
> And I shall conqueror be.
>
> I sink in life's alarms
>
> When by myself I stand;
>
> Imprison me within Thine arms,
>
> And strong shall be my hand.

Matheson understood the inner struggle to be a sign of Christ's presence:

> Lord, it is on my sea that Thou walkest; it is on the billows of my soul that Thou drawest near. The first proof of Thy presence is inward storm. It is by the rolling of the waves of conscience that I know Thee to be nigh . . . When Thy feet touched the waters my storm arose—the storm of my conscience . . . The cry has come from the Christ within me; the suppliant for Thy mercy has the sign of communion.[156]

For Matheson, the stormiest spot is not in the waves but in the soul.[157] It is the human heart which stands in need of the peace which Christ brings. "I can bear the storm on the sea if the calm has entered my soul."[158] In the Gospel account of the healing of the paralyzed man, Jesus said, "Your sins are forgiven." Matheson said that, on the face of it, Jesus' instruction to the man is irrelevant. However, Jesus sought to give rest to the man's soul: "What better prelude to a medical cure than a flash of sunshine in the soul; what better preparation for a physical improvement than a state of inward rest!"[159] Inner healing is what Jesus gave. In comparison to the wonder of the ocean, the "little stream in the heart of a man" leads to a higher plane, a greater reality.[160] The peace of God

---

154. Matheson, *Messages of Hope*, 82.

155. Matheson, *Messages of Hope*, 224.

156. Matheson, *Messages of Hope*, 115.

157. Matheson, *Messages of Hope*, 143.

158. Matheson, *Messages of Hope*, 144.

159. Matheson, *Messages of Hope*, 150.

160. Matheson, *Messages of Hope*, 158.

is to be found in life's trials: "the peace of God descends on every man as it descended on Jesus—in the midst of the waters."[161]

Each evening after his secretary left, after his sister had gone to bed, Matheson lay in bed: in meditation, he rested in God. Matheson described the Bible as "the biography of Divine Love."[162] Drawing together the Books of Genesis (3:24) and Revelation (11:7), he said that Love "begins with movement and its ends in rest."[163] Like the calm of Isaac, the rest which God offers is not rest from struggle but rest *in* struggle.[164] Paul was able to claim that in all things we are conquerors because we are blessed in tribulation and persecution. Matheson said: "It is much to be poor in spirit, to be meek, to be merciful, to be peaceable, to be pure in heart—but to be all these things through struggle, this is holiness indeed."[165] It is a sense of spiritual calm to which the psalmist refers in Psalm 23: "Thou prepares a table before me in the presence of mine enemies." Matheson commended the earliest days of the Papacy for its holiness. Without an army, territory, military followers or the desire to enter battle, he said that in contrast to the powers of the world, the Papacy believed in holiness because it possessed and was possessed by the Spirit of God.[166]

Silence

Alongside his focus on the inner life and immortality, Matheson regularly returned to the importance of silence and solitude in the spiritual life:

> Meet me alone, O Lord, meet me alone! Let me feel for one moment the awful dignity of my own soul . . . Bring me out from the hiding place of the fig leaves! Let me hear Your voice in the Garden speaking to me—to me alone! Is it not written, 'When they were alone, He expounded all things to His disciples'?
>
> Meet me on my own threshold. Meet me when the sun has gone down, when the crowd has melted, when the pulse of the city beats low. Meet me in the stillness of my own heart, in the quiet of my own room, in the silence of my own reflective hour. Reveal to me my greatness! Flash your light upon the treasures hid in my field! Show me the diamond in my dust! Bring me the

161. Matheson, *Messages of Hope*, 174.
162. Matheson, *Leaves for Quiet Hours*, 22.
163. Matheson, *Leaves for Quiet Hours*, 22.
164. Matheson, *Moments on the Mount*, 154.
165. Matheson, *Moments on the Mount*, 156.
166. Matheson, *Messages of Hope*, 252–253.

pearl from my sea! When you have magnified my soul, I shall
learn my need of You![167]

It is in the silence of night, "in the void—in the solitude of night,"[168] that
Matheson was able to follow God most easily. Matheson understood that
often it is the times when God seems farthest from us that God is nearest
to us: "I can see that the hour when I seemed to be most distant from the
Father's eye was just the hour in which He was in closest contact with
my soul."[169] For Matheson, not only is the soul the seat of prosperity and
adversity, the site of wrestling between the lower and higher self, it is also
the place in which the absence and presence of the Divine are true at the
same time: "There, in what appeared to me the silence and the solitude, the
chords of my heart were being strung for richest music, and the pulses of
my heart were being quickened for social life—the life of the city of God
... Therefore my walk through the wilderness was a walk with Him ... The
Lord was in that place and I knew it not."[170]

It was in the wilderness, in the silence and solitude, that Matheson
said he most felt his nothingness. He felt that nothingness because "for the
first time, I had felt the power of God."[171] It is in the stillness of solitude
that one must enter communion with oneself, examine one's own nature
and pursue self-forgetfulness. The struggle within is a silent struggle. The
communion which God requires of us is communion with oneself: "Commune with thine own heart; what converse so silent as that?"[172] Matheson
wrote of silent communion in the stillness of night: "Only in thine own
heart canst thou see thyself truly reflected, therefore, it is with thyself that
thy Father bids thee commune. 'Commune upon thy bed;' not alone with
thine own heart, but with thine own heart in the stillest locality—in the silence of the midnight hour, where there is no distraction, and where there
is no deception."[173] It seemed that Matheson struggled through many
hours of spiritual anguish from the time he was left alone by his assistant
and sister each evening to his rising each morning. Matheson's repeated
reference to meditation in the small hours suggests that it was a frequent
occurrence. Though he found God in the silence, the solitude and his own
darkness, it is true that he found much of these times a struggle in which

167. Matheson, *Portraits of Bible Men* vol. 3, 87–88.

168. Matheson, *Searchings in the Silence,* 111.

169. Matheson, *Moments on the Mount,* 174.

170. Matheson, *Moments on the Mount,* 174.

171. Matheson, *Moments on the Mount,* 176.

172. Matheson, *Moments on the Mount,* 214.

173. Matheson, *Moments on the Mount,* 215.

he wrestled within himself, groped for God and sought Divine peace for his soul. He found those earliest hours to be a time when he could be most honest with himself and with God. "When thou art alone with God the crowd melts away, and thou art to thyself an universe . . . Commune with thine own heart, O my soul."[174] "The heart of thy Father beats for thee beneath every cloud as well as in every sunbeam; the blessing of thy Father is in thy night as well as thy day."[175] Matheson believed that meditation on the cross, on the suffering of Christ led to a sensitizing of oneself to the suffering of others. The fire of the burning bush, of God's mysterious presence and concern "opened the door of thy sympathy, and thy spirit passed through—passed into the heart, into the life of thy brother man to bear his burden and to carry his cross."[176]

Matheson said that our judgement before Christ is a personal, intimate and secret matter. In his reflection on the woman accused of committing adultery (John 8:9), Matheson noted that it was only when the crowd departed and the woman was left alone with Jesus that she began to feel her sinfulness. "She stood alone in the Courts of the Lord *with* the Lord; she could only measure herself by *Him*."[177] Matheson said that to be alone with Jesus is to have "thy judgment-day."[178] Judgment will not be a public affair, but a private encounter: "Practice being alone with Christ! . . . Practice that solitude, O my soul! Practice the expulsion of the crowd! Practice the stillness of thine own heart! Practice the solemn refrain, "God and I! God and I!" . . . Thou shalt be both condemned and pardoned when thou shalt meet Jesus alone!"[179] Matheson said that "the climax of every emotion is silence."[180] He believed the greatest praise in heaven would be silence, a moment in which words and music would be inadequate. Citing the Book of Revelation (8:1), he wrote:

> Carlyle has said, "Speech is silver, but silence is golden." I think the harps in the new Jerusalem are never so golden as when nobody strikes their chords. Did you ever ask yourself when it was that according to the Book of Revelation there was "silence in heaven for the space of half an hour." It was when the seventh seal was opened and the prayers of the saints ascended as

---

174. Matheson, *Moments on the Mount*, 215.

175. Matheson, *Moments on the Mount*, 257.

176. Matheson, *Moments on the Mount*, 258.

177. Matheson, *Times of Retirement*, 262.

178. Matheson, *Times of Retirement*, 262.

179. Matheson, *Times of Retirement*, 261–62.

180. Matheson, *Messages of Hope*, 161.

incense to the Father. In other words, the moment of silence was the moment of ecstatic praise; thanksgiving expressed itself in speechless adoration.[181]

Immortality

Matheson lived the inner life. He spoke often of the inward eye and, through his meditations, sought and experienced the presence and peace of God. For Matheson, it is the Spirit of God within us which assures us of our immortality. When he described his personal experience of atheism, he said that he believed in neither God nor immortality. As his theology developed, immortality became a central feature of his faith. For Matheson, it is because humanity has the immortal Spirit within that we already possess immortality. Immortality is not something we gain in death; we are immortal now. In this section I shall briefly discuss the concept of immortality in historical context. I shall discuss Matheson's understanding of immortality in his earlier work, *Natural Elements of Revealed Theology*; immortality in the sermons of John Caird and others, and immortality in Matheson's meditations spanning his ministry.

Albert Schweitzer said that it was "as the religion of immortality that Christianity was consecrated to take the place of the slowly dying civilization of the ancient world."[182] Immortality lies at the heart of the Christian faith. In his Gifford lectures (1901–1902), William James said that for most people religion meant immortality: "God is the producer of immortality; and whoever has doubts of immortality is written down as an atheist without further trial."[183] One hundred years before Matheson, in 1777, Hume said perhaps in jest that "the mere light of reason" made belief in immortality difficult: "It is the gospel, and the gospel alone, that has brought life and immortality to light."[184] When asked by Boswell about the possibility of immortal life, Hume said:

> It was possible that a piece of coal put upon the fire would not burn; and he added that it was a most unreasonable fancy that he should exist for ever, that immortality, if it were at all, must be general; that a great proportion dies in infancy before being possessed of reason; yet the trash of every age must be

181. Matheson, *Messages of Hope*, 162.
182. Baillie, *And the Life Everlasting*, 89.
183. James, *Varieties of Religious Experience*, 445.
184. Baillie, *And the Life Everlasting*, 48.

preserved, and that new universes must be created to contain such infinite numbers . . . [185]

Alongside the skepticism of Hume, the Victorian era was enthralled by the supernatural. Sermons on immortality were preached against a backdrop of séances, serialized adventure stories set in the Valley of the Kings, replete with mummies, and some finding "the ghostly face of a dead relative staring out of a photograph."[186] In 1864, just four years before Matheson was ordained, in *Astounding Disclosures in Connection with Spiritualism and the Spirit World*,[187] we read: "Strange voices—voices not of this world—stole into the room, the gas turned alternately blue and crimson, and the place was suffused with an unearthly glare."[188]

Matheson said that immortality was inextricably tied to life in Christ. Christianity revealed "God in immortality, or, which is the same thing, immortality in God."[189] Matheson contrasted Christian immortality with that of Platonism and, from Eastern thought, the transmigration of the soul. In Platonism, Matheson noted that "the dissolution of the body [is] the liberation of the soul."[190] Transmigration of the soul means that "a higher spiritual life" is achieved by "a simple process of transition, by a mere change of locality."[191] In the ancient world, the hour of death is "the harbinger of the spiritual life."[192] By contrast, Matheson stated:

> Christian immortality is not a life which death brings to the soul, it is a life which belongs to the soul, and which, therefore, death is unable to destroy. The continuity of life in this system is never for a moment broken. Death introduces no pause in the march of human existence; it is simply jostled out of the way in its attempt to oppose its march. The immortality exists within the soul as its birthright, not merely outside the soul as its destiny.[193]

For Matheson, immortality is a life which belongs to the soul; it is our birthright. We do not inherit immortality through a change in external conditions but through inner transformation. Our spiritual prosperity and purity

185. Wilson, *God's Funeral*, 29.

186. Brown et al., *The Victorian Supernatural*, 2.

187. Brown et al., *The Victorian Supernatural*, 7.

188. Brown et al., *The Victorian Supernatural*, 7.

189. Matheson, *Elements of Revealed Theology*, 169.

190. Matheson, *Elements of Revealed Theology*, 172.

191. Matheson, *Elements of Revealed Theology*, 173–174.

192. Matheson, *Elements of Revealed Theology*, 174.

193. Matheson, *Elements of Revealed Theology*, 174.

require "the possession of that inward abiding life which is in the highest sense its own conception of immortality."[194] Matheson acknowledged that, within the popular mind, it may be that immortality is something which awaits us in "some far and unknown future."[195] However, he stressed that the eternal, by virtue of being eternal, is "a present possibility . . . It does not need a future condition of things to bring it nearer."[196] Matheson understood heaven and hell to be "in the first instance present atmospheres."[197]

Union with the Eternal assures humanity of its immortality. Drawing from the Gospels and the writings of Paul, Matheson said:

> Every man who is in union with the divine Head is declared in the most unequivocal language to be already in possession of immortality, of eternity, of the state popularly called the future: "This is life eternal, to know Thee." "He that hath the Son hath life." "Hereby we know that we have passed from death unto life." "Ye are dead, and your life is hid with Christ in God." "I am the resurrection and the life; he that believeth in me shall never die." "There are some standing here who shall not taste of death until they see the kingdom of God come with power."[198]

For Matheson, union between Christ the Head and the members of His Body was "so close, so deep, so intimate, that the rising of the one must of necessity mean the rising of the other."[199] Confidence in the Church stemmed from the fact that it is a living body and the Head of the body was "already lifted from the grave."[200] Using the terms immortality and resurrection interchangeably, Matheson said that it was the "vital union" with the Head which meant that the Church was already "in possession of His immortality . . . partaker of His resurrection . . . recipient of eternal life [and] raised together with Him."[201] Matheson commended the Anglican Church for its doctrine of the Communion of Saints, a doctrine of union, which "enables the souls on earth to hold communion with the spirits that have passed beyond it."[202]

194. Matheson, *Elements of Revealed Theology*, 176.
195. Matheson, *Elements of Revealed Theology*, 177.
196. Matheson, *Elements of Revealed Theology*, 178.
197. Matheson, *Elements of Revealed Theology*, 178.
198. Matheson, *Elements of Revealed Theology*, 179.
199. Matheson, *Elements of Revealed Theology*, 181.
200. Matheson, *Elements of Revealed Theology*, 182.
201. Matheson, *Elements of Revealed Theology*, 182.
202. Matheson, *Elements of Revealed Theology*, 185.

Matheson was a man of his time. In *Scotch Sermons* (1880), Caird selected two sermons on the theme of immortality for inclusion in the publication of which he was editor. Entitled "Eternal life," both sermons were based on the same text: "And this is life eternal, that they might know thee, the only true God, and Jesus Christ, whom thou hast sent" (John 17:3). The first, written by Adam Semple of Huntly, differentiated Christian immortality from the prolongation of life, noting that "bare life is not necessarily a blessing."[203] Semple defined eternal life as a state of the soul in which we have "knowledge of the only true God, and of Jesus Christ whom He has sent."[204] For Semple, knowledge of God was not a body of facts which is mere information and alien to the soul, something that can be known by atheist and Christian alike, but rather was that of which we read in the Fourth Gospel; knowledge was "living principles, vivifying and transforming the soul which possesses them."[205] Like Semple, Matheson understood eternal life as being within, an inward power that transforms the soul. For Semple, when the soul assimilated the facts or possessed knowledge, the soul and the facts become one and the same,[206] like the imagination ruling the poet's soul.[207] Once we apprehend the nature of God, the all-embracing tenderness of Divine love in every episode in our own lives, then "we cannot but render back to God the love He has lavished on us."[208] For Semple, it was not enough to recount the miracles and parables; in fact, these outward forms may even obscure Christ.[209] In words Matheson himself could have written, Semple said: "Not by familiarity with the record of Christ's outward life, not by the knowledge of what is patent to the eye, but by communion with the inward life—that communion which imbues us with the living Spirit—does Christ become known to such."[210] Once the mind of Christ is in us, we can live for our fellow human being and, in so doing, "breathe that spirit of self-sacrifice which produced its noblest fruit in the death of Christ . . ."[211] Semple's theology of union is nowhere more boldly stated than in this sermon: "To know Christ is, if we dare say it, to be Christ."[212]

203. Semple, "Eternal Life," 325.

204. Semple, "Eternal Life," 325.

205. Semple, "Eternal Life," 327.

206. Semple, "Eternal Life," 327.

207. Semple, "Eternal Life," 328.

208. Semple, "Eternal Life," 330.

209. Semple, "Eternal Life," 331.

210. Semple, "Eternal Life," 331.

211. Semple, "Eternal Life," 332.

212. Semple, "Eternal Life," 332.

Like Caird and Semple, Matheson dismissed the "compensation" argument. He readily acknowledged that the one who does good or refrains from evil without the promise of heaven is in a morally higher position than the one whose motivation is hope of gaining heaven.[213] For Matheson, it is "the strength of the present life," not the promise of a reward which influences and enables us to live a higher moral life.[214] It is the "inward power of holiness" which secured virtue: "The man who is holy through the power of Christian immortality, is holy through the love of holiness, pure through the power of purity, good through the vital strength of the very life of goodness."[215] In what is a remarkable admission, Matheson stated that even if the Son of Man be a mythical theory, it would lose none of its power because the portraiture was perfect and, above all, the picture had "revealed the infinite value of a human soul."[216] Semple echoed the arguments of Matheson against future compensation being a possible motivation for the spiritual and moral life. Eternal life, said Semple, "is not a glory which only after death will crown the successful endeavors of the faithful; but it is the purity, the well-doing, the holiness itself."[217]

The second sermon chosen by Caird for *Scotch Sermons* was written by Patrick Stevenson of Inverarity. Stevenson began by acknowledging that many Victorians regard humanity as little more than "an automaton," a life form which ends with the body's death.[218] He argued that only people with a spiritual faculty are able to experience the spiritual life, and life eternal. Pointing the reader to union with Christ, Stevenson said, the "Heavenly Father desires, working within the laws of nature, mind and spirit, to educate up to his likeness."[219] Stevenson placed humanity's experience of heaven and hell within the present moment: "So profound is the belief of humanity that whatever else heaven and hell may be, and wherever else they may be found, they are cognizable from time to time, in strange alternation, in the experience of the individual soul, as, on the one hand, it suffers itself to be degraded; or, on the other, to be raised in sympathy with what is noble and loving."[220] In his sermon to the University of Glasgow on "Spiritual Rest," Caird told the students that "the heaven which God's presence

213. Matheson, *Elements of Revealed Theology*, 190.

214. Matheson, *Elements of Revealed Theology*, 191.

215. Matheson, *Elements of Revealed Theology*, 191.

216. Matheson, *Elements of Revealed Theology*, 192.

217. Semple, "Eternal Life," 334.

218. Stevenson, "Eternal Life," 365–66.

219. Stevenson, "Eternal Life," 370.

220. Stevenson, "Eternal Life," 369.

brings is already in local contiguity to saint and sinner alike."[221] He said: "What keeps the sinner out of it is not material but moral barriers: break down these, and heaven's sweet rest would stream into the spirit."[222] In his repudiation of the compensation argument, Caird said that moral action which needed to be sustained by the hope of reward, either in this world or the next, is "not the purest."[223] Instead, Caird drew attention to the results which flow from "a pure and holy life."[224] Personal gain was to eternal life a contradiction in terms: "To seek something else by means of it, to cultivate religion for the sake of material or other benefits, is an impossible and self-contradictory notion, for of love divine, still more than of love human, it holds good, that it needs no pleasure or reward to create it, and no compensation for the sacrifices to which it may lead."[225]

Matheson used the story of the raising of Lazarus to illustrate that Jesus was not talking about a concept of resurrection for the future but that it can be seen and experienced in this life. To Martha, Jesus said, "If you believe, you will see the glory of God."[226] In raising Lazarus, Jesus made possible "a higher and a holier" thought about death: death is not the "suspension of life" but the "transition of life."[227] Matheson had Jesus say that one need not "wait for the last day . . . I am come to replace your thought of resurrection by my thought of immortality."[228] Matheson stressed that heaven is to be experienced now; immortality is possible in this life. Put succinctly of Jesus: "He was not immortal because He rose; He rose because He was immortal."[229] "Christ is, in the deepest sense, the cause of His own rising; in Christ, and not in His rising, lies our vision of immortality."[230] In fact, the resurrection, traditionally understood, is almost superfluous:

> As I stand in the great gallery and read the Face of Jesus, as I mark the expressions of that Face through all the scenes from Galilee to Calvary, I feel that He is already immortal. I feel, so far as my sense of His immortality is concerned, that I need no testimony from the open grave. It would not disconcert me, on

221. Caird, *Sermons*, 179.

222. Caird, *Sermons*, 179.

223. Caird, *Fundamental Ideas of Christianity*, vol. 2, 287.

224. Caird, *Fundamental Ideas of Christianity*, vol. 2, 287.

225. Caird, *Fundamental Ideas of Christianity*, vol. 2, 292.

226. Matheson, *The Portrait of Christ*, vol. 2, 157.

227. Matheson, *The Portrait of Christ*, vol. 2, 157.

228. Matheson, *The Portrait of Christ*, vol. 2, 157.

229. Matheson, *The Portrait of Christ*, vol. 2, 332.

230. Matheson, *The Portrait of Christ*, vol. 2, 334.

this point, if a new and earlier Bible were found which closed
its record at the Cross of Calvary. I should still feel that in this
Portrait of the Son of Man I had the highest possible incidence
of the existence of a soul invulnerable by death.[231]

The tears Jesus sheds over Lazarus were not for Lazarus *per se*, but because
people did not understand the nature of death: death is not suspension, but
transition. Drawing himself into meditation, as if feeling the tears of Jesus
on his own face, with a sense of cleansing, Matheson prayed:

> Thy tears fell on me. Thy tears were the showers of Thy compas-
> sion for my dead hope, for my dim sight, for my buried faith, for
> my forgetfulness of the glory of the Father. And the shower of
> sorrow was a shower of blessing; it was the tears of the protest-
> ing rainbow in the evening sky. In the hour of my life's despair,
> ever let such drops descend on me![232]

In the Garden of Gethsemane, Matheson draws the reader into the
suffering of Jesus. We are to "draw aside the veil" and, in union with Jesus,
we are to "share the night" and know for ourselves the pain He endured.[233]
The Father will ask, "Did I not see thee in the Garden with Him?"[234] It was
His sense of immortality, "a soul to whom the other world has always been
the real world and this the land of shadows," that made Him confident and
secured His inner peace in His hours of Passion.[235] For Matheson, it was
Christ's "sense of holiness" which sustained Him,[236] "it was the holiness that
sustained the wilderness and the cross."[237] Christ's holiness is free of egotism
and self-importance.[238] In Gethsemane, Christ's agony was not for Himself,
but for the world; His suffering arose from the rift between the world and
the Father: "The cry of Gethsemane is His cry for communion with the
world—with those whom the Father had not yet given Him. It comes from a
void in His heart. He possesses something which He wants to share; it pains
Him to possess it alone."[239] Jesus maintained His inner peace under ques-
tioning by Pilate and Caiaphas, a peace which, in prayer, Matheson himself

231. Matheson, *The Portrait of Christ*, vol. 2, 335.

232. Matheson, *The Portrait of Christ*, vol. 2, 160.

233. Matheson, *The Portrait of Christ*, vol. 2, 239.

234. Matheson, *The Portrait of Christ*, vol. 2, 248.

235. Matheson, *The Portrait of Christ*, vol. 2, 240.

236. Matheson, *The Portrait of Christ*, vol. 2, 244.

237. Matheson, *The Portrait of Christ*, vol. 2, 332.

238. Matheson, *The Portrait of Christ*, vol. 2, 245.

239. Matheson, *The Portrait of Christ*, vol. 2, 246.

found: "I shall know Thy strength by my unaccountable peace, by my inex-plicable calm."[240] Christ is to be known as "king" not by the ear, but by the heart.[241] On the cross, the vision of Jesus was beyond this world; it was never "a starless night."[242] In what might be described an ecstatic, mystical experi-ence, Matheson was himself caught up in a vision of the beauty of the cross, of Christ's hours on Calvary. Rather than the ghastliness of a brutal death, it was for Matheson a moment of "universal communion," in which represen-tatives from the whole of humanity are present: slave, peasant, priest, scribe, soldier, merchant, disciple and women.[243] The exchange which Jesus had with the malefactor, the criminal who asked Jesus to remember him, is the epitome of what it means to be a follower of Jesus. Where Peter had failed, the criminal's "spiritual life was born on Calvary; he was the first leaf of that winter tree."[244] Within the nameless criminal, there was "an inner life which unconsciously waited and thirsted."[245]

In his reflection on Genesis 1:26, that humanity is made in the image of God, Matheson pondered what it meant to be human. In comparison to the vastness and complexity of the physical universe, he found in the soul of humanity love and immortality:

> There are seasons in which I ask myself, what is my petty life amid the vastness of the stars? But love makes me stand erect. It gives me a sense of immortality, of imperishableness. It lifts me above all material things, however magnificent. It tells me there is room in the inn amid the guests of my Father . . . It makes me say, "What a piece of work man is!"[246]

It is the "ideal man," the Christ within us, which makes us feel immor-tal.[247] We are not "a living thing" but "a living soul."[248] In the Parable of the Prodigal Son, Matheson said that the prodigal began to want, not because there was insufficient swine-husks, but because he was a living soul. As a living soul, "all wealth of creation would be swine-husks to thee. All the kingdoms of the world would be dross to thee . . . Thy demand exceeds thy

240. Matheson, *The Portrait of Christ*, vol. 2, 279.
241. Matheson, *The Portrait of Christ*, vol. 2, 278.
242. Matheson, *The Portrait of Christ*, vol. 2, 296.
243. Matheson, *The Portrait of Christ*, vol. 2, 302.
244. Matheson, *The Portrait of Christ*, vol. 2, 306.
245. Matheson, *The Portrait of Christ*, vol. 2, 308.
246. Matheson, *Leave for Quiet Hours*, 6.
247. Matheson, *Searchings in the Silence*, 108.
248. Matheson, *Heart Chords; My Aspirations*, 3.

supply, and predicts thy immortality."[249] For Matheson, in the Sermon on the Mount, in the Beatitude "Blessed are they that mourn: for they shall be comforted," Jesus was not referring to natural bereavement but worldly unrest. Our mourning is "the inability to be satisfied with the possessions of life . . . Our very unrest is a badge of dignity; it proves that we are above our surroundings."[250] In a sense, our suffering is a grace of God: "It is because I have a higher home than earth that I cannot be filled by earth. It is because the far country is far from adequate to my nature that I find myself in want within it. The greatest comfort *is* my famine. It is the pledge of my immortality."[251]

Matheson was wrapped in a sense of God's presence, a presence which he described as immortality: it gave him an unshakable belief not only that eternity is now but that this will always be. His unrest was "the harbinger of holy calm!"[252] The hunger of the Prodigal Son was the reason he would not perish: "It is thy hunger keeps thee alive as an immortal."[253] To know God is to experience life eternal.[254]

Matheson directly linked immortality with the spirit of sacrifice. In Genesis, "the secret of Abel's immortality" is sacrifice.[255] Abel's immortality makes him "a living figure" whose name stretches across six millennia.[256] His strength or immortal quality is his heart: "he manifested his love by sacrifice . . . It is in the spirit of moral sacrifice that the proof of thy future lies."[257] The sacrificial spirit is "itself independent of time and space and change . . . it is truly called 'life eternal' for years cannot touch it."[258] Matheson said that the spirit of sacrifice was "impervious to time, and so it is the pledge of immortality . . . In the moment of thy surrender [my soul], thou shalt become green with immortal youth. In the hour of thy self-forgetfulness thou shalt have passed already from death unto life, for Calvary is the shadow of Olivet, and the spirit of Abel is the Spirit of Christ."[259] In his meditation,

---

249. Matheson, *Heart Chords; My Aspirations*, 3.

250. Matheson, *Heart Chords; My Aspirations*, 25.

251. Matheson, *Heart Chords; My Aspirations*, 26.

252. Matheson, *Heart Chords; My Aspirations*, 26–27.

253. Matheson, *Heart Chords; My Aspirations*, 32.

254. Matheson, *Heart Chords; My Aspirations*, 53.

255. Matheson, *Heart Chords; My Aspirations*, 108.

256. Matheson, *Heart Chords; My Aspirations*, 108.

257. Matheson, *Heart Chords; My Aspirations*, 109.

258. Matheson, *Heart Chords; My Aspirations*, 109.

259. Matheson, *Heart Chords; My Aspirations*, 110.

The Ground of Immortality (1884),[260] Matheson said that humanity enjoyed immortality because humanity has God within. Matheson said that the confidence of the prophet Habakkuk rested in the knowledge that God resides in humanity: "Art Thou not from everlasting, O Lord my God, mine Holy One? we shall not die" (Habakkuk 1:12). He said the same meaning is found in the Gospel of John and Colossians: "Because I live, ye shall live also" (John 14:19); "I live, yet not I, but Christ liveth in me" (Galatians 2:20); and "Christ in you, the hope of glory" (Colossians 1:27) Humanity's immortality is God's immortality.[261] Drawing on the creation narrative Matheson said: "He is not outside of thee. He has breathed into thy nostrils the breath of His own life, and it is by that breath that even now thou livest. It is by that breath that even now thou art victor over death from moment to moment, from hour to hour, from day to day."[262]

Day by day Matheson pleaded for the Spirit of Christ to reveal "Thy presence within me."[263] Matheson understood resurrection to mean immortality. Resurrection after death would make no sense because we possess God's immortality now in this life. Matheson prayed, "Reveal to me that the power of Thy presence is the power of my resurrection, the certitude of my immortality."[264] In what is a significant statement of his theology, Matheson said:

> Teach me that the state after death exists already before death, that I need not taste death until I have seen the kingdom of God. Teach me that my immortality is not to come, that it is here, that it is now. Teach me that the life eternal is not merely the life *beyond* the grave, but the life on this side of the grave. Reveal to me that I am *now* in eternity, that I am breathing the very air of those that have passed the gates . . . Let me feel that I am already immortal; that death could no more destroy *my* life than it could destroy Thine, because mine *is* Thine.[265]

There can be no mistake that this position was and is not the prevailing view in the Church of Scotland. Matheson favored oneness with the Divine to the extent that there was no need for a special event after death.

In his prayer accompanying his reflection on Enoch, the one who walked with God, Matheson said, "My soul, thy walk with God is thy

260. Matheson, *Moments on the Mount*, 46.

261. Matheson, *Moments on the Mount*, 47.

262. Matheson, *Moments on the Mount*, 47.

263. Matheson, *Moments on the Mount*, 47.

264. Matheson, *Moments on the Mount*, 47.

265. Matheson, *Moments on the Mount*, 48.

evidence of immortality . . . Thou hast transcended the seen and temporal; thou hast entered the unseen and eternal, thou hast passed from death unto life."[266] He told his reader, "Thy hope of glory is Christ already in thee. Thou art immortal before death."[267] Bringing together immortality and sacrifice, Matheson said that humanity did not need to wait for death to enter eternity. In a moment of intimate encounter, Matheson said of Jesus: "He told me that I need not wait till the last hour in order to find eternity, that I might find it now. He told me that God's presence could be reached without dying, that the grandest death of the spirit was the life of love, that the most reasonable service for a man was to present his body as a living sacrifice, holy, acceptable unto God."[268] In prayer, Matheson commended his spirit into the hands of the Father.[269] In a creative meditation on spiritual resurrection,[270] Matheson brought together three stories from the Gospels and one from the Book of Ezekiel. In his description of the stories, there is an increasing degree of disintegration of the body. For Jairus' daughter, the disintegration or "corruption" of the body has only begun while the young man of Nain has died and is on the road to burial. Lazarus, the brother of Martha and Mary, has already been buried and the corruption is "almost perfected." The final stage is that of Ezekiel's vision of dry bones: disintegration is complete. However, in his meditational prayer, Matheson affirmed his belief in the soul and its immortality: "My soul, never lose thy hope *in* the soul."[271] It was a powerful and creative piece of writing to bring these passages together: the effect is cumulative and persuasive.

Matheson said, "the spirit cannot die, whether in the body or out of the body. Do not believe in the sleep of the soul; the soul never sleeps."[272] In the face of death, Matheson reminded his readers of the words of the angel at the tomb of Christ: "He is not here, He is risen." Matheson said, "Death applies not to the spirit, and the spirit is the man."[273] Matheson repeated the words of Jesus to Martha with conviction, authenticity and sincerity: "for he that liveth and believeth in me shall never die at all."[274] Each of us, he

---

266. Matheson, *Moments on the Mount*, 17.

267. Matheson, *Moments on the Mount*, 17.

268. Matheson, *Moments on the Mount*, 82.

269. Matheson, *Moments on the Mount*, 83.

270. Matheson, *Moments on the Mount*, 103.

271. Matheson, *Moments on the Mount*, 103.

272. Matheson, *Moments on the Mount*, 247.

273. Matheson, *Moments on the Mount*, 248.

274. Matheson, *Moments on the Mount*, 248.

said, is "the child of resurrection."[275] He asked, "What communion has the cemetery with life, what intercourse has the spirit with death?" Matheson answered: "If the departed should meet thee, it will not be in the graveyard; it will be in those moments when thou art furthest from the graveyard. Not from out the tombstone shall their voices come, but through the thoughts that make thee forget the tombstone; not from the symbols that are memories of death, but through the hopes that tell of immortality."[276] For Matheson, God is found in light and darkness. Darkness and death are not to be feared: "the shadow of death is itself to be the light that thou seekest."[277] It was from his vision of death (Job 12:22) that Job glimpsed "the clearest sight" of his immortality.[278] Darkness, death and life's shadows are not moments of God's absence, God's "hidings," but are "revelations of the face of God; they come to thee as messengers of light."[279] This is a very profound and probing spirituality, one which is not easily deflected when faced with suffering and death. One can hear the extent to which Matheson trusted in God and had a sense of being firmly held in the darkness. It may be that the darkness of suffering and death, the complete need to trust in that which one cannot see or comprehend, was strengthened by Matheson's blindness. He understood his own life of darkness, his own sense of isolation, as instructive of human suffering and the experience of death, of being cut off from the world of life and light: "How could trust exist if there were no darkness? It is the darkness that lights thee, it is from the shadows that thy spiritual nature is illuminated. From the sense of human emptiness thou reachest that prophetic hunger which is certain to be filled; thy life rises, phœnix-like, from the ashes of thy dying, and out of thy deepest darkness God says, 'Let there be light.'"[280] If the end of life points to immortality, so too does the beginning of life: "the helpless cry of infancy says more to the human soul" about God and immortality than does the sun, however powerful its energy and light.[281] All arguments in favor of immortality count as nothing compared to "immortality begun."[282] Each of us is on a personal ascension, a journey into God. Our life is an experience of Jacob's ladder, a binding together of heaven and earth; the summit is the Throne of God.

275. Matheson, *Moments on the Mount*, 248.

276. Matheson, *Moments on the Mount*, 249.

277. Matheson, *Moments on the Mount*, 166.

278. Matheson, *Moments on the Mount*, 166.

279. Matheson, *Moments on the Mount*, 167.

280. Matheson, *Moments on the Mount*, 167–68.

281. Matheson, *Moments on the Mount*, 250.

282. Matheson, *Moments on the Mount*, 250.

Matheson said: "The more life is in me, the nearer I am to the Throne; my revelation grows not by what I get from without but by what I gain from within."[283] For Matheson, to know God is life eternal: "this unspeakable glory may be mine—be mine now, here, in the midst of the present world: 'He that followeth me shall not walk in darkness, but shall have the light of life.'"[284] It is our thirst for Christ which reveals to us our immortality: our cry for God is the voice of God within us: "Thy conscious want is thine open door, thy sense of sin is thy height of Pisgah, and thy vision of the world's gathering shadow is made by the light of life eternal."[285]

For most of his public ministry, Matheson returned to his sense of immortality. It is a distinguishing feature of his spirituality. It was something he saw, something he experienced as now, and it was something he felt. It was closely linked to his understanding of sacrifice, which he believed to be the very nature of reality, present from the foundation of the world. In his posthumously published work, *Messages of Hope*, Matheson argued that immortality rests on God's justice. This is a different line of argument from that taken in his earlier work, which centered on the breath of God and the experienced encounter. Matheson cited the psalmist who said, "Remember how short my time is; wherefore hast Thou made all men in vain!" (Psalm 89:47). This is "the earliest Bible cry for immortality."[286] Matheson's argument was that without life beyond death this life would be a waste of humanity's potential. Humanity is different from the animals, from the bee, the lark and the ox, because they are satisfied by this world. Matheson said that it was our incompleteness which was the source of our hope.[287] He wrote:

> It is not my fear that cried to Thee; it is my sense of justice and my wish to vindicate *Thy* justice. If earth met all my needs, I *accept* the day of death . . . It is in defense of Thee that I seek a life beyond. I cannot bear to see the wasted gifts upon the shore . . . Forbid that I should think Thou hast made my life in vain.[288]

In his later publications, *Rests by the River* and *Messages of Hope*, Matheson moved to some extent to a more prosaic or measured style of writing. By this stage in his life, he was no longer preaching and had perhaps lost some of the spiritual energy, focus and discipline of communicating

283. Matheson, *Moments on the Mount*, 251.

284. Matheson, *Moments on the Mount*, 251.

285. Matheson, *Moments on the Mount*, 252.

286. Matheson, *Messages of Hope*, 97.

287. Matheson, *Messages of Hope*, 99.

288. Matheson, *Messages of Hope*, 99.

the spirituality of the Gospel to a congregation. He was also ageing and his health was impaired. In a meditation on immortality Matheson for the first time spoke of the resurrection beyond death. He made no reference to experiencing God now. While he may have been aware of his own decline and approaching death, it is noteworthy that he looked to the future for the resurrection rather than immortality in the present moment. There is a lifelessness and orthodoxy about *Man's Need for Immortality*[289] that we do not encounter in his earlier work. Published posthumously, the content may not have been what he would have chosen himself. There is also a notable increase in meditations which are pastoral in nature.

In his meditation on the death of Moses Matheson sought to provide comfort for those readers who had lost loved ones and for whom there had been no body over which to grieve, something which had made bereavement all the more distressing and painful. In the Book of Deuteronomy we read that Moses died and was buried by God; no one knew the place of his burial. Matheson wrote, "Ye that weep for the unfound dead, ye that lament the burial rites denied, know ye not that there are graves which are consecrated by God alone!"[290] In a poetic and sensitive passage, he said: "Is not that bleak hillside God's acre evermore! Is it not as holy to you as if you had brought sweet spices to the tomb! It has no chant but the winds, no book but the solemn silence, no bell but some wild bird's note, no wreath but the wreath of snow; yet there is no more sacred spot in all the diocese of God."[291] Besides the stories of Enoch, Elijah and Samuel, in the Old Testament Matheson said that to find intimation of immortality, of the resurrection life, we need look further than that Moses was buried by God. Matheson asked of God, "Why should He hold the dust of Moses dear if He had obliterated his *spirit!*"[292] In a rare example of drawing from the poets of his day, Matheson briefly cited some lines of poetry from Byron and Tennyson. His purpose was to contrast the shared insight of the poets with that of the psalmist. Byron and Tennyson both suggest that nature, the hills and rivers, were permanent in contrast to humanity, which was fleeting and transitory. Quoting from Psalm 102:26, 27, Matheson argued that it was the spirit, not nature, which was permanent. Re-writing Tennyson's original lines, Matheson said that it was the brooks which come and go, but humanity remained forever: "Brooks may

289. Matheson, *Messages of Hope*, 97.
290. Matheson, *Messages of Hope*, 51.
291. Matheson, *Messages of Hope*, 51.
292. Matheson, *Messages of Hope*, 52.

come and brooks may go, but soul goes on for ever."[293] Matheson said that "the permanence attributed to each natural form is an illusion cast by the shadow of the soul's own immortality."[294]

He said that the favorite word of the Fourth Evangelist is "life." John, he said, spoke from personal experience. Life for John meant eternal life: "He felt every morning as if he were born afresh into the world. He felt something within him like the springing up of living waters. Nay, he felt as if he had already passed the rubicon of death and had even now entered the world of the immortals."[295] For John, the name and thought of Jesus brought him alive: "the eye sparkled; the cheek mantled; the pulse quickened; the room became radiant . . . the hours received wings."[296] The intensity of Christ's Spirit which brought John alive was found in the soul of Matheson: like many mystics, he is animated and intoxicated by the name of Jesus. With John in mind, Matheson prayed, "My spirit, like his, may leap at the sense of a presence—Thy presence."[297] John told his readers not to love the world because it is fleeting: "Men speak of earthly vanity; but its vanity is its fleetingness. The defect of its pleasures is that they vanish. Free them from this vanity, O Lord! Redeem them from the taint of perishableness! Breathe into them Thine own eternal life! Perpetuate them with Thy presence, immortalize them with Thine indwelling!"[298] In his mediation on Psalm 139:9, 10, Matheson wrote of a connection of persons between this life and the next. Connection is possible because in heaven and on earth we are one with the Eternal. "What a comfort to be told that, with all our seeming separation, we are still inmates of the same house—the house of God!"[299] The absolute separation of two souls is "an impossibility."[300] Believing in the possibility of communication between souls in this world and the next, Matheson said, "I should say, 'Convey into the heart of my friend the impression that he is still remembered by me, still loved by me, still longed for by me.'"[301] For Matheson, the Divine is "the only presence that annihilates distance . . . Death itself cannot separate what is in the hollow of Thy hand . . . I commit my

293. Matheson, *Messages of Hope*, 66.

294. Matheson, *Messages of Hope*, 66. In his poem, *The Brook*, Tennyson has the brook sing, 'And out again I curve and flow To join the brimming river, For men may come and men may go, But I go on for ever.'

295. Matheson, *Messages of Hope*, 73.

296. Matheson, *Messages of Hope*, 74.

297. Matheson, *Messages of Hope*, 76.

298. Matheson, *Messages of Hope*, 139–140.

299. Matheson, *Messages of Hope*, 196–197.

300. Matheson, *Messages of Hope*, 197.

301. Matheson, *Messages of Hope*, 197.

message to *Thee* . . . Breathe it into the breast of my brother!"[302] In no sense does Matheson endorse the popular Victorian practice of séance, but he did offer pastoral comfort to those suffering the death of a loved one. His belief that messages may be conveyed to a loved one in heaven, dwelling in life beyond this life, cannot be thought mainstream in the Church of Scotland, then or now, but it was his sense of oneness, of union with the Divine and so with others that shaped his thinking. He does not offer an example from personal experience of such communication.

While not mainstream in the Church of Scotland, in his prayer *A Veil Thin as Gossamer*, Macleod wrote:

> Be Thou, triune God, in the midst of us as we give thanks for those who have gone from the sight of earthly eyes. They, in Thy nearer presence, still worship with us in the mystery of the one family in heaven and on earth.
>
> . . .
>
> If it be Thy holy will, tell them how we love them, and how we miss them, and how we long for the day when we shall meet with them again.
>
> . . .
>
> Strengthen [the bereaved] to go on in loving service of all Thy children. Thus shall they have communion with Thee and, in Thee, with their beloved. Thus shall they come to know, in themselves, that there is no death and that only a veil divides, thin as gossamer.[303]

In his meditation on the Ascension of Jesus, Matheson asked why it was that Jesus returned to Bethany before leaving this world. For Matheson, the name of Bethany was suggestive of the events that occurred there. He pointed to the family of Mary, Martha and Lazarus and recalled the fellowship which Jesus enjoyed in their home and the raising of Lazarus: "Bethany sums up His whole revelation—the brotherhood in life and the brotherhood in death . . . the Christ in human joy and the Christ in human sorrow."[304] Matheson understood that the Ascension took place at Bethany because in Bethany we have a story of eternal life, of immortality in this life.

302. Matheson, *Messages of Hope*, 198–199.

303. MacLeod, *The Whole Earth Shall Cry Glory*, 60.

304. Matheson, *Messages of Hope*, 230–31.

6

Self-Forgetfulness

IN HIS GIFFORD LECTURES,[1] Matheson's academic mentor, John Caird, departed from the atonement theology of Calvinism while, at the same time, like Matheson, stressed humanity's participation in the will of God, in order that humanity may be one with God. For Caird, it is not that Christ's perfect righteousness is "ascribed" to us but that "the essential principle of the life of Christ becomes by faith the essential principle of our own."[2] While the desire to maintain God's grace to us is seen as being "absolute and unmingled,"[3] that is, not conditional on human merit or dependent on human effort, nevertheless, without humanity's intense co-operation, faith becomes "nothing more than a passive reception of a boon that has been already won for us."[4] Such an external operation would leave humanity unchanged. Our salvation would be independent of moral activity and would "supersede any demand for moral goodness or holiness of life."[5] For Matheson, salvation of the soul is internal, a transformation of the inner life. Caird said that, by definition, atonement means union with God and such union can only be possible with our explicit co-operation and our desire to will the will of God. A spiritual blessing needs to be understood and grasped by our intelligence, conscience and the energy of the soul.[6] With strong overtones of mystical unity and oneness, Caird said that the atoning sacrifice of Christ required of us "Nothing less than the absolute surrender of the soul to God, the renunciation of self, and the identification of our whole life and being with that perfect ideal which is presented to us in the life and death of Christ. It is only

1. In 1890, John Caird was appointed Gifford Lecturer at Glasgow.
2. Caird, *Fundamental Ideas of Christianity*, vol. 2, 226.
3. Caird, *Fundamental Ideas of Christianity*, vol. 2, 227.
4. Caird, *Fundamental Ideas of Christianity*, vol. 2, 228.
5. Caird, *Fundamental Ideas of Christianity*, vol. 2, 228.
6. Caird, *Fundamental Ideas of Christianity*, vol. 2, 229.

another name for that which the great Christian Apostle so often represents as a dying to self, and living to Christ."[7]

Drawing on the inspiration of Paul and pointing us to mystical union, union to the point of losing oneself altogether, Caird said that: "The distinctive principle of the Christian life is an annulling of the life of self and of all selfish desires and impulses, and the blending of my will with the mind and will of Christ so absolute that, in a sense, my private, particular self may be said to have become extinct and my very being to be absorbed and lost in His."[8]

In this chapter I shall discuss the place of self-forgetfulness in a number of Matheson's publications: *Studies of the Portrait of Christ, My Aspirations, Moments on the Mount, Times of Retirement*, and *Messages of Hope*. Matheson understood holiness to mean a self-sacrificial spirit, a spirit of self-forgetfulness. I shall give a brief historical account of kenotic theology in the nineteenth century, discuss Matheson's similarity to Caird, and I shall conclude this chapter with a discussion of the extent to which Matheson found God in sacrifice and suffering.

Matheson had a true regard for Judaism though, as a Hegelian, he understood that the Jewish religion could only ever be a preparation for Christianity. His pleasure, he said, would not be complete until Christ was shared with the Jews.[9] Matheson looked to Abraham as a man of holiness, as being greater than holy law.[10] In our inner journey, holiness is the learned ability to die to self; the Christian life means "a dying in Him."[11] The keynote in the life of Jesus and in the follower is "self-forgetfulness."[12] Humanity has greater needs than mere bread: humanity is to love the Father for the Father's own sake. The Father is to be "reverenced for His holiness."[13] Sacrifice must be "unconscious of itself, must deny its own existence."[14] "Holiness, to be holiness, must be spontaneous."[15] The model for the Christian is no different from that of Jesus: Christ's first act is one of "self-emptying. He must forget everything but the love of God and

---

7. Caird, *Fundamental Ideas of Christianity*, vol. 2, 230.

8. Caird, *Fundamental Ideas of Christianity*, vol. 2, 230.

9. Matheson, *The Portrait of Christ*, vol. 1, 26.

10. Matheson, *The Portrait of Christ*, vol. 1, 30–31.

11. Matheson, *The Portrait of Christ*, vol. 1, 37.

12. Matheson, *The Portrait of Christ*, vol. 1, 50.

13. Matheson, *The Portrait of Christ*, vol. 1, 43.

14. Matheson, *The Portrait of Christ*, vol. 1, 47.

15. Matheson, *The Portrait of Christ*, vol. 1, 48.

man."[16] The desire "to satisfy the holiness of the Father . . . was the boldest idea that ever entered into the heart of man."[17] Holiness was the test John the Baptist set himself in finding the Messiah.[18] Matheson wrote: "The testimony of the Spirit is the 'standard of Messianic holiness.' Test his claims by goodness. Leave in abeyance any external test—whether miracle or pedigree. Consider only the extent, the intensity, the abidingness of his virtue."[19] In prayer, Matheson desired that, in the gallery of the heart,[20] he would be able to follow Christ, that Christ would reveal to him "the power of self-forgetfulness" and that Christ would teach him that "the burial of self is the road to resurrection."[21] In similar terms to Caird,[22] Matheson cited the story of Nicodemus, in which he said that to be born of the Spirit meant to do the Father's will because it was one's own.[23] The miracles of Jesus, apart from that at Cana in Galilee, were acts of selflessness. The miracles of sympathy were "spontaneous outpourings of His heart coming forth because He cannot help it; this is the feature about them with which the Father is well pleased."[24]

During the years of his spiritual recovery, Matheson said that the work of Thomas à Kempis, *The Imitation of Christ*, stood next to the Bible as a spiritual and mystical work. In à Kempis, in his chapter titled *On the Royal Road of the Holy Cross*, he wrote:

> In the Cross is salvation; in the Cross is life; in the Cross is protection against our enemies; in the Cross is infusion of heavenly sweetness; in the Cross is strength of mind; in the Cross is joy of spirit; in the Cross is excellence of virtue; in the Cross is perfection of holiness . . . There is no other way to life and to true inner peace, than the way of the Cross, and of daily self-denial.[25]

For Matheson, as for à Kempis, the Cross is the supreme symbol of self-denial, self-forgetfulness.

For Matheson, the Sermon on the Mount was about self-forgetfulness. Through countless variations, the central theme is in "one

---

16. Matheson, *The Portrait of Christ*, vol. 1, 49.

17. Matheson, *The Portrait of Christ*, vol. 1, 177.

18. Matheson, *The Portrait of Christ*, vol. 1, 55.

19. Matheson, *The Portrait of Christ*, vol. 1, 56.

20. Matheson, *The Portrait of Christ*, vol. 1, 74.

21. Matheson, *The Portrait of Christ*, vol. 1, 75.

22. Caird, *University Sermons*, 70.

23. Matheson, *The Portrait of Christ*, vol. 1, 85.

24. Matheson, *The Portrait of Christ*, vol. 1, 98.

25. À Kempis, *The Imitation of Christ*, 85.

word—self-forgetfulness."[26] It is through the death of the ego that the human soul is able to spiritually grow and realize itself in this life:

> The Kingdom of heaven, the inheritance of the earth, the satisfaction of the spirit, the vision of God, the reputation of being called the children of God, the privilege of illuminating the world—these are among the summits at which the human soul is permitted to aim. But how is it to gain them? In the same way as, according to Paul, the Son of Man reaches His own glory—by the act of self-burial.[27]

Matheson distinguished self-forgetfulness from self-restraint. Holiness is the pursuit of the "glory of another, of a higher object: You will only forget your self when you 'glorify your Father.'"[28] The old religious system, that of the Law, was restraint rather than forgetfulness: it was external, not inner transformation. The Law led to self-imprisonment while Jesus came to set the prisoner free.[29] Christ points to the "unselfishness of love."[30] Our highest motive in prayer is "submission to self-sacrifice."[31] For Matheson, Jesus never tired of "emphasizing the inwardness of the kingdom."[32] Those who died to self, those who were humanitarian by their action, are the greatest in the kingdom.[33] Christ is enthroned by virtue of His selfless, self-forgetful humanity, not by any notion of "supernaturalness."[34]

In the mystical tradition emphasis is placed on overcoming the ego, our selfishness, pride and small self. "What one does for the glory of the Father is never looked upon as a source of fame."[35] Matheson believed that the pride of the Greek was culture and the pride of the Jew was religion. In both cases, Jesus pointed to "the moral of self-forgetfulness, 'Except a corn of wheat fall into the ground and die, it abideth alone.'"[36] We overcome our selfishness in the presence of Jesus and thereby allowing the love of Jesus to fill us with His selflessness. In speaking to himself and the reader, Matheson prayed:

---

26. Matheson, *The Portrait of Christ*, vol. 1, 201.

27. Matheson, *The Portrait of Christ*, vol. 1, 202.

28. Matheson, *The Portrait of Christ*, vol. 1, 203.

29. Matheson, *The Portrait of Christ*, vol. 1, 204.

30. Matheson, *The Portrait of Christ*, vol. 1, 205.

31. Matheson, *The Portrait of Christ*, vol. 1, 206.

32. Matheson, *The Portrait of Christ*, vol. 1, 314.

33. Matheson, *The Portrait of Christ*, vol. 1, 316.

34. Matheson, *The Portrait of Christ*, vol. 1, 316.

35. Matheson, *The Portrait of Christ*, vol. 2, 193.

36. Matheson, *The Portrait of Christ*, vol. 2, 199.

> Come, then, and sit first at the feet of Jesus! Come, fill thy heart beforehand with thoughts of beauty! Come, and empty thy spirit of its pride! Come, and disburden thy mind of its care!
>
> . . .
>
> Come, above all, and be filled with a larger love—the love for humanity itself, the hope for thy brother-man![37]

Matheson wrote of the love of Jesus and of allowing ourselves to sit at the feet of Jesus. We find this same mystical intimacy in à Kempis:

> They who love Jesus for His own sake, and not for the sake of comfort for themselves, bless Him in every trial and anguish of heart, no less than in the greatest joy. And were He never willing to bestow comfort on them, they would still always praise Him and give Him thanks.
>
> Oh, how powerful is the pure love of Jesus, free from all self-interest and self-love![38]

For Matheson, it is not selfishness which desires immortality but unselfishness. It is because "I want eternally to love that which is lovely—eternally to love Thee."[39] Matheson's definition of a saint, of a saint's immortality is that the saint knows that love, peace, friendship and sacrifice are everlasting: "This is the saint's rest!"[40] The failing in Judas was a failing of the "power of the internal," the diligence of the heart.[41] He was overpowered by jealousy, driven by a concern for himself, not love of another. At the close of the Last Supper, in meditation, Matheson prayed, "Let me walk with Thee, O Lord, on the way from that Upper Room; let me enter into Thine unselfish spirit."[42] On the cross, "the tribute dearest to the Father . . . was not the prostration of a body but the surrender of a will."[43] The Risen Christ, whom the disciples encounter, recognize "the Broken Body—the Body broken for them;" in that, it is Christ's sacrificial love which they remember.[44]

37. Matheson, *The Portrait of Christ*, vol. 2, 131.
38. à Kempis, *The Imitation of Christ*, 83.
39. Matheson, *The Portrait of Christ*, vol. 2, 144.
40. Matheson, *The Portrait of Christ*, vol. 2, 145.
41. Matheson, *The Portrait of Christ*, vol. 2, 217.
42. Matheson, *The Portrait of Christ*, vol. 2, 232.
43. Matheson, *The Portrait of Christ*, vol. 2, 321.
44. Matheson, *The Portrait of Christ*, vol. 2, 353.

Kenosis: Historical Context

In his Baird Lectures and *Studies of the Portrait of Christ* Matheson employed kenotic theology. Kenotic theology has been defined as the "attempt within the bounds of Chalcedonian orthodoxy to construe the incarnate person of Christ in a way that would account for his full humanity and complete person . . ." [45] Kenosis is derived from the Greek verb *kenoein* meaning to empty. Kenotic theology is "inspired by Philippians 2:6–11, which speaks of Christ as one who 'being in very nature God' still 'emptied himself' or 'made himself nothing.'"[46] Other prominent passages of Scripture used in kenotic theology include *"For you know the generous act of our Lord Jesus Christ, that though he was rich, yet for your sakes he became poor, so that by his poverty you might become rich"* (2 Corinthians 8:9); *"And Jesus increased in wisdom and in years, and in divine and human favor"* (Luke 2:52); and,

> In the days of his flesh, Jesus offered up prayers and supplications, with loud cries and tears, to the one who was able to save him from death, and he was heard because of his reverent submission. Although he was a Son, he learned obedience through what he suffered; and having been made perfect, he became the source of eternal salvation for all who obey him . . . (Hebrews 5:7–9)

Evans states that "these particular passages highlight a characteristic that is pervasively present in the entire narrative of Jesus' life and death."[47]

Evans says that the self-emptying of God "does not stop with Christ's becoming human but goes to the extreme of 'taking the very nature of a servant' and becoming 'obedient to death, even death on a cross.'"[48] The nineteenth century saw something of a "stampede"[49] of kenotic models of the Incarnation. In part, the stampede was an attempt to "eliminate what were considered the debilitating paradoxes of the two-nature model."[50] By the beginning of the twentieth century, it was felt that the kenotic venture had run aground because it could not achieve what it set out to do while maintaining the Chalcedonian orthodoxy.[51] However, at its height, kenotic theology could be found in many quarters. One scholar goes so far as to say that: "The kenotic endeavor was a movement of such mass and distinction

---

45. Thompson, "Nineteenth Century Kenotic Christology," 74.

46. Evans, *Exploring Kenotic Christology,* 195.

47. Evans, *Exploring Kenotic Christology,* 196.

48. Evans, *Exploring Kenotic Christology,* 196.

49. Thompson, "Nineteenth Century Kenotic Christology," 76.

50. Thompson, "Nineteenth Century Kenotic Christology," 110.

51. Thompson, "Nineteenth Century Kenotic Christology," 111.

as to constitute 'the fourth great attempt at theological explanation of the being of Christ—after the biblical, conciliar, and scholastic endeavor."[52] Hegel's system is characterized as "an all-inclusive kenotic theology, since he made the self-divesting of the Unitarian God and the finitization of the absolute Spirit central in his philosophy."[53]

In the nineteenth century significant names in kenotic theology include Gottfried Thomasius (1802–1875), J. H. August Ebrard (1818–1888), Wolfgang Friedrich Gess (1819–1891), and Charles Gore (1853–1932). In the Scottish context, two prominent names are the theologian William Milligan (1821–1893) and George Matheson. Thomasius states that "*assumtio* of human essence does not by itself completely express the concept of Incarnation, but that the latter must be conceived at the same time as divesting of the divine."[54] By self-determination, Christ among us was not omnipotent, omnipresent or omniscient.[55] Ebrard said that the "omni-attributes" were only available to Christ in "an applied, space-time form."[56] Gess, described as "the most consistent of the nineteenth century kenoticists," wrote:

> In order to effect the Incarnation the Logos relinquishes all divine attributes, power, prerogatives, and glory. The pre-existent Word becomes flesh, literally. Having been transferred into a human soul, the Son gains consciousness of his divine identity and mission only in the gradual course of human development, a life of faith lived in complete dependence on God the Father in the power and energies of the Spirit, a life which also included the possibility of a fall into sin.[57]

Critics, such as Francis J. Hall, asked, "Was He God or not?" Hall argued that if Christ failed to possess any of the Divine attributes at any point, then Christ was not God.[58] In a similar vein, years later, William Temple asked, "What was happening to the rest of the universe during the period of our Lord's earthly life?"[59] Similarly, the "paradox of the stone" poses much the same question: can God create a stone which God could not then move? Defending the Chalcedonian formula, Hall stated his case against kenoticism clearly: "The doctrine of the Trinity is violated by kenoticism.

52. Thompson, "Nineteenth Century Kenotic Christology," 76.

53. Thompson, "Nineteenth Century Kenotic Christology," 77.

54. Thompson, "Nineteenth Century Kenotic Christology," 80.

55. Thompson, "Nineteenth Century Kenotic Christology," 84.

56. Thompson, "Nineteenth Century Kenotic Christology," 86.

57. Thompson, "Nineteenth Century Kenotic Christology," 87.

58. Thompson, "Nineteenth Century Kenotic Christology," 96.

59. Thompson, "Nineteenth Century Kenotic Christology," 97.

Whatever the Trinity is It is eternally. The three persons are co-eternal and co-equal. But if the Son of God was at any time lacking in Divine attributes He was not then co-equal with the Father and the Holy Spirit.[60] Writing in the twenty-first century, Evans argues that it is the doctrine of the Trinity which makes possible the giving up of divine power, at least by one of the Persons of the Trinity. Evans argues that if God were a unity, "the divine being could not possibly limit himself, for if he did, he would be giving up control of the universe."[61] However, as a Trinity, the Son can give up divine power while the Father and the Holy Spirit continue to "providentially guide creation."[62]

Towards the end of the nineteenth century, Gore was becoming the dominant figure in Anglican theology.[63] In stark contrast to Hall, Gore wrote of Christ: "He never exhibits the omniscience of bare Godhead in the realm of natural knowledge; such as would be required to anticipate the results of modern science and criticism . . . Indeed, God declares His almighty power most chiefly in His condescension, whereby He 'beggared Himself' of Divine prerogatives to put Himself in our place."[64] Gore said that God beggared Himself; in other words, the Self-emptying God does more than refrain from using divine power. Published 1889 midway between Matheson's Baird Lectures and his *Studies of the Portrait of Christ, Lux Mundi: A Series of Studies in the Religion of the Incarnation* was written by students of T H Green, many of whom were theologians lecturing at Oxford University. The writers argued that sacrifice was as central to incarnation as it was to atonement. Gore wrote: "The incarnation is the supreme act of self-sacrificing sympathy, by which one whose nature is divine was enabled to enter into human experience. He emptied himself of divine prerogative in so far as he was involved in really becoming a man, and growing, feeling and suffering as a man."[65] Kenotic theology means that, "In facing the frustrations and even terrors of human experience, Christ must depend entirely on the Father and the comfort of the Spirit."[66] An early criticism of *Lux Mundi* came in the April 1890 edition of *Church Quarterly Review*. Darwell Stone said that the writers of *Lux Mundi* had eroded the distinction between revelation and reason and

---

60. Thompson, "Nineteenth Century Kenotic Christology," 98.

61. Evans, *Exploring Kenotic Christology,* 213–214.

62. Evans, *Exploring Kenotic Christology,* 214.

63. Ramsay, *From Gore to Temple,* vii.

64. Ramsay, *From Gore to Temple,* 6.

65. Bradley, *The Power of Sacrifice,* 180.

66. Evans, *Exploring Kenotic Christology,* 203.

so "blurring the line between the distinctive inspiration of Scripture and the phenomenon of genius in the human race."[67]

Gore's contention was that humanity's sin was real: it was within our nature; it was not imputed. Therefore, humanity's recovery from sin had to be inward, an "inward infusion" of Christ's life, and not "an external imputation of His merits."[68] Gore stressed that Christ is in us: "We are grafted into Him, as branches in the vine. His life runs in the veins of our human spirits. He is growing in us, and we shall (if we abide in Him) one day have grown up into the fullness of his stature."[69] Gore said that Christ is "formed within" us.[70] Interpreting Philippians 2:5, Gore said that the eternal Son of God "laid aside" the attributes of divinity which would have prevented him "living a truly human life—such as omniscience."[71] Gore believed that he was returning to the Christology of the first six centuries. This is in contrast to Friedrich Loofs who stated that theologians of the early church never contemplated "the actual supersession of the divine form of existence by the human—a real 'becoming-man', that is, a trans-formation on the part of the Logos."[72] Similarly, Giorgiov states that the kenosis of the Patristic period was a "*krypto-kenosis,* a mere concealment or veiling of Christ's divine activities."[73]

Gore stressed the humanity of Jesus. More than Christ's teaching about God or the kingdom of God, it was "The Man" which left the greatest impression on His followers: "the dominant influence on the disciples" was "of God resident in Him."[74] Gore wrote: "The self-sacrifice of the Incarnation appears to have lain in great measure, so far as human words can express it, in His refraining from the divine mode of consciousness within the sphere of His human life, that He might really enter into human experience."[75] In becoming human, God submitted God's Self to the condition of human life and, Gore argued, in the past too much emphasis had been put on God behind the "veil of humanity" rather than the fact that "God was really made man."[76] While Temple was later to say that Gore implied "a change in the eternal

---

67. Ramsay, *From Gore to Temple,* 8.

68. Waddel, *Charles Gore: Radical Anglican,* 41.

69. Waddel, *Charles Gore: Radical Anglican,* 41.

70. Waddel, *Charles Gore: Radical Anglican,* 42.

71. Waddel, *Charles Gore: Radical Anglican,* 43.

72. Loofs, "Kenosis," 249.

73. Giorgiov, "Christology of Charles Gore," 47-66.

74. Waddell, *Charles Gore: Radical Anglican,* 43.

75. Waddell, *Charles Gore: Radical Anglican,* 49.

76. Waddell, *Charles Gore: Radical Anglican,* 55.

Word," Gore moved the argument away from the mechanics of metaphysics towards to nature of God's Self, God's true character:

> In seeking to realize the meaning of the Incarnation, we are bound to recognize that within that sphere what we behold is not God in the whole of His attributes merely veiling Himself in humanity, but God having abandoned what was inconsistent with a really human experience, in order that by such self emptying His real self, which is love, might be truly manifested . . .[77]

Earlier in the century, the Danish philosopher Søren Kierkegaard had said that:

> God can enter more deeply into the limited world of the one he wishes to have a relationship with, because God has what he might call a superior ability to limit himself: "For this is the boundlessness of love, that in earnestness and truth and not in jest it wills to be the equal of the beloved. . ."[78]

Kierkegaard had argued that, "If God limits himself, this is not a loss of omnipotence, but an exercise of it."[79]

Throughout the nineteenth century, theologians and clerics wrestled with the concept of sacrifice. Kenoticists came to see sacrifice as "a universal principle emanating from God and animating the whole of his creation."[80] With the spread of evolutionary theory, it came to be seen that "all life on earth depended on struggle, surrender and self-limitation."[81] Nineteenth century kenotic theology was also responding to its inheritance from the previous century of divine immutability: the sovereign, omnipotent watchmaker was no longer a viable model. Added to that, there was growing unease concerning "the concept of propitiation on both moral and ethical grounds."[82] Horace Bushnell (1802–1876) wrote his book, *God in Christ* (1850): "Out of a determination to be rid of propitiary and substitutionary notions of atonement and to show that suffering does not appease God but rather it expresses God—displays in open history the unconquerable love of God's heart."[83]

---

77. Waddell, *Charles Gore: Radical Anglican,* 56.

78. Evans, *Exploring Kenotic Christology,* 205.

79. Evans, *Exploring Kenotic Christology,* 208.

80. Bradley, *The Power of Sacrifice,* 161.

81. Bradley, *The Power of Sacrifice,* 162.

82. Bradley, *The Power of Sacrifice,* 162.

83. Bradley, *The Power of Sacrifice,* 163.

In his book, *The Vicarious Sacrifice* (1866), Bushnell stated, "There is a cross in God before the wood is seen upon Calvary."[84] For Bushnell, sacrifice was "the means that God has provided by which his creatures, self-centered and sin-laden as they are, can come back to him."[85] The Brighton preacher and Anglican cleric, F W Robertson (1810–1853), to whom Matheson was often compared, described sacrifice, conscious and unconscious, as "the grand law of the universe."[86] Robertson said: "Christ came into collision with the world's evil . . . He approached the whirling wheel and was torn in pieces. He laid His hand upon the cockatrice's den, and its fangs pierced him. It is the law which governs the conflict with evil. It can only be crushed by suffering from it."[87] Robertson said that "the whole of the life of God is sacrifice of self . . . Creation itself is sacrifice—the self-impartation of the divine Being."[88] In the same manner in which Gore had spoken of Christ in us, formed in us, so Robertson said that the Christian's life is sacrifice: it occurs "spiritually in the life of all in whom the Crucified lives. The sacrifice of Christ is done over again in every life which is lived, not to self but to God."[89] For Robertson, Christ's sacrifice, the manifesting of that sacrifice, is repeated afresh in the life of every Christian. In writing of Paul, T H Green said that the apostle "developed the notion of a perpetual renewal of the death and resurrection of Christ taking place within the individual soul."[90] For Green, God is to be found in the "higher self" which is reached through "self-sacrifice and self-denial."[91] In Scotland, the parish minister and professor of Biblical Criticism William Milligan echoed the concept of the inner Christ when he said, "One with Him, we die with Him, rise in Him. We are in Him from the beginning to the end of our spiritual experience."[92]

Alongside Robertson, F D Maurice (1805–1872) described sacrifice as "the doctrine of the Bible, the doctrine of the Gospel"[93] while claiming that "the idea of sacrifice as in any sense propitiatory, or indeed vicarious . . . [is] profoundly unbiblical."[94] Maurice said that true sacrifice is: "The sacrifice

84. Bradley, *The Power of Sacrifice*, 163.
85. Bradley, *The Power of Sacrifice*, 164.
86. Bradley, *The Power of Sacrifice*, 166.
87. Bradley, *The Power of Sacrifice*, 167.
88. Bradley, *The Power of Sacrifice*, 168.
89. Bradley, *The Power of Sacrifice*, 169.
90. Bradley, *The Power of Sacrifice*, 177.
91. Bradley, *The Power of Sacrifice*, 178.
92. Bradley, *The Power of Sacrifice*, 185.
93. Bradley, *The Power of Sacrifice*, 169.
94. Bradley, *The Power of Sacrifice*, 170.

which manifests the mind of God, which proceeds from God, which accomplishes the purposes of God in the redemption and reconciliation of His creatures, which enables those creatures to become like their Father in Heaven by offering up themselves."[95] Maurice spoke of the inner life and the need for the Christian to discover one's own poverty. Sacrifice does not so much mean the giving up of things, but rather the giving up of self.[96] He said, "God is the Author of every true sacrifice; that it originates in His will, and therefore fulfills His will."[97] This is similar to Caird when he wrote of the mind and will of God becoming our own as our own.[98] Like Matheson and P. T. Forsyth, Maurice employed the imagery of the Lamb taken from the Book of Revelation:

> The Will that rules the universe, the Will that has triumphed and does triumph, is all expressed and gathered up in the Lamb that was slain . . . The principle of sacrifice has been ascertained once and for ever to be the principle, the divine principle; that in which God can alone fully manifest His eternal Being. His inmost character, the order which He had appointed all creatures, voluntary and involuntary, to obey.[99]

The Aberdeen-born Congregational minister P T Forsyth said that "Christ's sacrifice began before He came into the world, as His Cross was that of a lamb slain before the world's foundation. There was a Calvary above which was the mother of it all."[100] For Forsyth, Christ "limits Himself in the freedom of holiness for the purposes of His own end of infinite love."[101] Like Gore, Forsyth places the character of God, God's love, above God's attributes. In 1876, in a sermon described by Michael Ramsay as "one of the greatest of all time," one of the contributors to *Lux Mundi*, Henry Scott Holland (1847–1918) described the formation of the earth, the cooling of its crust from "the primeval fireball" as indicative of the "law of surrender, of self-sacrifice" hidden and implicit within nature itself.[102] Like Matheson, Holland spoke of holiness and by it he meant nothing less than the union of God's creatures with God.[103] For Holland, the root of all

95. Maurice, *Doctrine of Sacrifice*, xlvi.

96. Bradley, *The Power of Sacrifice*, 171.

97. Bradley, *The Power of Sacrifice*, 171.

98. Caird, "Union with God," 32.

99. Bradley, *The Power of Sacrifice*, 172.

100. Bradley, *The Power of Sacrifice*, 184.

101. Bradley, *The Power of Sacrifice*, 184.

102. Bradley, *The Power of Sacrifice*, 181.

103. Bradley, *The Power of Sacrifice*, 182.

religion, not simply that of Christianity, lies in the discovery that we are not our own; we belong to God.[104]

Matheson and Kenotic Theology

Matheson's theology stands within nineteenth century kenotic theology. The sentiments of Gore, Robertson, Milligan and the others are found throughout Matheson's work. The basic question in kenotic theology is the extent to which the humanity of Jesus forced Him to empty Himself of divine powers. Traditionally understood, the self-emptying of deity was true in the sense that, while remaining unimpaired, the divine accepted union with a physically limited humanity. In the nineteenth century in psychology consciousness was understood as central to humanity. As omniscient and human, did Jesus have two centers of consciousness? Thomasius said that Christ had a sleeplike unconsciousness of the divine nature during his life on earth. Gore maintained that Christ was both God and human but that the relation of the two natures was "different at different epochs. Before the resurrection He, very God, acts under conditions of manhood; since His glorification, He, very man, is living under conditions of Godhead."[105] Gore makes the point that Paul in using these words (self-emptying, making himself poor), is "not thinking of any particular aspect of the human life of Jesus, such as the limitation of His knowledge; but he regards the Incarnation in itself as having involved in some sense the abandonment of riches which belong to the previous divine state of the Son."[106] P T Forsyth argued that God can limit God's Self: "Among the powers of the Omnipotent must be the power to limit Himself."[107] Forsyth distinguished between "emptied Himself" and "humbled Himself;" the former was before Christ was born and the latter He lived during His earthly life.[108] H. R. Mackintosh was later to suggest that rather than the abandonment of attributes, we can conceive the Son as possessing concentrated potency rather than actuality; in other words, Christ only used His divine attributes which were necessary for His vocation. Mackintosh said that Christ had a filial consciousness, which was a perfect relationship with the Father.[109] The main appeal for Matheson of kenotic theology was religious and spiritual rather

104. Bradley, *The Power of Sacrifice*, 183.
105. Gore, *The Incarnation*, 177.
106. Gore, *The Reconstruction of Belief*, 521.
107. Forsyth, *God the Holy Father*, 33.
108. Forsyth, *God the Holy Father*, 38.
109. Mackintosh, *The Person of Christ*, 28.

than metaphysical: the concept of sacrifice, self-denial, was a moral act, an act of love, the truest reflection of the Divine nature. Matheson understood kenosis as moral, though he did not involve himself in the minutiae of the theological discussion of the period.

In his meditation on the Last Supper, Matheson understood the words of Jesus to be spoken in the present tense. On the night before He died as throughout His life, Jesus had been "yielding up flesh and blood by a sacrifice of the will."[110] Christ's sacrifice at the table was in the present moment; Jesus was not waiting for death to begin His work. At the Supper Jesus looked forward to a fuller communion in His Father's Kingdom in which He and the disciples would enjoy a "permanent communion."[111] In similar language, Milligan spoke of the sacrificial nature of Communion and its importance as the greatest point of union within the life of the Church. He said that 'the communion table, "more than any other spot" is "the meeting-place of heaven and earth": "In the sacrament of the Supper the Church realizes to a greater extent than in any other of her ordinances both her own deepest, that is her sacrificial life in her glorified Lord, and His peculiar presence with her as her nourishment and strength and joy."[112] For Matheson, sacrifice for it to be sacrifice must be "unconscious of itself, must deny its own existence."[113] To be a follower of Jesus means to be Christ-like: Christ's first act is one of "self-emptying. [The follower] must forget everything but the love of God and man."[114] In his pursuit of personal union with God, Matheson craved intimacy to the point of self-annihilation. He prayed, "Extinguish my torch in Thy glory!" In healing the sick, Matheson said that Jesus sought union with the one who was sick. He said, "It was one step of humiliation to assume the likeness of Man; but it was another and a deeper step to assume the likeness of men."[115] Matheson sought complete self-forgetfulness in his relationship with God and humanity. That same desire is found in à Kempis: "Desire to die on the Cross with Him. For if you die with Him, you will also live with Him."[116]

At the heart of the mystical life is union with the Divine. Central to our union with God is our need to let go of self and to model the self-lessness of Jesus. At the end of his fifth lecture of the Baird lectureship,

---

110. Matheson, *The Portrait of Christ*, vol. 2, 227.

111. Matheson, *The Portrait of Christ*, vol. 2, 228.

112. Bradley, *The Power of Sacrifice*, 186.

113. Matheson, *The Portrait of Christ*, vol. 1, 47.

114. Matheson, *The Portrait of Christ*, vol. 1, 49.

115. Matheson, *The Portrait of Christ*, vol. 1, 170.

116. À Kempis, *The Imitation of Christ*, 85.

Matheson again stressed that, in Christ, we see "the divine joy of sacrifice, the glory of self-forgetfulness [and] the certainty of finding the life which for another we have consented to lose."[117] The surrender of the individual will is "the height of sorrow": "the natural heart" is the life of "blessedness" for the follower of Jesus; "the crucifixion of self magnifies the personal life and brings joy to the individual heart."[118] The essence of Christianity is the "belief in the power of the Cross—the belief in the survival of that which is the opposite of selfishness and the crucifer of the selfish man."[119] À Kempis said, "In the Cross is salvation . . . There is no salvation of soul, nor hope of eternal life, save in the Cross."[120] For Matheson, Jesus' life was "a ladder of descent."[121] In prayer, Matheson said, "Inspire me with Thy power to descend the ladder of human experience. Let me come after Thee in the downward steps of sacrifice."[122] It is our acquiescence, not resignation, to the divine will, "Thy will be done," that marks our union with God and the climax of human existence. Creation, the "grand plan of evolution," is that we "grow upwards towards a type of sacrifice, towards a joy which is deeper than the personal joy, and whose very life is purchased by the crucifixion of personal interest."[123]

Sacrifice lies at the center of Mathesonian theology: sacrifice is the manifestation of love. In the late twentieth century, V. H. Vanstone argued that the supreme illustration of love's self-giving or self-emptying is the surrender in God of God's fullness in order to create in God's Self, "the emptiness of need."[124] Vanstone affirmed that the nature of God is love and that it is the character of love to sacrifice itself for the other. However, along with others, Vanstone believed that God had to create that need within God's Self as an act of will. Fiddes argues that God chooses to be a God of love: "in choosing to be a God with the needs of love, God willingly renounces self-sufficiency."[125] In his Gifford Lectures, Caird argued that God's love and sacrificial self-emptying was more than an act of will; it was the very nature of God: "There must be in the very being and life of God that which calls for the existence of a finite world, and in the finite world that which has its

117. Matheson, *Elements of Revealed Theology*, 164.

118. Matheson, *Elements of Revealed Theology*, 164.

119. Matheson, *The Old Faith Live*, 391.

120. À Kempis, The Imitation of Christ, 85.

121. Matheson, *The Portrait of Christ*, vol. 1, 71.

122. Matheson, *The Portrait of Christ*, vol. 1, 74–75.

123. Matheson, *Elements of Revealed Theology*, 165.

124. Evans, *Exploring Kenotic Christology*, 217.

125. Fiddes, "Creation out of Love," 182.

explanation and origin, not in the mere will and pleasure, but in the inner being and life of God."[126] Caird argued that the life of the finite is essential to God's being and life. There would be something lacking in the completeness of the Divine Being if the finite did not exist and "with reverence be it said, God would not be God without it."[127] Caird argued that to think of God as "an abstract, self-identical, self-sufficing Infinite" would be to make God less than human: Divine self-sufficiency would deprive God of "the highest element of the life and blessedness of a spiritual nature, the element of love."[128] For Caird, sacrificial love is the primary way to conceive of God:

> We have not yet surrounded the depths of what we express by the word until we think of a love which no ingratitude can exhaust, no unworthiness can alienate, no meanness of infamy and degradation render hopeless of its object, or place it beyond the range of reconciliation and forgiveness; nay, more than that, till we can think of a love which, undeterred by the unworthiness of its object, will bear any hardship with and for it, and for which there is no measure of pain and sorrow and sacrifice to which it will not submit for the restoration of that object to goodness and happiness.[129]

Similarly, for Matheson, sacrifice epitomizes the very essence of God: sacrifice is that which is most true about God. Bradley writes of Matheson:

> He takes the sacrificial nature of the Son as being revelatory of the nature of the Father . . . in seeing God not simply as the author of life through sacrifice but as the personification of the sacrificial spirit. He wrestles with the notion in one of his prayers: "If Thou art love, then, Thy best gift must be sacrifice; in that light let me search Thy world. It has pains wrapped up in every pleasure, and who can explain them? Only Thyself—the Spirit of sacrificial love."[130]

Drawing together revealed theology with natural theology, Matheson wrote: "That which we call the revealed is seen to exist before the natural, and that which we call the natural is seen to exist only as the evolution of the revealed, for at those foundations of the world which we term the power of nature, there is already working that thought which is to close the drama—the

126. Caird, *Fundamental Ideas of Christianity*, vol. 1, 129.

127. Caird, *Fundamental Ideas of Christianity*, vol. 1, 130.

128. Caird, *Fundamental Ideas of Christianity*, vol. 1, 160.

129. Caird, *Fundamental Ideas of Christianity*, vol. 1, 161–62.

130. Bradley, *The Power of Sacrifice*, 187.

Lamb that is slain."[131] Matheson's use of Revelation 13:8 signifies "the power of sacrifice as the central animating principle in the life of the universe."[132] Elsewhere we read: "All things shine by passing into the life of others: the seed into the flower, the sun into nature, the sea into the reflections of light. Each stage of human life expands by sacrifice of the self-will."[133] Of Christianity, Matheson was able to conclude that human suffering does not point to a distant God but rather to "the immanent presence of the divine."[134] Matheson wrote with an intensity which revealed his closeness to Christ. We are never left feeling that sacrifice was a subject in which he was interested but distant and detached. On the contrary, it was in large measure kenotic theology which gave him a sense of Christ within him. He had suffered so much, lost so much: a theology of sacrifice made sense to him, not only intellectually about the nature of the universe, but within his own experience and life. For Matheson, to have discovered God present in suffering and sacrifice and suffering foundational to the character and nature of God, was a sign of God's presence and love. This must have comforted him deeply. Kenotic theology brought the Divine into his soul, into the darkness of his world. It filled his darkness with light.

Suffering and Sacrifice

Matheson understood holiness to be the spirit of self-forgetfulness. Suffering and sacrifice were more than moments in which God could be encountered. For Matheson, in a mystical sense, suffering and sacrifice were the means of encountering the Eternal. He understood sacrifice to be the very essence of the nature of the love of God. In his sacred song titled "The Divine Plan of Creation," based on the verse, "The Lamb slain from the foundation of the world" (Revelation 13:8), Matheson wrote:

> Thou hast, O Lord, a wondrous plan
>> To build a tower to reach the skies;
> Its base is earth, its progress man,
>> Its summit sacrifice.

131. Matheson, *Elements of Revealed Theology*, 166.
132. Bradley, *The Power of Sacrifice*, 187.
133. Bradley, *The Power of Sacrifice*, 187–88.
134. Matheson, *Elements of Revealed Theology*, 167.

'Tis only for the summit's sake

    Thou layest the foundation-stone;

The mornings of creation break

    For sacrifice alone.

Thou wouldst not have prepared one star

    To float upon the azure main,

Hadst Thou not witnessed from afar

    The Lamb that should be slain.[135]

In this section I shall discuss Matheson's reflections on sacrifice through the biblical stories of Aaron, Moses and Jesus, the stories of the rich young ruler, the testimony of the Roman soldiers at the foot of the Cross and in the Book of Revelation. The sacrifice of self, including God's Self, is the pinnacle of reality. On the Cross, Jesus gave up His strength and might; God gave up His strength and might. In praise of the Divine, in his reflection on the Beatitude, "Blessed are the meek: for they shall inherit the earth" (Matthew 5:5), Matheson wrote: "I stand amazed in the presence of that might which could empty itself of all might. Thou art more wonderful to me in Thy cross than in Thy crown. Thou art greater to me in which Thou hast given up than in what Thou possessest. Thy glory is Thy shame. Majesty is Thy self-surrender. Thy Kinghood is Thy service."[136]

As he gazed on Christ, the Crucified One, "Look unto me, and be ye saved," (Isaiah 45:22) Matheson said that, gazing on Christ, we are healed and our ego or small self is lost in God:

> They tell me that the mesmeric gaze can cure pain; it will be so with my gaze on Thee. Let but mine eye be rivetted on Thee, and the wounds of the serpent will be all forgotten. There will be no more pain, because there will be no more self. I will have thenceforth no life but Thine . . . Let my natural heart behold Thee and die! . . . Let there rise the new man that only lives in Thee.[137]

For Matheson, it is the surrender of the human will which delights the Father; once Christ came, all other sacrifices were superfluous.[138] Like Christ in the Garden of Gethsemane, the cup which God gives us to drink

---

135. Matheson, *Sacred Songs*, 13–14.

136. Matheson, *Heart Chords; My Aspirations*, 28–29.

137. Matheson, *Heart Chords; My Aspirations*, 55–56.

138. Matheson, *Heart Chords; My Aspirations*, 56.

is "a cup for the will . . . The real battlefield is in the silence of the spirit; conquer *there* and thou *art* crowned."[139] When we have made the sacrifice of will we have finished the work God gave us to do (John 17:4).[140] It is when we are able to forget self and "enter into communion with [Christ's] cross of universal sympathy," when we are able to "carry in thy breast the care of thy brother," that we learn what it means when Jesus said, "My yoke is easy and my burden is light" (Matthew 11:29).[141] In his reflection on Aaron, "The rod of Aaron brought forth buds" (Numbers 17:8), Matheson said that only the rod of Aaron, "the empire of the priesthood, the power of sacrifice" flourished.[142] In prayer, Matheson bids his soul to go down to meet a fellow human being in the valley, in the place of their error and sinfulness and restore them through the spirit of meekness, the spirit of self-sacrifice, from the level of common and conscious weakness.[143] In the prophecy of Isaiah, in which every valley shall be exalted and every mountain and hill made low, Matheson wrote, "To me outward things are now high and inward things lowly," but there will be a time when this is reversed: "The poor in spirit were once the men of the valley; Thou hast made them the men of the mountain."[144] In prayer, he said: "Inspire me, O Lord, with this heroism of the valleys. Help me to see the elevation of lowly things. Reveal to me the Divine beauty of meekness, of patience, of forgiveness. Show me thine own power—the power of the Cross . . . Let me learn the life of death, the victory of self-surrender, the joy of sacrifice."[145]

Alongside self-surrender and sacrifice, Matheson believed that suffering could be a doorway into the Divine. He understood the suffering of Christ to be the supreme point of union between Jesus and every other human being because suffering and death are universal.[146] The spirit of sacrifice, of self-forgetfulness, is "independent of time and space and change . . . It is truly called 'life eternal', for years cannot touch it."[147] "In the moment of thy surrender thou shalt become green with immortal youth."[148] It is the moment of surrender, of perfect self-forgetfulness, the moment when there

139. Matheson, *Heart Chords; My Aspirations*, 59.

140. Matheson, *Heart Chords; My Aspirations*, 60.

141. Matheson, *Heart Chords; My Aspirations*, 75–76.

142. Matheson, *Heart Chords; My Aspirations*, 85.

143. Matheson, *Heart Chords; My Aspirations*, 86–87.

144. Matheson, *Heart Chords; My Aspirations*, 92.

145. Matheson, *Heart Chords; My Aspirations*, 93.

146. Matheson, *Heart Chords; My Aspirations*, 96–97.

147. Matheson, *Heart Chords; My Aspirations*, 109–10.

148. Matheson, *Heart Chords; My Aspirations*, 110.

is no more sea, no division between one person and another that humanity comes together in unity.[149] In prayer, Matheson craved to overcome his
isolation, weary of himself, of the battle within him. He prayed to be saved
from himself; he sought God's peace, God's unspeakable joy.[150] He understood that union with God meant taking up the Cross: "Give me Thy spirit
of sacrifice, that I may be elevated above my own fears. Unite me to the great
continent, the brotherhood of human souls, that the storms of my island
life may be lulled to rest; then shall I be able in my heart to say, 'There is no
more sea.'"[151] At times, Matheson used the metaphor of water differently.
On occasion, the ocean was an image of the depth and breadth of God's love
while, on other occasions, the sea was a barrier, something to be overcome.
The sea could be a metaphor of separation of humanity from God and from
one human being to another. Matheson looked forward to the vision in the
Book of Revelation in which there will be no more sea and so to a time
when the life and will of humanity will be one with the Divine. Matheson
understood the death of Jesus to be a self-offering. Jesus was not a victim;
He was not compelled to die.[152] There is no hint of penal substitutionary
atonement. In Jesus, Matheson saw the self-surrendering power of love of
the Father, to which we may offer our own life in service.[153] The Cross is not
a source of shame but a power, a glory, to be replicated in our life: We gaze
on Thee till we shall catch Thine impress, till we shall be transformed into
Thine image from glory to glory, till we shall say, not with resignation but
with acquiescence, 'Thy will be done.'"[154]

In Moses, in the refusal of the lawgiver to be called the son of Pharaoh's
daughter, Matheson said that Moses had rejected the "cup of worldly glory"
but instead accepted the "cup of spiritual sacrifice."[155] Moses had chosen
to "go down into the valleys to suffer affliction with the people of God."[156]
Matheson prayed he might join his heart to the heart of God, that he too
might stand alongside those who suffer, those who had "never seen the glory
of the mountain's brow."[157] Matheson said that "Love's joy is the surrender of

---

149. Matheson, *Moments on the Mount*, 32–33.

150. Matheson, *Moments on the Mount*, 33.

151. Matheson, *Moments on the Mount*, 34.

152. Matheson, *Moments on the Mount*, 65.

153. Matheson, *Moments on the Mount*, 66.

154. Matheson, *Moments on the Mount*, 66–67.

155. Matheson, *Moments on the Mount*, 91.

156. Matheson, *Moments on the Mount*, 92.

157. Matheson, *Moments on the Mount*, 92.

itself; the joy of lovelessness is the keeping of itself."[158] In his meditation on the words of Samuel, "Behold, to obey is better than sacrifice," (1 Samuel 15:22) Matheson distinguished between the ritual sacrifice of religion and sacrifice of the will. With these words, Samuel had become a Christian. Samuel had said that the point of religion, the crown of religion, was not "sacrifice, pain, the sense of privation and suffering" but "to obey, to yield the will, to surrender the life, to have a heart harmonious with the thing commanded."[159] Matheson prayed: "When I shall touch Thee, there shall be no more penance, no more night, no more sea, no more sacrifice. I shall have reached that perfect obedience which is perfect love, and therefore perfect painlessness."[160] For Matheson, self-forgetfulness meant overcoming the ego. The request of the Risen Christ to Peter, "Feed my lambs," is a call to the lead disciple to be "the least proud, the most self-forgetting," the one who descends to "the lowliest valleys," and the one who, above all others, "must lose through the very power of thy love all sense of thine own power."[161] Peter's greatest thought is not thought for himself but for "the burden of humanity, the bearing of [Christ's] cross."[162] In the Gospel of John, the woman at the well said to Jesus, "Sir, thou hast nothing to draw with" (4:2). In his accompanying meditation, Matheson drew a parallel between the drawing of water, the bucket travelling up and down within the well, with the withdrawing or shrinking of Jesus in order that people, when He is lifted up, may be drawn upward to Him.[163] Overcoming the ego, humility and the life of self-forgetfulness are the withdrawing of Jesus: "The greatest compliment you can put to man or woman is to say that they attract without adornment."[164] The beauty offered by Jesus, "Son of the Highest," is His all-consuming love:

> It is in a soiled garment that Thou hast solicited my love. Thou hast offered me no gifts of material glory. Thou hast asked me to share Thy poverty. Thou has said: ' . . . Wilt thou go with me where the hungry cry for bread, where the sick implore for health, where the weary weep for rest . . . Wilt thou walk with me through the lanes and alleys where the poor meet and struggle and die?[165]

158. Matheson, *Moments on the Mount*, 114.

159. Matheson, *Moments on the Mount*, 118.

160. Matheson, *Moments on the Mount*, 119.

161. Matheson, *Moments on the Mount*, 164.

162. Matheson, *Moments on the Mount*, 164.

163. Matheson, *Times of Retirement*, 35.

164. Matheson, *Times of Retirement*, 35.

165. Matheson, *Times of Retirement*, 36–37.

Matheson's consciousness of Jesus saturated his soul. He opened the above passage on social concern with the words, "Wilt thou follow me down the deep shadows of Gethsemane, up the steep heights of Calvary?" Matheson ended his meditation acknowledging that Jesus had drawn his heart to heaven without the aid of earth.[166] Matheson believed that the greater our exposure to humanity and humanity's diverse story and experience, the more likely we are to be forgetful of ourselves. Whether we are too confident or too shy, in both cases we are primarily concerned with self: the greater our environment the more likely we are to smash the mirror of self.[167] It is when Christ enters into the soul that we open ourselves to others and reach our fullest potential.[168] Matheson prayed, "Let there be a crucifying of my egotism! Let me break the mirror ere I go!"[169] If we speak to display ourselves the listener will miss "the stamp of unselfishness" on our forehead; they will read "the stamp of egotism" and fail to see "Christ in you."[170] For Matheson, "What God's light reveals is myself."[171]

In heaven, we each rise in order with Christ being the first (1 Corinthians 15:23). Matheson said that that order is not in any sense worldly reward or status but according to personal sacrifice, to love and self-forgetfulness: "Come 'they that are Christ's'—they that have washed their robes in the blood of self-forgetfulness."[172] He wrote:

> I should learn to domineer in a week. But to serve, to help, to minister, to perform menial offices, to retire in the shade that another's light may shine—that needs a long education . . . The front flowers are Thy Gethsemane flowers—Thy Passion flowers. My place in the New Jerusalem will be determined by my conquest of exclusiveness; and nothing conquers exclusiveness like pain. They who have passed through the furnace of earth come out to Thee unbound. They are freed from the shackles of all caste; therefore thy are the prime-*ministers* of Thy Kingdom.[173]

Matheson contrasted the ritual of other world faiths, in particular the demands of an ascetic lifestyle, with the test of self-emptying which he found in Jesus. Instead of going to the mountain top where his neighbor is

166. Matheson, *Times of Retirement*, 37.

167. Matheson, *Times of Retirement*, 72.

168. Matheson, *Times of Retirement*, 73.

169. Matheson, *Messages of Hope*, 247.

170. Matheson, *Messages of Hope*, 246.

171. Matheson, *Messages of Hope*, 201.

172. Matheson, *Times of Retirement*, 90.

173. Matheson, *Times of Retirement*, 90–91.

unseen, Matheson said we are told to seek "a sacrificial mission . . . where people gather, where the crowds jostle, where man competes with man."[174] We find this same sentiment in the words of George MacLeod written over half a century later:

> I simply argue that the Cross be raised again at the center of the market place as well as on the steeple of the church. I am recovering the claim that Jesus was not crucified in a cathedral between two candles, but on a cross between two thieves; on the town garbage heap; at a crossroads so cosmopolitan that they had to write his title in Hebrew and in Latin and in Greek (or shall we say in English, in Bantu and in Afrikaans?) at the kind of place where cynics talk smut, and thieves curse, and soldiers' gamble. Because that is where He died. And that is what He died about.[175]

Matheson said that it is easy to be humble while alone before God but to be humble:

> when Lazarus is begging at thy gate—this is the victory over pride—this, this is humility! To be poor in spirit in the presence of the kingdoms of earth, to be meek in the presence of the crouching, to be merciful to faults beneath thy nature, to make peace when thine adversary is weak, to mourn thy shortcomings when thou art the magnet of attraction to hundreds—this is the blessing of the mount, for this is the humility of the plain![176]

The truth of human life is that "every one of us only *begins to live* by the act of *dying*."[177] À Kempis said, "Be assured of this, that you must live a dying life. And the more completely a man dies to self, the more he begins to live to God."[178] It is not self-denial *per se* that makes one great.[179] We overcome self with our sacrificial, self-forgetful union with Christ: "Feel thyself a member of His body! Identify thy interests with the interests of Him! Let there beat one pulse between thee and thy Lord! Let His grief by thy grief; let His joy be thy joy! Let thy prayer be the Lord's Prayer, His six golden wishes thy six golden desires in life!"[180] The act of dying, of sacrificial, self-forgetfulness is to

174. Matheson, *Times of Retirement*, 229.
175. MacLeod, *Only One Way Left*, 103.
176. Matheson, *Times of Retirement*, 230.
177. Matheson, *Times of Retirement*, 131.
178. À Kempis, *The Imitation of Christ*, 88.
179. Matheson, *Times of Retirement*, 132.
180. Matheson, *Times of Retirement*, 133.

be carried into the home. "The deeds of silent sacrifice, the homes of humble piety, the acts of covert kindness" are examples and sources of human greatness.[181] A humble life is worth a future world because it is in "the sphere of the humble" where worlds are made.[182] In 1955, Macleod similarly spoke of God found "in ordinary life: among the tables and trays and chairs and windows that surround our lives; the innumerable contacts that form our everlasting nows."[183] Through care for others, we overcome our own selfish care and weariness: "let me listen to the murmurs of the sick, and mine will be mute."[184] In prayer, Matheson said, "May the pain of the Son of Man be my panacea for pain!"[185] We are to gaze on the Son of Man and by so doing overcome the shallowness and selfishness of the ego. Matheson prayed: "Thou hast prayed that all may be one with Thyself. Teach me the manliness of ministration, the heroism of helpfulness, the sovereignty of serving, the lordship of loneliness, the kinghood of compassion, the strength of stooping, the scepter of unselfishness, the crown of crucifixion . . ."[186] Matheson's motivation for the overcoming of selfishness was "the enlargement of the soul."[187] The soul has a mirror which is "Selfishness."[188] "Wealth is not bad till it glorifies thy mirror, till thou sayest with triumph, 'I am exalted above my fellows.'"[189] In his meditation on Isaiah 58:8, "Thy righteousness shall go before thee; the glory of the Lord shall be thy rearward," Matheson stressed the plea of the prophet to care for the poor. Providing it is sought for the sake of the sufferer, the prophet said that "such a life of sacrifice is of more value than the keeping of sacred days or the attendance at holy festivals."[190]

Matheson dismissed the compensation argument: while the face of God shines upon those who live the life of sacrifice, it is not for personal gain that one cares for others.[191] He said: "There is joy in heaven to a sacrificial soul; but I would not have that soul keep the joy of heaven before its eyes. I would have it, when it serves the beggar, forget the golden streets and the pearly gates and the unsetting suns and the crystal rivers and the living

181. Matheson, *Messages of Hope*, 8.

182. Matheson, *Messages of Hope*, 9.

183. MacLeod, *Only One Way Left*, 24.

184. Matheson, *Messages of Hope*, 13.

185. Matheson, *Messages of Hope*, 14.

186. Matheson, *Messages of Hope*, 33–34.

187. Matheson, *Messages of Hope*, 43.

188. Matheson, *Messages of Hope*, 43.

189. Matheson, *Messages of Hope*, 44.

190. Matheson, *Messages of Hope*, 53.

191. Matheson, *Messages of Hope*, 54.

fountains. I would have it remember only the claims of love."[192] For Matheson, sin is "a state of love . . . the love of a person—myself."[193] At Pentecost, it was significant for Matheson that the disciples were together in one place: we are to be one of one heart with our fellow human beings. Matheson said that the Lord's Prayer begins "Our Father," not "My Father."[194] We are called to stand in the place where humanity stands and the measure of our prayer is not what is asked but for whom it is asked.[195] In his meditation on the story of the rich young ruler (Mark 10:20—21), Matheson said that the point is not that the young man give his wealth away under instruction but instead out of love. In prayer, he said, "I will not pray, 'Bind my hands that I hurt not my brother'; my cry will be, 'Loose my hands that I may *serve* him.'"[196] In his meditation on the rich young ruler, à Kempis asked what the young man needed: "What is this? That he forsake himself and all else, and completely deny himself, retaining no trace of self-love. And when he has done all that he ought to do, let him feel that he has done nothing."[197] When Christ healed others, it was not out of self-interest or glorification of self but rather for the sake of the other.[198] In prayer, Matheson said, "May I give to my brother because his thirst makes a thorn in me! May I give because my pity is a pain to me, my sorrow a soreness, my compassion a cross!"[199] At the wedding in Cana in Galilee, it was selflessness, not for personal benefit, that Mary asked Jesus for the provision of more wine. Her primary concern was for the wedding guests and the dignity of the families: "Unselfishness in little matters is the top of the sacrificial hill."[200]

For many people, their faith in Christ is "clouded . . . Christ is shaded to the eye" but nevertheless "love reigns. And love purifies."[201] Matheson defended the service and sacrifice offered by those who do not explicitly follow Jesus. In prayer, to God the Father he said, "Tell me that the roll of Thy disciples is larger than the communion roll, that the names written in heaven exceeded the names signed on earth!"[202] In his sacred song titled "One in

192. Matheson, *Messages of Hope*, 54.

193. Matheson, *Messages of Hope*, 86.

194. Matheson, *Messages of Hope*, 169.

195. Matheson, *Messages of Hope*, 171.

196. Matheson, *Messages of Hope*, 187–88.

197. À Kempis, *The Imitation of Christ*, 84.

198. Matheson, *Messages of Hope*, 227.

199. Matheson, *Messages of Hope*, 228.

200. Matheson, *Messages of Hope*, 239.

201. Matheson, *Messages of Hope*, 190.

202. Matheson, *Messages of Hope*, 192.

Christ," based on Ephesians 1:10, "That in the dispensation of the fullness of times He might gather together in one all things in Christ," Matheson wrote:

> Gather us in, Thou Love that fillest all,
> Gather our rival faiths within Thy fold,
> Rend each man's temple and bid it fall
> That we may know that Thou hast been of old;
> Gather us in.
>
> Gather us in: we worship only Thee;
> In varied names we stretch a common hand;
> In diverse forms a common soul we see;
> In many ships we see one spirit-land;
> Gather us in.
> . . .
> Thine is the mystic life great India craves,
> Thine is the Parsee's sin-destroying beam,
> Thine is the Buddhist's rest from tossing waves,
> Thine is the empire of vast China's dream;
> Gather us in.
>
> Thine is the Roman's strength without his pride,
> Thine is the Greek's glad world without its graves,
> Thine is Judea's law with love beside,
> The truth that censures and the grace that saves;
> Gather us in.
>
> Some seek a Father in the heavens above,
> Some ask a human image to adore,
> Some crave a spirit vast as life and love:
> Within Thy mansions we have all and more;
> Gather us in.[203]

203. Matheson, *Sacred Songs*, 36.

For Matheson, in his meditation on Abraham, Lazarus and Dives (Luke 16: 31), the sin or failing of Dives was not unbelief but his failure in charity.[204] No miracle, "no apparition from the dead" could turn selfishness into love.[205] What is needed lies within: a change of heart. "Christ is an attitude of the heart—a sacrificial attitude."[206] For Matheson, it is significant that in the only recorded occasion when Jesus acts as host it is to bring together and serve at the same table disciples and publicans. Matheson thanked Christ for this revelation: "the brotherhood of man."[207] He said that not everyone is ready to participate in the Sacrament or hear the Word preached: "Thy house is larger than our temple. Thy table is wider than our communion."[208] For love to be love it must be unforced. In humanity, this requires a "*tempering* of the power of God;" a withdrawing that love can act freely.[209]

In his meditation on Christ on the cross, Matheson applauded the compassion and charity of those who offered the dying Christ a drink of vinegar mixed with gall. As a narcotic, the intention of those at the foot of the cross was to relieve Christ's suffering. Too readily do we divide the world into Christians and non-Christians. Referring to the Parable of the Sheep and the Goats, Matheson wrote: "I am told that at the Day of Judgment those will be on the right hand who gave Him drink, and those on the left hand who did not. But here on earth He has received drink from those apparently on the left hand—Roman soldiers have sought to assuage His sufferings!"[210] Those who helped Jesus owed allegiance not to Him but to Caesar. "They have not yet bowed to His crown; but they are loyal to His cross."[211] Matheson said, "Never forget that in the hour and the power of sacrifice you are obtaining a greater privilege than ever you bestow."[212] In the story of the feeding of the four thousand, sacrifice is again Matheson's central insight. Jesus gave the loaves to His disciples to distribute to the crowd. He said that Jesus could have given out the broken bread but, had He done so, the disciples would have lost out on the most important aspect of the story, namely, the breaking of the bread. Matheson said that more than the broken bread itself, "the

204. Matheson, *Messages of Hope*, 215.

205. Matheson, *Messages of Hope*, 216.

206. Matheson, *Messages of Hope*, 246.

207. Matheson, *Messages of Hope*, 220.

208. Matheson, *Messages of Hope*, 220.

209. Matheson, *Messages of Hope*, 223.

210. Matheson, *Messages of Hope*, 249.

211. Matheson, *Messages of Hope*, 250.

212. Matheson, *Messages of Hope*, 282.

breaking of the bread [is] the greater blessing of the two."[213] It is the symbol and ritual of sacrifice, of self-giving.

For Matheson, there was a dual emphasis on union with Christ: union meant union with the life of Jesus, with Jesus Himself and a self-giving to others in service, working to care for the needs of others and seeking to relieve the suffering of others. In losing oneself in others, we find our fuller humanity. Matheson held both of these emphases together convincingly without accentuating one over the other. He avoided a gospel which sought Jesus and celebrated His life at the expense of social justice and he avoided a gospel of social justice which lost its spirituality and personal relationship with Jesus.

In tones reminiscent of Caird, the union which Matheson sought was to be one with Christ's spirit of self-forgetfulness: "Teach me to lose self-will, that I may be strengthened by a higher will. Let my life be buried in the love of Thee, hid in the sense of Thy presence, absorbed and lost and over-shadowed in Thine all-excelling glory."[214] The sacrifice which God desires is "the delight of a human heart . . . the offering of a freewill, the surrender of a voluntary life."[215] God desires not "my experience of Gethsemane, but my will; not my experience of suffering, but my power to rejoice in Him in *spite* of my experience of suffering."[216] "Love can sing in the night the joys of morning."[217] Matheson desired nothing more than to be a recipient of the Divine Spirit; he said, "Breathe on me . . . I shall learn that dying is life, that loss is gain, that perfect sacrifice is fullness of joy."[218] Matheson returned to the theme that the joy of God is to be found in our experience of suffering. It is not that we are to seek suffering but that it is possible, if not a gift, that God can be encountered in the midst of suffering. In a passage which may be autobiographical, Matheson reflected on God's love:

> It seeks me in my poverty that it may dower me with its wealth,
>
> it seeks me in my loneliness that it may glad me with its fellowship,
>
> it seeks me in my weariness that it may inspire me with its strength,
>
> it seeks me in my deformity that it may crown me with its beauty;
>
> it chooses me in my furnace of affliction . . .
>
> I accept Thy glorious offer of union with my nothingness.[219]

213. Matheson, *Messages of Hope*, 288.

214. Matheson, *Moment on the Mount*, 165.

215. Matheson, *Moment on the Mount*, 177.

216. Matheson, *Moment on the Mount*, 178.

217. Matheson, *Times of Retirement*, 259.

218. Matheson, *Moments of the Mount*, 178.

219. Matheson, *Moment on the Mount*, 266.

In these lines, we see Matheson's spiritual poverty, his humility, his sense of union with the immensity of God, but we hear the deeper darkness of his soul, deeper than that of his physical blindness. His biographer, Donald Macmillan, seldom if ever hints at the incredible suffering in Matheson's soul. Macmillan said that Matheson's physical blindness was the making of the man and, while that may be true, that sentiment does not fully convey Matheson's years of loss and agony which he felt and to which he gave voice in his meditations. Matheson also believed that to carry great burdens and still carry on, to endure grief and still work and to suffer deep anguish and still perform one's daily tasks was "a Christ-like thing" to do. On the one hand, these words seem immensely courageous and spiritually inspiring but on the other hand, applied unthinkingly, they could be pastorally insensitive and destructive: this seems unlikely given Matheson's otherwise tender sensitivity to the suffering of others. In prayer, he said, "Men ask for a rainbow in the cloud; but I would ask more from Thee. I would be, in my cloud, myself a rainbow—a minister to others' joy."[220] This is an extremely profound sentiment. Matheson turned suffering around: the darkness, however harrowing, is a place of encounter and with Christ we are the place of healing to ourselves. This suggests that Matheson believed that, because the Divine dwelt in his soul, he was the rainbow in his own cloud of suffering. We need to learn to trust in the Sacred within and draw strength from our meditations, from our sense of oneness with the Divine. In his sacred song entitled "The Revelation of Divine Silence" based on the words of Jesus, *If it were not so, I would have told you* (John 14:2), Matheson said that the silence of God is itself the revelation of God's presence and care:

> If there dwell within my soul
>
> A longing deep and high,
>
> And if no bell shall toll
>
> To contradict its cry,
>
> The silence has become
>
> Itself my sign from heaven
>
> That in my Father's home
>
> The boon I ask is given.[221]

For Matheson, union with the Divine exists not only in a mystical or ontological sense but also in its character and essential nature. In the story of Christ with Cleopas and his friend, Christ is known in the breaking of

---

220. Matheson, *Times of Retirement*, 170.
221. Matheson, *Sacred Songs*, 146–147.

the bread. The life of Christ in heaven, the life of the Risen Christ, is one with the life of Jesus on earth: Jesus is "the path of sacrifice, the hour of humiliation: 'He was known of them in breaking of bread.'"[222] It is in our sacrifices for others that we will encounter Christ. If we are to see the Risen Christ then we must be like Him in sacrificial spirit: "He keeps the mark of the nails, He remains a high priest for ever. If thou wouldst know Him, it must be through that priesthood; if thou wouldst recognize Him, it must be through the mark of the nails borne in thine own body."[223]

Matheson avoided a secular reduction of the Gospel to social work alone because his account of one's caring for others was steeped in his awareness of Jesus. In caring for others, our bodies are torn like the body of the dying Jesus. Matheson was intensely aware of Jesus, in himself, in the spirit of others and in the world around him. In prayer, he spoke of the life of his soul in Jesus.[224] Matheson's inner sense of the Divine is all-pervading. We find the same intense sentiment of desire for Jesus in à Kempis. In his chapter on the inner life, à Kempis wrote:

> Had you but once entered perfectly into the Heart of Jesus, and tasted something of His burning love, you would care nothing for your own gain or loss; for the love of Jesus causes a man to regard himself very humbly. The true, inward lover of Jesus and the Truth, who is free from inordinate desires, can turn freely to God, rise above self, and joyfully rest in God.[225]

The final word belongs to Matheson. In his blindness, in his soul, Matheson found Jesus to be a constant companion, a very present reality in the commonplace; in his moments of highest meditation and in his times of suffering. Matheson brought immortality in the midst of the Christian life, made it an everyday encounter, and from the breath of God within him, saw God as all in all. He wrote: "Build up my waste places, O my God! Crown my crosses; gild my Gethsemanes; beautify my Bethanys; wreathe my reverses; make steps of my sorrows; bring treasures from my trials; strike music from my mourning; reveal that my road to Paradise was the pathway of my pain! I shall learn the glory of obedience when I see my desert's bloom."[226]

---

222. Matheson, *Moments on the Mount*, 157.

223. Matheson, *Moment on the Mount*, 159.

224. Matheson, *Times of Retirement*, 204.

225. À Kempis, *The Imitation of Christ*, 69.

226. Matheson, *Messages of Hope*, 294.

Conclusion

IN MY BOOK, I have shown that George Matheson was a mystic. As a minister in the Church of Scotland, in a denomination distinguished for Calvinism and legal probity, Matheson's spiritual life and theology were shaped by his insatiable desire for union with the Divine. From the deep soil of silence and daily solitude, Matheson encountered the Immortal within. Through imaginative engagement with the Bible, seeking meaning beneath the surface of Scripture, his religion was one of direct spiritual experience. Matheson's physical blindness significantly enabled his insight into the Eternal and the nature of things. Matheson saw inwardly with the third eye or the eye of the heart.

The Roman Catholic theologian Karl Rahner has said that "The Christian of the future will be a mystic or will not exist at all."[1] In future, faith will be primarily experiential or there will be no faith. The task of the Church is to facilitate encounter with the Eternal through its spiritual practice. Matheson's daily practice of meditation, of shutting out the world, is vital if the Church, including the Church of Scotland, is to have something unique to offer society which, to a large extent, is materialist and secular. If the Church is able to cultivate and nurture among its members a fruitful spiritual relationship with the Living God it may have a future as an institution and, more importantly, as an instrument of the Infinite. Matheson's appropriation of Spencer's Inscrutable Force may assist the Church in its dialogue with those who today defend the concept of transcendence but dismiss the possibility of God.

Matheson's creative and sometimes unique interpretation of familiar biblical texts has been a rich discovery. Taken together with his mystical emphasis on union with God, the inner life (overcoming the ego), the immortality of the soul and the foundational importance of (self-) sacrifice, Matheson's theology is one of the heart which penetrates to the heart of the

1. Rahner, *The Practice of Faith*, 22.

gospel. Matheson's relationship with Jesus is personal, intimate and life trans-forming. Life lived in and with the Divine is the meaning of life which the Church has to offer a world which, to some extent, believes the universe to have no purpose. Matheson argued that Christianity is not the only route to God. Like Matheson, the Church today needs to honor the Divine in the faith and followers of the other major world religions. The urgency for genuine inter-faith conversation and commitment to joint action for justice, for indi-viduals and the planet, has never been greater. Part of that story of justice is our God-given responsibility for the care and well-being of animals.

Matheson's life and ministry have much to offer the Church of Scot-land today, including the practice of closing our eyes to the attractions of the world and so deepen our relationship with the Sacred.

Bibliography

Abbot, Lyman, and Francis Brown, eds. *The Prophets of the Christian Faith*. London: Macmillan, 1896.

Adeney, W. F. "Immortality." *Christianity and Evolution: Modern Problems of the Faith*, edited by George Matheson et al., 111–28. Nisbets Theological Library. London: Nisbet, 1887.

Altholz, J. L. "The Warfare of Conscience with Theology." In *Religion in Victorian Britain*, edited by Gerald Parsons, 4:150–69. 4 vols. Manchester: Manchester University Press, 1988.

Anonymous. *Scotch Sermons*. London: Macmillan, 1880.

Augustine. *Confessions*. Edinburgh: T. & T. Clark, 1876.

Bailey, Peter. "Leisure: Merrie to Modern." In *The Victorian World*, edited by Martin Hewitt, 619–35. Routledge Worlds. London: Routledge, 2012.

Baillie, John. *And the Life Everlasting*. Oxford University Press, 1961.

———, ed. *The Cambridge Companion to Biblical Interpretation*. Cambridge Companions to Religion. Cambridge: Cambridge University Press, 1998.

Beiser, Frederick C., ed. *The Cambridge Companion to Hegel and Nineteenth-Century Philosophy*. Cambridge Companions to Philosophy. Cambridge: Cambridge University Press, 2008.

Bradley, Ian. *O Love That Wilt not Let Me Go: George Matheson*. London: Fount Paperbacks, 1990.

———. *The Power of Sacrifice*. London: Darton, Longman & Todd, 1995.

Brett, R. L., ed. *Poems of Faith and Doubt*. London: Arnold, 1980.

Brown, Nicola, et al., eds. *The Victorian Supernatural*. Cambridge: Cambridge University Press, 2004.

Caird, John. "Corporate Immortality." In *Scotch Sermons*, no editor, 1–17. London: Macmillan, 1880.

———. *The Fundamental Ideas of Christianity*. Glasgow: MacLehose, 1899.

———. *An Introduction to the Philosophy of Religion*. Glasgow: MacLehose, 1904.

———. *Sermons*. Edinburgh: Blackwood, 1893.

———. "Union with God." In *Scotch Sermons*, Anonymous, 18–25. London: Macmillan, 1880.

———. *University Sermons*. Glasgow: MacLehose, 1898.

Cantor, Geoffrey, and Sally Shuttleworth. *Science Serialized: Representations of the Sciences in the Nineteenth Century*. Cambridge: MIT Press, 2004.

Chadwick, Owen. *The Secularization of the European Mind in the 19th Century*. Gifford Lectures. Cambridge: Cambridge University Press, 1975.

———. *The Victorian Church Part II*. 2 vols. Ecclesiastical History of England. London: Black, 1970.

Chapman, Charles. "Evolution and the Biblical Representations of God." In *Christianity and Evolution: Modern Problems of the Faith*, edited by George Matheson, 167–95. Nisbet's Theological Library. London: Nisbet, 1887.

Collini, Stefan. "Arnold." In *Victorian Thinkers*, edited by A. L. Le Quesne et al. Oxford: Oxford University Press, 1993.

Cox, Jeffrey. "Worlds of Victorian Religion." In *The Victorian World*, edited by Martin Hewitt, 433–48. Routledge Worlds. London: Routledge, 2012.

Drummond, Andrew L., and James Bulloch. *The Church in Late Victorian Scotland, 1874–1900*. Edinburgh: St Andrew Press, 1978.

Eliot, T. S. *Collected Poems 1909–1962*. London: Faber & Faber, 1974.

Evans, C. Stephen, ed. *Exploring Kenotic Christology: The Self-Emptying of God*. Oxford: Oxford University Press, 2006.

Fergusson, David, ed. *The Blackwell Companion to Nineteenth-Century Theology*. Blackwell Companions to Religion. Malden, MA: Blackwell, 2010.

Fiddes, Paul. "Creation out of Love." In *The Work of Love: Creation as Kenosis*, edited by John Polkinghorne, 167–91. Grand Rapids: Eerdmans, 2001.

Flint, Kate. *The Victorians and the Visual Imagination*. Cambridge: Cambridge University Press, 2000.

Forsyth, P. T. *God the Holy Father*. London: Independent Press, 1954.

Fyffe, Aileen. *Science and Salvation: Evangelical Popular Science Publishing in Victorian Britain*. Chicago: University of Chicago Press, 2004.

Giorgiov, Adrian. "The Kenotic Christology of Charles Gore, P. T. Forsyth and H. R. Mackintosh." *Perichoresis* 2 (2004) 47–66.

Gore, Charles. *The Incarnation of the Son of God*. Bampton Lectures. New York: Scribner, 1891.

———. *The Reconstruction of Belief*. London: Murray, 1951.

Happold, F. C. *Mysticism: A Study and an Anthology*. Harmondsworth, UK: Penguin, 1963.

Hedley, Douglas. *Coleridge, Philosophy and Religion: Aids to Reflection and the Mirror of the Spirit*. Cambridge: Cambridge University Press, 2000.

Helmer, Christine. "Schleiermacher." In *The Blackwell Companion to Nineteenth Century Theology*, edited by David Fergusson, 31–57. Blackwell Companions to Religion. Malden, MA: Blackwell, 2010.

Helmstadter, R. J., and Bernard Lightman, eds. *Victorian Faith in Crisis*. London: Macmillan, 1990.

Hewitt, Martin, ed. *The Victorian World*. Routledge Worlds. London: Routledge, 2014.

Hill, John Charles. *Innellan*. Glasgow: Kirkwood, 1943.

Hollywood, Amy, and Patricia Z. Beckman, eds. *The Cambridge Companion to Christian Mysticism*. Cambridge Companions to Religion. Cambridge: Cambridge University Press, 2012.

Hull, John. *Touching the Rock: Notes on Blindness*. London: SPCK, 1990.

Huxley, T. H. *On the Physical Basis of Life*. Yale College, 1869. New Haven: Chatfield, 1870.

James, William. *The Varieties of Religious Experience: A Study in Human Nature*. 1902. Reprint, London: Folio Society, 2008.

Jasper, David. "Literary Readings of the Bible." In *The Cambridge Companion to Biblical Interpretation*, edited by John Barton, 21–34. Cambridge Companions to Religion. Cambridge: Cambridge University Press, 1998.

à Kempis, Thomas. *The Imitation of Christ*. London, UK: Penguin, 1952.

King, Ursula. *Christ in All Things: Exploring Spirituality with Teilhard de Chardin*. London: SCM, 1997.

Lamm, Julia A. "Romanticism and Pantheism." In *The Blackwell Companion to Nineteenth-Century Theology*, edited by David Fergusson, 165–86. Blackwell Companions to Religion. Malden, MA: Blackwell, 2010.

Larsen, Timothy. *A People of One Book: The Bible and the Victorians*. Oxford: Oxford University Press, 2011.

———. *Crisis of Doubt: Honest Faith in Nineteenth-Century England*. Oxford: Oxford University Press, 2006.

Law, Graham. "Periodicalism." In *The Victorian World*, edited by Martin Hewitt, 619–35. Routledge Worlds. London: Routledge, 2012.

Lightman, Bernard. "The Creed of Science and its Critics." In *The Victorian World*, edited by Martin Hewitt, 440–65. Routledge Worlds. London: Routledge, 2014.

Lightman, Bernard. "Scientists as Materialists in the Periodical Press: Tyndall's Belfast Address." In *Science Serialized: Representations of the Sciences in the Nineteenth Century*, edited by Geoffrey Cantor and Sally Shuttleworth, 199–237. Cambridge: MIT Press, 2004.

Livingston, James C. "Natural Science and Theology." In *The Blackwell Companion to Nineteenth-Century Theology*, edited by David Fergusson, 141–64. Malden, MA: Blackwell, 2010.

———. *Religious Thought in the Victorian Age: Challenges and Reconceptions*. New York: T. & T. Clark, 2007.

Le Quesne, A. L., et al. *Victorian Thinkers*. Oxford: Oxford University Press, 1993.

Loofs, Friedrich. "Kenosis." In *Encyclopaedia of Religion and Ethics*, edited by James Hastings, 7:680–87. 13 vols. Edinburgh: T. & T. Clark, 1914.

MacDonald, George. *A Dish of Orts, Chiefly Papers on the Imagination, and on Shakspere*. London: Sampson, Low, Marten, 1895.

Mackintosh, H. R. *The Doctrine of the Person of Christ*. Edinburgh: T. & T. Clark, 1913.

MacLean, Norman. *Set Free*. London: Hodder & Stoughton, 1949.

MacLeod, George F. *Only One Way Left* in *Daily Readings with George MacLeod*. London: Fount Paperbacks, 1991.

———. *The Whole Earth Shall Cry Glory*. Bristol, UK: Purnell, 1985.

MacMillan, D. *The Life of George Matheson, D.D., LL.D., F.R.S.E.* London: Hodder & Stoughton, 1910.

Macquarrie, John. *Two Worlds Are Ours: An Introduction to Christian Mysticism*. London: SCM, 2004.

Magee, Glenn Alexander. "Hegel and Mysticism." In *The Cambridge Companion to Hegel and Nineteenth-Century Philosophy*, edited by Frederick C. Beiser, 253–80. Cambridge Companions to Philosophy. Cambridge: Cambridge University Press, 2008.

McGinn, Bernard, ed. *The Essential Writings of Christian Mysticism*. New York: Modern Library, 2006.

————. *The Foundations of Mysticism: Origins to the Fifth Century*. London: SCM, 1991.

McKay, Johnston. *The Kirk and the Kingdom: A Century of Tension in Scottish Social Theology, 1830–1929*. Edinburgh: Edinburgh University Press, 2012.

Mander, W. J. *British Idealism: A History*. Oxford: Oxford University Press, 2011.

Matheson, George. *Aids to the Study of German Theology*. Edinburgh: T. & T. Clark, 1874.

————. *Can the Old Faith Live with the New? Or the Problem of Evolution and Revelation*. Edinburgh: Blackwood, 1885.

————. *Growth in the Spirit of Christianity from the First Century to the Dawn of the Lutheran Era*. Edinburgh: T. & T. Clark, 1877.

————. *Heart Chords: My Aspirations*. London: Cassell, Petter, Galpin, 1883.

————. *The Lady Ecclesia: An Autobiography*. New York: Dodd Mead, 1897.

————. *Leaves for Quiet Hours*. New York: Armstrong, 1904.

————. *Messages of Hope*. London: Clarke, 1908.

————. *Moments on the Mount: A Series of Devotional Meditations New*. New York: Armstrong, 1884.

————. *Natural Elements of Revealed Theology*. London: Nisbet, 1881.

————. *Portraits of Bible Men*. Vol. 3. 1910. Reprint, Grand Rapids: Kregel, 1996.

————. *The Psalmist and the Scientist, or, the Modern Value of the Religious Sentiment*. New York: Dodd Mead, 1887.

————. *Rests by the River*. London: Hodder & Stoughton, 1906.

————. *Sacred Songs*. Edinburgh: Blackwood, 1904.

————. *Searchings in the Silence*. London: Cassell, 1894.

————. *Spiritual Development of St Paul*. Edinburgh: Blackwood, 1890.

————. *Studies in the Portrait of Christ*. Vol. 1. London: Hodder & Stoughton, 1899.

————. *Studies in the Portrait of Christ*. Vol. 2. London: Hodder & Stoughton, 1900.

————. *Times of Retirement: Devotional Meditations*. New York: Revell, 1901.

————. *Voices of the Spirit*. New York: Armstrong, 1888.

Matheson, George, et al. *Christianity and Evolution: Modern Problems of the Faith*. Nisbet's Theological Library. London: Nisbet, 1887.

Maurice, F. D. *The Doctrine of Sacrifice Deduced from the Scriptures*. Cambridge: Macmillan, 1854.

Melnyk, Julie. *Victorian Religion: Faith and Life in Britain*. Victorian Life and Times. London: Praeger, 2008.

Miles, Margaret. *Desire and Delight: A New Reading of Augustine's Confessions*. New York: Crossroad, 1992.

Miller, J Hillis. *The Disappearance of God: Five 19th Century Writers*. New York: Schocken, 1965.

Moffatt, James. *Handbook to the Church Hymnary*. Oxford: Oxford University Press, 1927

Mozley, James Bowling. *Eight Lectures On Miracles: Preached before the University of Oxford in the Year 1865 on the Foundation of the Late Rev. John Bampton*. London: Rivingtons, 1872.

Muir, A. F. "Has Evolution a Claim to a Place in the Christian System?" In *Christianity and Evolution: Modern Problems of the Faith*, edited by George Matheson et al., 250–76. Nisbet's Theological Library. London: Nisbet, 1887.

Newell, John Philip. *A New Harmony: The Spirit, the Earth and the Human Soul.* San Francisco: Jossey-Bass, 2011.

Otis, Laura. *Literature and Science in the Nineteenth Century: An Anthology.* Oxford: Oxford University Press, 2002.

Otto, Rudolf. *The Idea of the Holy.* Translated by John W. Harvey. Oxford: Oxford University Press, 1923.

———. *Mysticism East and West: A Comparative Analysis of the Nature of Mysticism.* Translated by Bertha L. Bracey and Richenda C. Payne. New York: Macmillan, 1972.

Polkinghorne, John, ed. *The Work of Love: Creation as Kenosis.* Grand Rapids: Eerdmans, 2001.

Prickett, Stephen. "The Bible and Literary Interpretation." In *The Blackwell Companion to Nineteenth-Century Theology,* edited by David Fergusson, 395–411. Blackwell Companions to Religion. Chichester, UK: Blackwell, 2010.

Pulsford, William H. *Scenes in the Life of Jesus: Thirty-Six Lessons for Advanced Classes.* Boston: Unitarian Sunday School, 1895.

Ramsay, Arthur Michael. *From Gore to Temple: The Development of Anglican Theology between Lux Mundi and the Second World War 1889–1939.* London: Longman, Green, 1960.

Reardon, Bernard M. G. *Religion in the Age of Romanticism: Studies in Early Nineteenth Century Thought.* Cambridge: Cambridge University Press, 1985.

Richter, Melvin. *The Politics of Conscience: T. H/ Green and His Age.* Bristol, UK: Thoemmes, 1964.

Rogerson, John W. "The Bible and Theology." In *The Blackwell Companion to Nineteenth-Century Theology,* edited by David Fergusson, 455–67. Blackwell Companions to Religion. Chichester, UK: Blackwell, 2010.

St Aubyn, Giles. *Souls in Torment: The Conflict between Science and Religion in Victorian England.* London: New European Publications, 2010.

Schmidt, Leigh Eric. "The Making of Modern Mysticism." *Journal of the American Academy of Religion* 71 (2003) 273–302.

Semple, Adam, "Eternal Life." In *Scotch Sermons,* Anonymous, 324–35. London: Macmillan, 1880.

Smith, Mark A., "Religion." In *A Companion to Nineteenth-Century Britain,* edited by Chris Williams, 337–52. Blackwell Companions to British History. Oxford: Blackwell, 2004.

Smith, Roger. "The Physiology of the Will: Mind, Body, and Psychology in the Periodical Literature, 1855–1875." In *Science Serialized: Representations of the Sciences in the Nineteenth Century,* edited by Geoffrey Cantor and Sally Shuttleworth, 81–110. Dibner Institute Studies in the History of Science and Technology. Cambridge: MIT Press, 2004.

Stevenson, Patrick. "Eternal Life." In *Scotch Sermons,* Anonymous, 365–72. London: Macmillan, 1880.

Teilhard de Chardin, Pierre. *Writing in Time of War.* London: Collins, 1968.

Thomas, Keith, ed. *Victorian Thinkers.* Oxford: Oxford University Press, 1993.

Thompson, Thomas R. "Nineteenth Century Kenotic Christology: the Waxing, Waning and Weighing of a Quest for a Coherent Orthodoxy." In *Exploring Kenotic Christology: The Self-Emptying God,* edited by C. Stephen Evans, 74–111. Oxford: Oxford University Press, 2006.

Turner, Frank M. "The Victorian Conflict between Science & Religion: A Professional Dimension." *Isis* 69 (1978) 356–76.

Tyler, John Crew. *The Blind Seer.* London: Vision, 1960.

Vaughan, Robert Alfred. *Hours with the Mystics: A Contribution to the History of Religious Opinion.* London: Slark, 1888.

Waddel, Peter. *Charles Gore: Radical Anglican.* Norwich, UK: Canterbury, 2014.

Wallace, Alfred Russel. *Miracles and Modern Spiritualism.* London: Redway, 1896.

Watson, Roderick. *The Literature of Scotland.* 2 vols. New York: Palgrave Macmillan, 2007.

Wheeler, Michael. *Heaven, Hell and the Victorians.* Abridged ed. Cambridge: Cambridge University Press, 1994.

Williams, Chris, ed. *A Companion to Nineteenth-Century Britain.* Blackwell Companions to British History. Oxford: Blackwell, 2004.

Wilson, A. N. *God's Funeral.* London: Abacus, 2000.

———. *The Victorians.* London: Arrow, 2003.

Printed in Great Britain
by Amazon

10827548R00129